ARCHIVES OF FLESH

SEXUAL CULTURES

General Editors: Ann Pellegrini, Tavia Nyong'o, and Joshua Chambers-Letson

Founding Editors: José Esteban Muñoz and Ann Pellegrini

Titles in the series include:

Times Square Red, Times Square Blue
Samuel R. Delany

Queer Globalizations: Citizenship and the Afterlife of Colonialism
Edited by Arnaldo Cruz-Malavé and Martin F. Manalansan IV

Queer Latinidad: Identity Practices, Discursive Spaces
Juana María Rodríguez

Love the Sin: Sexual Regulation and the Limits of Religious Tolerance
Janet R. Jakobsen and Ann Pellegrini

Boricua Pop: Puerto Ricans and the Latinization of American Culture
Frances Négron-Muntaner

Manning the Race: Reforming Black Men in the Jim Crow Era
Marlon Ross

In a Queer Time and Place: Transgender Bodies, Subcultural Lives
Judith Halberstam

Why I Hate Abercrombie and Fitch: Essays on Race and Sexuality
Dwight A. McBride

God Hates Fags: The Rhetorics of Religious Violence
Michael Cobb

Once You Go Black: Choice, Desire, and the Black American Intellectual
Robert Reid-Pharr

The Latino Body: Crisis Identities in American Literary and Cultural Memory
Lázaro Lima

Arranging Grief: Sacred Time and the Body in Nineteenth-Century America
Dana Luciano

Cruising Utopia: The Then and There of Queer Futurity
José Esteban Muñoz

Another Country: Queer Anti-Urbanism
Scott Herring

Extravagant Abjection: Blackness, Power, and Sexuality in the African American Literary Imagination
Darieck Scott

Archives of Flesh

African America, Spain, and
Post-Humanist Critique

Robert F. Reid-Pharr

NEW YORK UNIVERSITY PRESS
New York

NEW YORK UNIVERSITY PRESS
New York
www.nyupress.org

References to Internet websites (URLs) were accurate at the time of writing. Neither the author nor New York University Press is responsible for URLs that may have expired or changed since the manuscript was prepared.

ISBN: 978-1-4798-8573-2 (hardback)
ISBN: 978-1-4798-4362-6 (paperback)

For Library of Congress Cataloging-in-Publication data, please contact the Library of Congress.

New York University Press books are printed on acid-free paper, and their binding materials are chosen for strength and durability. We strive to use environmentally responsible suppliers and materials to the greatest extent possible in publishing our books.

Manufactured in the United States of America

10 9 8 7 6 5 4 3 2 1

Also available as an ebook

For

Joanna Reid Bacote and Robert Lyons Pharr

CONTENTS

ACKNOWLEDGMENTS

As ever, I have relied fully on the kindness of friends and strangers. The first faltering words of *Archives of Flesh* were delivered at Oxford University while I was in residence in the winter of 2010 as the Drue Heinz Visiting Professor of American Literature. I thank Ron Bush for hosting me during my stay in Oxford. I later arrived at the American University of Beirut as the Edward Said Visiting Professor of American Studies and the College of William and Mary as the Sara and Jess Cloud Visiting Professor of English. In both instances I was privileged to encounter remarkably gifted students and breathtakingly generous colleagues. Among the folks at AUB whom I owe, and owe big, are Adam Waterman, David Wrisley, Robert Myers, and Patrick McGreevy. Adam, David, Robert, and Patrick are leaders among a group of intellectuals in Beirut who not only shepherded me through the complexities of Lebanese and American bureaucracy, but also entertained me, fed me, and put up with my bumbling attempts to bring this project to life. I would also like to thank Marj Henningsen, who adopted me when I arrived on campus, then sent me back to New York a better person than the one she first met. At the College of William and Mary I encountered even more brilliant students and generous colleagues, all of whom made me remember daily why I chose this profession. Great thanks are in order to Hermine Pinson and Susan Donaldson, who as chair of the English Department was unremittingly kind and efficient. My time at William and Mary also gave me the opportunity to reconnect with my college friends Scott Nelson and Cindy Hahamovitch. Scott and Cindy greatly inspired me when I was an undergraduate at Chapel Hill and they continue to inspire me today.

In 2010 I presented work from *Archives of Flesh* at Duke University in a wonderful seminar organized by the even more wonderful Karla Holloway. Robyn Wiegman offered a captivating response to my paper that still operates for me as a model of collegiality and intellectual rigor.

I was thrilled to have my friends Maurice Wallace, Wahneema Lubiano, Fred Moten, and Miles Grier in attendance at that session. Giovanna Covi approached me with an invitation to be one of the plenary speakers at the 2011 conference of the Associazione Italiana di Studi Nord Americani in Trento, Italy. I gladly acknowledge Giovanna's generosity. My dear friend Derek Brueckner organized a cold February 2012 visit for me at the University of Manitoba. I thank both Derek and his partner in crime, David Churchill, for their ongoing support. In 2013 I was honored to deliver the Sidney Kaplan lecture at the University of Massachusetts Amherst. Thanks to TreaAndrea Russworm for the invitation. That same year, Michael Bronski organized a talk for me at Harvard University under the auspices of the Committee on Degrees in Studies of Women, Gender, and Sexuality. I thank both Michael and the generous audience I encountered at Harvard. I gratefully acknowledge Paula Moya's gracious 2014 invitation to present work at Stanford University under the auspices of the Program in Modern Language and Thought. I also want to acknowledge Cam Awkward-Rich for his insightful response to my presentation. I am equally grateful for the invitation from Ezra Tawil to deliver a talk at the University of Rochester during the same year. At the University of Alabama at Tuscaloosa I presented a section of this book as the 2014 Robert Milton Young Memorial Lecture. I would like to acknowledge Yolanda M. Manora for organizing this event, one made more precious still by the presence of my mentor, Trudier Harris. Charles Rowell of the journal *Callaloo* invited me to *Callaloo* conferences at both Oxford and Emory Universities. My comments at Emory were later reproduced in *Callaloo* 38, no. 3 (Summer 2015). I am indebted to Charles and the many remarkable individuals who participated in those conferences. I am also grateful to Rinaldo Walcott and Cassandra Lord for their 2015 invitation to the outstanding Black Queer Human conference at the University of Toronto, where I delivered a portion of the conclusion to this book.

At home in New York I am supported by a group of colleagues who are somehow able to look past my many defects and peculiarities in order to encourage both the letter and the spirit of the work that I do. I am privileged to count Herman Bennett, Zee Dempster, Duncan Faherty, Ruth Wilson Gilmore, Eric Lott, Cindy Katz, Meena Alexander, Wayne Koestenbaum, and Kandice Chuh as colleagues, interlocutors, co-conspirators, and friends. Eric Lott deserves special thanks for both reading a draft of this book and holding my hand at one of the many points at which I lost my confidence. My dear friend Arnaldo Cruz-Malavé did the same. I thank them both for their kindness and generosity. Dagmawi Woubshet, Lyrae Van Clief-Stefanon, Margo Crawford, and José María Armengol Carrera read sections of the manuscript. Gwendolyn Shaw and Iemanjá Brown provided invaluable research assistance. I am humbled by their efforts on my behalf.

Khary Polk, Nathaniel Belcher, Tyler Schmidt, Patricia Dixon, Neil Goldberg, Jennifer Morgan, Emma Taati, David Bahr, Tavia Nyong'o, Jesse Schwartz, Justin Rogers-Cooper, and Eduardo Aparicio are constant sources of sustenance and encouragement. I wear their friendships like so many badges of honor. My many students inspire me more than I can express. I have been particularly moved by those individuals who have chosen to write their dissertations with me while I have tried to complete this project. Allen Durgin, Kristin Moriah, Velina Manolova, Lavelle Porter, LaRose Parris, Tristan Striker, Kristina Huang, Jason Baumann, Brian Baaki, Deberati Biswas, Tonya Foster, Timothy Griffiths, and Anahi Douglas have all given me the privilege of accompanying them on their own exciting intellectual and creative journeys. I look on in amazement as they produce work that is equal parts inspired, elegant, rigorous, fun, insightful, hopeful, sure, and true. The research and writing of *Archives of Flesh* were supported in part by grants from the Humboldt Foundation and the Professional Staff Congress of the City University of New York. I am proud to be associated with both institutions. Finally, completion of *Archives of Flesh* was greatly aided by a grant from the John Simon Guggenheim Memorial Foundation. I am both honored and thrilled by the foundation's acknowledgment and support.

Just as I began this project, my mother, Joanna Reid Bacote, died. Just as I was finishing this project, my father, Robert Lyons Pharr, did the same. If there are moments in these pages that are brave or generous, hopeful or incisive, iconoclastic or alive, they exist only because I have tried to produce work that equals the profound sense of ethics and possibility that my parents tried to give their children. I dedicate this book to them.

Introduction

Shuttles in the rocking loom of history,
the dark ships move, the dark ships move,
their bright ironical names
like jests of kindness on a murderer's mouth;
plough through thrashing glister toward
fata morgana's lucent melting shore,
weave toward New World littorals that are
mirage and myth and actual shore.

Voyage through death,
Voyage whose chartings are unlove.
—Robert Hayden, "Middle Passage"

Toward a new humanism. . . .
Understanding among men. . . .
Our colored brothers. . . .
Mankind, I believe in you. . . .
—Frantz Fanon, *Black Skin, White Masks*

I might as well begin with the truth. In 1971, bundled onto a bus, my satchel stuffed with pencils, paper, and the flushed hopes of neighbors and kin, I traveled beside my sister to one of the newly desegregated schools of North Carolina's Mecklenburg County. Shielded by childhood oblivion from the polite vulgarity and polished hostility that greeted us as we left the nondescript, working-class black enclave of Beatties Ford Park to etch our ever so light traces onto the history of a reluctant America, we entered into the drama of desegregation buffeted by hopes that the promise of liberal humanism that rang so triumphantly in American public discourse might indeed come soon, and very soon, to apply to all the country's citizens. In the 1970 *Swann v. Charlotte-Mecklenburg Board of Education* ruling, the Supreme Court offered a tentative, and explicitly

temporary, response to the cynicism that surrounded the interpretation and (non)enforcement of the 1954 *Brown v. Board of Education*
decision. The fact that in all its foundations and practices the United
States is a profoundly segregated society had become so apparent as to
make it clear that no institution in the nation is immune to the charge
of either white supremacy or mediocrity. Thus, the breathless self-
congratulation of liberal America notwithstanding, the United States
effectively remained as racially segregated in 1970 as it had been in 1954.
Until the *Swann* decision, Mecklenburg County's residential patterns
proved more than enough to maintain the system of dual education
(whites in county schools; blacks in city schools) that had existed since
the founding of the Charlotte city schools system in the latter part of
the nineteenth century. The decision was crafted to address this frankly
vulgar reality by mandating a complex system of busing to achieve racial
integration, sending tens of thousands of students rushing each morning to local stops where they boarded garishly yellow metal tubes of
hope and modernity, striving in their uncomfortable, stiff-backed seats
to achieve what their forebears could not.

In the process, Charlotte gained notoriety as one of the most advanced locations in the New South, the "city that made desegregation
work." Riding those buses, coveting hoarded resources, we crisscrossed
routes marking the resilience of a striving black working class struggling
against the no-nonsense will to maintain white privilege and distinction:
Beatties Ford Park to Long Creek; Hidden Valley to Newell to Northeast
to Albemarle Road; Hampshire Hills to Garinger. Becoming accustomed
to watching friendly, good-natured, and ostensibly liberal white people turn and run at the approach of black children overburdened with
slide rules and history books, we learned early and well not only how
little truth lay behind the oft-repeated rhetorics of fairness and color
blindness, but also that the modes of our education had been developed
precisely to squelch awareness of the forms of violent repression being
directed squarely in our direction. Entering in 1983 as a scholarship student into the University of North Carolina and eventually making my
way to New Haven for postgraduate studies, I was reminded each step of
the way of my luck and exceptionality, told to be proud and rejoice as I
left graduate school in 1994, energized and expectant, if more than a bit
apprehensive, with a newly minted Ph.D. shining warmly in my pocket.

The uncomfortable truth, however, the inconvenient reality that fuels the sense of irritation stretching through these pages, is that the story that I have just narrated is not the typically American tale of triumph over adversity, but instead a much less elegant, infinitely more pessimistic account of cynicism, hypocrisy, and disappointment. During the years of my university education, Charlotte's economy boomed, drawing impressive numbers of individuals from the Northeast and Midwest, who came to what they understood as a prosperous, sun-drenched southern city in which the most vulgar aspects of segregation had long been defeated. Imagining themselves as somehow exempt from any responsibility for the antique certainties of the so-called Old South, they chafed at the busing system that had been put into place by the *Swann* decision. In 1999, facing a challenge by a white parent whose daughter was denied a position in a magnet school because of her race, Judge Robert D. Potter of the U.S. District Court for the Western District of North Carolina ended mandatory court-ordered busing. The predictably disastrous results came almost immediately. Charlotte entered as fully as any American city into the laughing duplicity of post-racial white supremacy. Only six years after Judge Potter's ruling, Wake County Superior Court Judge Howard Manning accused the Charlotte-Mecklenburg school system of "academic genocide," pointing to the systematic herding of low-income students into cash-strapped, underperforming schools, citing four city high schools as particularly noxious examples of the city and county's failing public school students: Waddell, West Charlotte, West Mecklenburg, and Garinger (from which I had graduated in 1983).[1]

Hearing all this, you will perhaps have some sympathy for why I have so little patience for the reiteration of casual rhetorics of liberal humanism. Though the philosophical foundations of the profession to which I claim an awkward allegiance are built upon notions of logic, clarity, and fairness that presumably will eventually prove the lie of the most vulgar forms of racialism, I have never seen anything even remotely approaching a proper actualization of this ideal. According to the U.S. Department of Education's National Center for Education Statistics, as of 2011, 79 percent of full-time instructional staff in U.S. colleges and universities were white, 6 percent were black, 4 percent were Hispanic, 9 percent were Asian/Pacific Islander, and less than 1 percent were American Indian/Alaska Native. Among those individuals holding professorial titles,

84 percent were white, 4 percent were black, 3 percent were Hispanic, 8 percent were Asian/Pacific Islander, and again less than 1 percent were American Indian/Alaska Native.[2] Or to state the matter even more harshly, at the current rate of increase, it will take African Americans more than a century for their representation in the professoriate to reach parity with their numbers in the general population.

The idea that allegiance to Enlightenment ideals passed to us from the founders will inevitably result in the realization of a just and race-blind democracy has proven across multiple generations to be either a sloppy fiction or a bold lie. This notion, the almost religious certainty that the ravages of slavery, colonialism, and white supremacy notwithstanding, the basic philosophical, critical, and pedagogical structures that define what we euphemistically name humanism *must* eventually result in the full articulation of a common good, is itself established on profoundly unstable institutional and ideological conventions that privilege an essentially scholastic intellectualism, one in which it is perfectly acceptable to ignore the hostility to Africans and their descendants that is often quite bluntly stated in the works of Kant, Hume, Jefferson, Hegel, and Heidegger, not to mention their many students and interlocutors. Indeed, it is still the rare scholar who seeks to gauge the quality of humanist debate by direct reference to the lived realities of the communities that sponsor and support his work. Is he smart? Is she thorough? That it is so easy to answer these questions without taking into account the vigor, the genius, and the unremitting struggle of the colonized and the enslaved begs the question of whether progressive intellectuals should continue to sign off on notions of (e)quality and liberalism that effectively rob large swaths of the human population of their resources without bothering even to note the seriousness of the crime.

I will admit, then, that much of what paces and structures this work are equal measures of displeasure and distrust. Attempt to place the words *humanism, humanities, human sciences, universalism, cosmopolitanism, liberalism,* and *black* into the same sentence, and you are likely to find that the only concept strong enough to bind them is "failure." By noting my displeasure, I mean not only to remark my abandonment of forms of intellectualism that avoid questions of utility and historical urgency, but also to name the fact that in the midst of radical structural and demographic change, the philosophical and critical systems that support humanistic inquiry in both the United States and Europe are woefully inadequate. Thus the apparatus of distrust that I name and willfully exploit in these pages is built upon the simple suggestion that "humanism," the noble study of "Man," has a quite intelligible history, one based in a set of material realities that are not distinct from the histories of slavery and colonization that set sturdy-limbed southern children boarding buses and chasing hope though pleasant streets bordered by loblolly pines. The blunt question that one must ask is whether the cynical manner in which those hopes have been—and are—systematically blocked and mocked is indeed a proper representation of the reality of humanism and its most significant institutional articulations. Judge Potter's anti-busing decision was, after all, an affirmation of the "universalist" and "color-blind" ideals that presumably stand at the heart of the Enlightenment traditions that are so staunchly reiterated in dominant pedagogical structures.

It is here that the work I have undertaken diverges from that of a scholar like Cary Wolfe, who along with the feminist scholar of science and technology Donna Haraway has become a central figure in the articulation of what one might think of as the "post-humanist agenda." In his capacious 2010 study, *What Is Posthumanism?*, Wolfe rightly points to the fact that in the Western philosophical traditions that he examines, one achieves "the human" by "transcending bonds of materiality and embodiment altogether."[3] The pluralist impulse that is presumably the driving force in liberal humanism is itself dependent upon a pointedly aloof stance to both the material and the corporeal. The ideological apparatuses that structure Western humanism allow us to celebrate uniqueness and diversity without radically altering remarkably resilient structures of exclusion. Speaking of the legal efforts to alleviate the suffering of animals and the marginalization of people with disabilities, Wolfe writes that

> these pragmatic pursuits are formed to work within the purview of a liberal humanism in philosophy, politics, and law that is bound by a historically and ideologically specific set of coordinates that, because of that very boundedness, allow one to achieve certain pragmatic gains in the short run, but at the price of a radical foreshortening of a more ambitious and more profound ethical project: a new and more inclusive form

of ethical pluralism that is our charge, now to frame. (Wolfe, *What Is Posthumanism?*, 137)

I am altogether in agreement with Wolfe's arguments here. I am also equally convinced by his call for thorough—and potentially corrosive—examinations of the material, institutional, and disciplinary forms in which humanism is articulated, as well as his assertion that Disability Studies and Animal Studies have the ability to provide key models for moving the terms of post-humanist debate forward.

What troubles me about Wolfe's work, however, what provokes that necessary divergence to which I have just alluded, is the fact that not only does he never consider the multiple ways that the intellectual protocols of slavery and colonization have structured increasingly complex and novel manipulations of discourses of human subjectivity, but also that he rushes to dismiss the accomplishments of those intellectual insurgencies that have attempted to do just this work. In defending his turn to Animal Studies, Wolfe remarks offhandedly that

> the full force of animal studies—what makes it not just another flavor of "fill in the blank studies" on the model of media studies, film studies, women's studies, ethnic studies, and so on—is that it fundamentally unsettles and reconfigures the question of the knowing subject and the disciplinary paradigms and procedures that take for granted its form and reproduce it. (xxix)

True to his word, Wolfe then spends the remainder of *What Is Posthumanism?* making a very convincing argument about the necessity of Animal Studies and to a lesser extent Disability Studies in the articulation of the post-humanist critical project, without ever stopping to demonstrate either concern for or anything more than the lightest and most two-dimensional familiarity with "fill in the blank studies."

Where I lose contact with the guiding logic of Wolfe's work is in my inability to understand how in the absence of any consideration of the protocols of race and gender in the articulation of humanism he might achieve the fundamental "unsettling" that he desires. Indeed, he has fallen victim to the very ideological boundedness about which he warns his readers. In his rush to avoid the pitfalls of disciplinary provincialism, he clumsily forgets his own call for a critical practice that deeply considers "the institutional forces it is interested in and the modes and protocols of knowledge by which those materials are *disciplined*" (106). Wolfe is tone-deaf about the analytical and political labor that has most consistently and doggedly resisted the worst ideological and structural expressions of Western humanism, particularly labor enacted under the rubrics of postcolonial and African Diaspora Studies. Understanding this helps us to make sense of Wolfe's confusing silence regarding the remarkable achievements of generations of anti–white supremacist, anticolonialist thinkers, chief among them Frantz Fanon, who called for a radical restructuring of humanism nearly sixty years prior to the unveiling of Wolfe's own essentially closed efforts.

My criticisms of Cary Wolfe are meant to illustrate a particularly sorry reality in the dominant structures of American and European intellectual life. Our complex rhetorics of pluralism take place in contexts—and institutions—that gain much of their social capital by actively repressing truly democratic forms of study and debate. "The black" can be imagined much more simply and comfortably than he can be addressed. This sad truth is one of the factors that fuels the disappointment and distrust about which I spoke earlier. I can easily understand and sympathize, then, with the frustration of a scholar like Frank Wilderson when he argues that the pluralist rhetorics that are the hallmarks of liberal humanism are poor substitutes for much-needed structural change in American and European intellectual life:

> In sharp contrast to the late 1960s and early 1970s, we now live in a political, academic, and cinematic milieu which stresses "diversity," "unity," "civic participation," "hybridity," "access," and "contribution." The radical fringe of political discourse amounts to little more than a passionate dream of civic reform and social stability. The distance between protester and police has narrowed considerably.[4]

The sneering on display here is equal parts shocking, refreshing, provocative, *and* disappointing. Wilderson is right to call out the cynicism that accompanies so much of the rhetoric that he critiques. The essentially therapeutic modes with which conversations about pluralism and diversity take place in this country operate to forestall deeply needed structural change by assigning an almost metaphysical status to increasingly complex announcements of a never quite attainable beloved community in which the knottiest questions of resources and power are addressed through the deployment of murky rhetorics of mutual recognition and respect.

Strangely, however, Wilderson makes a very significant conceptual error, one remarkably similar to those made by Wolfe. For Wilderson, "the black" is a "paradigmatic impossibility in the Western Hemisphere, indeed the world." The black is "the very antithesis of a Human subject" (Wilderson, *Red, White, and Black*, 9). In one manner Wilderson is *almost* correct. As I will discuss in some detail, the black operates in Western humanism as a nonsubject who gives meaning to the awkward and untenable concept of "Man." The many articulations in "our" philosophical traditions that read Africans and their descendants as outside history (Hegel) or incapable of the finest procedures of human thought and affect (Jefferson) work to disavow the very possibility of black subjectivity. Moreover, as I have argued repeatedly, the racial liberalism of American and European institutional life, the tepid and slow diversification procedures announced so breathlessly in the grandest of our grand institutions, were never designed to effect anything approaching a broad-ranging reconsideration of the most basic of humanist ideologies and protocols.[5]

What confuses me about Wilderson's thinking, however, what makes me wonder whether I have misunderstood his methods and motivations, is his willingness to reiterate—and rely upon—spectacularly rigid conceptions of human subjectivity. For Wilderson, Western humanism is the only game in town. His theoretical models allow no room for contradiction or slippage. He insists upon the most harsh and provocative nomenclature, suggesting that the labels "black" and "African American" should be understood as nothing more than drained examples of sentimentalism and sophistry. The White, the Slave, and the Savage (the Native American) are the only figures with enough conceptual heft to become visible within the philosophical graph that Wilderson produces. I would argue, however, that these essentially political and ethical arguments are marred by Wilderson's unwillingness to pay attention to the complexity of American sociality, the uncanny messiness of American history. In his rush to produce a radical critique of rhetorics of pluralism, Wilderson has been duped by one of the masters' most powerful lies. The Western philosophical traditions to which we have all been forced to pay obeisance represent not vessels of truth per se, but instead the quite specific discursive protocols and institutional procedures by which examination and discussion of human being has been delimited.

While scholars like Orlando Patterson and his many students have demonstrated the most salient ideological structures of slave (non)identity, the ways the slave's natal alienation allows for the transmogrification of a fully socialized human individual into a thing, these ideological structures should never be taken to represent "the slave's" essence.[6] Generations of intellectuals—W. E. B. Du Bois, C. L. R. James, John Blassingame, Deborah Gray White, and many others—have demonstrated not only enslaved persons' awareness of their presumed status as chattel but also and quite importantly their resistance to this status, their self-conscious articulation of counternarratives of human subjectivity in which enslaved and colonized persons might be understood as both historical actors and proper subjects of philosophy.[7] I agree with Wilderson that part of what Black Studies must continue to do is to point out the white supremacist basis of much within the articulation of so-called humanism. Even more importantly, however, I am eager to examine the cultures of enslaved persons, colonized persons, and their descendants in order to begin a process of articulating forms of humanistic inquiry that move beyond the stale compromises and brittle ceremonies that typify so much in the current practice of the humanities and human sciences.

Here is where I stress the pressing need to imagine the beginnings of a post-humanist archival practice. I build upon the work of Wolfe, Wilderson, and the communities of scholars whom I take them to represent, by resisting at every turn the tyrannies of philosophy and sociology. I meet Wolfe's refusal to engage Black Studies and Wilderson's refusal of the very idea that "the black" *can* be studied by arguing that, though the conceits of humanism would have us believe that our ability to address human being must by necessity be a radically demarcated endeavor, the *lived* reality of black life demonstrates an unusually broad set of procedures that have challenged and critiqued not only white supremacy but also the smugness and certainty of the entire Western humanist apparatus.

In this way, my work is in conversation with that of Alexander Wehe-liye, who argues in *Habeas Viscus: Racializing Assemblages, Biopolitics, and Black Feminist Theories of the Human* that contemporary discussions surrounding human being, particularly those by Michel Foucault, Giorgio Agamben, Achille Mbembe, and Orlando Patterson, have been too quick to dismiss or ignore "the existence of alternative modes of life alongside the violence, subjection, exploitation, and racialization that define the modern human."[8] He rejects the essentially academic and two-dimensional concepts of human subjectivity that he finds in these men's work by turning to the self-consciously embodied critiques of black feminist theorists. Focusing on Hortense Spillers's useful distinction between the body and the flesh, Weheliye claims that flesh, that "zero degree of social conceptualization," that irreducibly human thing that cannot be properly corralled within the suffocating racialist and woman-hating strictures of Western humanism, might facilitate the excavation of "the social (after) life" of Agamben's bare life and Patterson's social death.[9] The flesh marks the site at which "lines of flight, freedom dreams, practices of liberation, and possibilities for other worlds" might be made visible (Weheliye, *Habeas Viscus*, 2).

One runs, however, directly into the question of how. How might we begin to access the tantalizing political/ethical/theoretical possibilities that Weheliye names? My tentative answer is to call not simply for a return to "the archive," but also for the invigoration of Critical Archive Studies; critical in the sense of operating to end the terror of white supremacy while also naming how the humanist split between Man and (not)man has been achieved and maintained. While I am certainly not hostile to the philosophical and critical methods advanced by Weheliye and Wolfe as they attempt to resist the erasure of the lived, embodied, fleshy reality of humans from the articulation of humanism, I nonetheless believe that the example of the interesting, provocative, but ultimately defeated work of a scholar like Frank Wilderson speaks to the need to look for methods of inquiry, ways of naming human being, that are not bounded by the very forms of philosophy and sociology from which black and female subjectivity are always already excluded. We have no choice but to develop critical methods established at precisely those many moments of illogic, indeed of wildness and bestiality, that one finds in humanist discourse. Or to return to the main rhetorical currents of this book, I will pay particular attention to those many instances where the specificities of "the flesh" are utilized to announce humanism's dream of transcendence. I will look for not only the many (ancillary, farcical, grotesque) images of black subjects in so-called Western modernity, but also the abundant evidence (at least for the wide-awake reader) of black individuals' having turned humanist discourse to their own purposes, having utilized the rhetorics of the flesh in order to access alternatives to the most vulgar of the humanist protocols.

* * *

In enacting these procedures, I turn to a remarkably rich, if largely unexamined, archive centered on many decades of intimate interaction between African American and Spanish intellectuals. My fascination with Spain and what I call the African American Spanish archive turns both on the central place of the Iberian Peninsula in the articulation of Western humanism and the impolite, joking, sarcastic, and mocking assumption by many African Americans and other people of color that scores of so-called white individuals (including Spaniards) have not properly established themselves on the right side of the (white) Man/ (black) animal binary.

Following the lead of Michel Foucault and Cedric Robinson, I point to the centrality of the Iberian Peninsula in the development of what eventually came to be known as globalization and humanism. For his part, Robinson is particularly eloquent about the ways early modern notions of progress and cosmopolitanism were caught up with the production and reproduction of white and Christian identity.[10] I rush to pair these observations with María DeGuzmán's claims in her remarkable study, *Spain's Long Shadow: The Black Legend, Off-Whiteness, and Anglo-American Empire*, that the clear evidence of Iberian cultural forms that predate our contemporary racialist conceits as well as the peninsula's strategic position at the crossroads of Europe, Africa, and the Middle East have been used by American racialists to call into question the so-called racial purity of Spaniards.[11] Swimming against the current, however, I would suggest that the "off-whiteness" that DeGuzmán names signaled for African American intellectuals a species of Spanish promise and possibility, an opening by which the vulgar fiction of white superiority might be mitigated through access to not yet properly defeated Spanish flesh. Thus speaking out of school, I would remind my readers of some naughty truths. Slavery and colonization produced the wealth that allowed for the development of capitalism and spawned the ideological protocols that produced ridiculously clumsy concepts of racial and ethnic difference. At the same time, however, they also produced any number of (un)bounded, (un)authorized counternarratives, in which the many contradictions of racialism and capitalism were made patently visible.

I take inspiration here from work of the Jamaican novelist, critic, and philosopher Sylvia Wynter, who, following Foucault and the anthropologist Jacob Pandian, suggests not only that the Man/human split is a relatively recent invention but also that the conceptual tear that it represents—white, Western, propertied, universal Man versus non-white, Eastern, property-less, local female animal—is itself a product of the post-1492 need to put key ideological, discursive, and aesthetic structures at the service of modes of capital accumulation that were at once vigorously acquisitive and none too sentimental about the vicious exploitation of fellow members of the species.[12] Thus for Wynter, "the systemic revalorization of Black peoples can be fundamentally effected only by means of the no less systemic revalorization of the human being itself, *outside* the necessarily devalorizing terms of the biocentric descriptive statement of *Man*." It is not enough simply to name yet again the ridiculousness of still quite vibrant discourses of race. Instead we are called to disrupt the basic conceits regarding the proper structures of our most precious modes of intellectual labor. The key work is not so much to deliver "manhood" to "the blacks" as it is to rescue all of us, Africans, Europeans, Americans, and Asians alike, from the stranglehold of a stunningly calcified understanding of human being in which we name and evaluate our aesthetic structures via metrics designed to remark just how far we have traveled along the great chain of being: from hairy beasts with their faces bent to the ground to denatured, no longer quite animal beings fretfully eager to distinguish ourselves from species kin in order to maintain fictions of a disembodied transcendence.

My critique of a critic like Cary Wolfe turns, then, on the fact that even as he rightly notes that humanism is flawed to the extent that it is built upon an indissoluble distinction between "Man" and animal, he nonetheless seems incapable of recognizing that this idea reaches its highest—and most bizarre—level of clarity at those many moments in which some human animals are understood to be more human than others. I want to be clear, however, that the archival work that I propose, the awkward pairing of Spanish and African American intellectualism that makes up the bulk of this study, is intended to help make plain both the functioning and the *dis*-functioning of these structures, the ways cultures of slavery, white supremacy, and empire work not only to normalize the social and ideological domination of Africans, Asians, and aboriginals, but also to provoke awareness among slaves and slavers alike of shared humanity, common subjectivity, and modern person-hood released from the restraints of the local and the native. As Marcus Rediker and Stephanie Smallwood remind us, the enslaved necessarily established new ideologies of belonging and kinship, turning the "neutral" phrase "shipmate" into a mark of endearment and the slur "Igbo" (outsider, stranger) into a label of struggle and aspiration.[13]

I must remind you, however, that even as we joyously celebrate the victories of our enslaved ancestors, even as we take satisfied stock of how far we have come, we must studiously avoid the triumphalist narratives that are the hallmarks of humanist discourse. I can offer no stories of success and nobility, no salutary tales of the gallant victory of black will over the vulgarities of slavery and the slave trade. Following the lead of Sylvia Wynter, I will not rehash plots that return us to the very Cartesian division of mind and body by which the enslaved and the colonized have been so vigorously insulted. Instead I ask that we consider the idea that the process of extracting the new from the husk of the old was accomplished by both the mind *and* the flesh. I want to remain alert to the details of how (black human) bodies were not only abused by slavers but also utilized by the enslaved themselves as key sites of resistance and change. Struggling to remain sensitive to the ways the essentially provincial concept of (white, Western, propertied) Man has been established as universal precisely through the willful erasure of the profound violence that attended—and attends—the articulation of humanism, Wynter pushes her readers to understand that the story of Western humanism is not distinct from the story of capitalist/colonialist/white supremacist expansion. In my specific efforts to imagine a modern, future-oriented, and indeed post-humanist Black Studies, I must oppose the continued refutation of the animal in the human/animal binarism. I must attempt to rescue the flesh from the dream's much-celebrated despotism; must ask what a project of black liberation *not* built on the "need" to prove that we are indeed men might entail.

Discussing Hegel's *Phenomenology of Mind*, Frantz Fanon reminds us that "Man is human only to the extent to which he tries to impose his existence on another man in order to be recognized by him."[14] Amplifying this line of thought, Giorgio Agamben offers a succinctly stated diagnosis of the generative tension between the concept of "Man" and the (human) animal body that supports this concept:

> Man exists historically only in this tension: he can be human only to the degree that he transcends and transforms the anthropophorous animal which supports him, and only because, through the action of negation, he is capable of mastering, and eventually, destroying his own animality (it is in this sense that Kojeve can write that "man is a fatal disease of the animal").[15]

The strange neologism "anthropophorous" holds one's attention in this passage. Agamben names the Man-bearing animal, a creature that though proximate to and intimate with Man should never be seen or hailed. To do so would risk revealing the obvious lie of a fundamental distinction between Man and Man bearer. It would disrupt the "action of negation," the pursuit of mastery and destruction that Agamben suggests as a primary engine of modern society.

While I am convinced by Agamben's arguments, I also find myself fretting about the targets and the modes of his address. Spectral figure of a profoundly flawed articulation of modernity or not, Man stands as the undisputed subject of these sentences. Man exists. He transcends and transforms; masters and destroys. It seems, in fact, that Man's neverending attempts to confront and destroy animality sponsor the flexibility, creativity, and vigor necessary for his ever-proliferating creative projects. In contrast, the anthropophorous animal does only one thing. It supports. Irritatingly, it consistently fails to perform the only other task that has ever been asked of it. It will not die. What Agamben misses here is an opportunity to reimagine this essentially Hegelian narrative of slave and master so as to allow for the possibility of a much more complex and productive relation between Man and anthropophorous animal. Even as he advances a self-consciously progressive philosophical and ethical project, he still cannot imagine a conception of history in which the anthropophorous animal, the slave, the flesh, might be recognized as an actor. Agamben is trapped within the very Man-made rhetorics and ideologies that he is attempting to disrupt. This is why I turn to what one might think of as an extra-philosophical archival project in my efforts to reconsider Black Studies' relationship to humanism. That is to say, an intellectual tradition built upon the need to support the aspirations of a people thought to be hyper-embodied and bestial is defeated from the outset if it resists only the content and not the form of these slurs.

I beg your forbearance as I turn to a set of images that offer remarkable visual clues to the infinitely productive, always fraught ideological assemblies that draw together Atlantic slavery, white supremacy, capital accumulation, and nativity. The first, José de Ribera's *Maddalena Ventura, con su marido* (1631), commonly referred to as *La mujer barbuda* (*The Bearded Woman*), is a large (49.6' x 76.34') painting of Maddalena Ventura, her husband, and her child, who became public phenomena in the early part of the seventeenth century after Maddalena, aged thirty-seven, began to grow a heavy beard, eventually attracting the attention of the Duque de Alcalá, who commissioned Ribera to paint the Abruzzo-born woman (see figure I.1).

I am wholly taken by both the painting's confrontational iconicity and its sheer animality. Standing solidly at "dead" center, Maddalena, with her heavy beard, muscled hands, and most especially her ripe (erect?) breast, suggests exactly the masculinist fears of a dominant/dominating femininity that have cut such a decisive path through all discussions of (African) American society and culture. To borrow a phrase from Hortense Spillers, the image of Maddalena reveals a suppressed "law of the mother" that both supports and threatens modern structures of patriarchy (Spillers, "Mama's Baby"). The point is reiterated by the spectral presence of Maddalena's husband. Dressed in black, his face emaciated and drawn, his hands nearly hidden, he recedes in the face of his wife's white-clad, gold-trimmed vibrancy. While Ribera clearly continues both the realism and the sobriety of Caravaggio, he also affects a decidedly forward-looking, inviting, and opulent mood within the painting. I first encountered the work hanging prominently in the Museo Nacional

Figure I.1. José de Ribera, *Maddalena Ventura, con su marido* (1631). Hospital de Tavera, Toledo (Spain). Fundación Casa Ducal de Medinaceli.

del Prado. It was a crowd favorite, eliciting a sort of bemused, titillated horror among the museum's visitors. "*Bruto!*" the Italians complained. "*¡Bárbaro!*" the Spaniards countered. In either case, one was left with the sense that something fascinatingly ill-disciplined had taken place. I would argue, in fact, that the painting's prominence in the Prado, smug symbol of Spain's presumably stable and established traditions, was designed less to celebrate the genius of Ribera than to tame and domesticate La Mujer Barbuda's radicalism, her hysteria.

José de Ribera, known in Italian as Giuseppe de Ribera or Lo Spagnoletto (the little Spaniard), has imaged a sort of modern and secular transmogrification. Unlike those moments when, seated uncomfortably in a cathedral, one takes the blood of Christ between the lips and feels the texture of his flesh between the teeth, there is only the most vexed sense of antiquity in this painting. It may repeat some essential truth, but it does so mechanically. There is no attempt to revivify some elemental presence. Instead what Ribera notes is the creation of new forms of human subjectivity, the self-reproducing automaton, the automatic. The seed of the husband does not spring fully formed from the crucible of the wife. The steady advance of the modern belies the need for patriarchal interposition. As with the (modern) slave, antique narratives of descent and primogeniture must be reconstructed in order to establish the ideological ground on which all modern subjectivity rests. It is in this sense that I nominate the child that Maddalena holds in her arms as the most truly beastly figure in the familial tableau that Ribera creates. Wrapped in red, its greedy lips pursed and ready to take its mother's overripe breast, the child stands decidedly apart from its father. The old man's darkness disappears in the pink, light-framed visage of his offspring. Facing the infant is the carcass of what appears to be a quail, suggesting that the production of this child was done in the presence of destruction, the literal death of the natural, the disavowal of the flesh.

Again following the extremely useful clues provided by Cedric Robinson, I would remind you that the so-called Spanish Golden Age (*siglo del oro*), the period from the fifteenth to the seventeenth centuries that witnessed both Columbus's "discovery" of the Americas and the phenomenally productive practices of Ribera, El Greco, Velázquez, Cervantes, and de Vega, hardly represented a moment of stability within "Spanish" culture. On the contrary, the very notion of a Golden Age was based on the *diminution* and *suppression* of cultural complexity, at least so far as it worked to celebrate the Reconquista that culminated with the expulsion of Prince Boabdil from Granada, the last of the Muslim strongholds on the Iberian Peninsula. Still, this was hardly a moment in which an emergent Spanish people might take pride in the achievement of economic, political, or cultural independence. Instead, as Robinson reminds us, much of the newfound Iberian confidence and prosperity was based upon the often heavy-handed interventions of Genoese traders. There is, in fact, an extremely strange and shockingly effective sleight of hand that has allowed a once living man, Cristoforo Colombo, to be simultaneously transformed into the Spanish national hero Cristóbal Colón and the father of Anglo-American colonization, Christopher Columbus (Robinson, *Black Marxism*, 106–9).[16]

Without belaboring the point, I would submit that what is so disturbing about *Maddalena Ventura, con su marido* is the fact that it so ably demonstrates what one might call a sense of cultural/ideological dislocation underwriting the productions of Golden Age intellectuals like Ribera. Though born in Valencia, Ribera spent his apprenticeship in Rome and Naples, then part of the Spanish empire, eventually becoming deeply enmeshed in Neapolitan cultural and intellectual life. Tellingly, the celebrated artist would never return to live in his Iberian birthplace. Instead he remained in Italy, courting the patronage of the Spanish elite. He established his career at precisely that place where artistic production intersected with the exigencies of capital accumulation and the newly developed philosophical/ideological structures (humanism) that attended it. Though much of the criticism of *Maddalena Ventura* turns on either explication of Ribera's style or consideration of the work's gender politics (including the possibility of Maddalena's hormonal imbalance), I prefer to maintain my focus on the question of how Ribera narrates dynamic procedures of both *re*-spatialization and re-corporealization, procedures that included not only the Reconquista, but also the (dis)establishment of a complex of "fixed" ethnic and national boundaries.

I ask now that you focus your attention on the blessed/benighted face of America, the very child whom I take Maddalena to be holding in her arms, the child whom she shields from the dark, disapproving visage of her European husband. In particular, I would note the fact that the Spanish Golden Age was also the age of Spanish Empire, an empire whose greatest treasures were quite decidedly American. After the unification of the kingdoms of Castile and Aragon with the marriage of the Catholic monarchs Isabella and Ferdinand, the newly established community of "Spaniards" set about both to Christianize the peninsula and to build upon recently acquired—or at least recently modernized—abilities at conquest and annexation. Columbus's adventures of 1492 led to Spain's domination of much of the Caribbean and even more impressively the usurpation of huge swaths of the Inca and Aztec Empires of North, South, and Central America. The development of the modern Spanish nation absolutely depended on the extraction of value in the form of natural resources and human labor taken from its many colonies, particularly those of the Americas. The gold of the Golden Age was mined on the "uncharted," "unspoiled" side of the Atlantic by communities of Africans, aboriginals, and mestizos, slaves and free persons alike, who produced for Spain the wealth and leisure necessary to create artists and intellectuals on the order of a Velázquez or a Goya.

What I argue against, however, is the deeply embedded assumption that enslaved and colonized people offered nothing other than labor. I chafe at the idea that "physical" labor, the act of tilling a field, digging a mine, or suckling a child, is in fact less creative, less cerebral, less imaginative than the labor of painting a portrait or writing a sonnet. When I make the claim that Americans, including African Americans, were central to the production of Spain, I mean to suggest something much more provocative than simply the known fact that colonizers and enslavers successfully monetized the labor of black and brown bodies. Instead, to say that "Africa and America produced Spain" disrupts the clumsy ways even contemporary scholars continue to narrate world economic, social, and cultural history such that progress always flows from a magical, always already developed Europe to an inevitably and irredeemably underdeveloped periphery. At the same time, however, I suggest that the cultural apparatuses that produced the fledgling Spanish nation were structured in rather precise relation to the complex interplay of race, caste, class, language, and gender that remain quite obvious in the so-called New World.

These realities become starkly apparent when one turns toward the gem of the Spanish New World colonies, "New Spain," a location that more or less corresponds to present-day Mexico. Entering into the Spanish orbit at the beginning of the sixteenth century, New Spain not only became the largest and most prosperous of the Spanish colonies, but also one of the most ethnically and racially diverse. African slaves were key players in the creation of Spanish wealth, so much so that their presence, alongside that of the colony's aboriginal subjects, both deeply fascinated and intensely troubled the "white" elites of the peninsula. The importance of blacks and browns to the articulation of an emergent "white" and "Spanish" identity necessitated the deployment of modes of normalization and control that would allow for the continuation of the thin fiction of a (white) European Spain while nonetheless continuing—and accelerating—the practices of cultural and economic dispersal that stood at the center of the empire's rapid economic and cultural development.

Among the most significant responses to this phenomenon were the hundreds of *casta* (caste) paintings that were produced in seventeenth- and eighteenth-century New Spain. Often extremely decorative and luxuriant, the paintings at once reproduced and extended the anxieties we saw on display in Ribera's *Maddalena Ventura, con su marido.* The concern with production and reproduction is ever-present in the images. Father, mother, and child, light, dark, and mixed, are unendingly examined, giving voice to a developing/modernizing racialism (white and black produce mulatto; mestizo and Indian produce coyote; white and mulatto produce *morisca*) as well as the fascination with both the danger and vibrancy of Spanish colonialism.

Both a master of style and iconography and a self-conscious promoter of the interests of colonial artists, Miguel Cabrera (1695?–1768?) was easily one of the most accomplished of the *casta* artists in eighteenth-century New Spain.[17] Cabrera assiduously struggled to rescript the distinction between colony and metropole, suggesting that the luxury, exuberance, and most especially the originality of New Spain were absolutely necessary for the production of an expansive and self-confident imperial culture. He evinced a surprisingly effective aesthetic naïveté, working throughout his career not to obscure but instead to make patently apparent the intimate connection between colonization and humanism. In a 1763 masterwork entitled *De español y negra, mulata* (*From Spaniard and Black, Mulatta*), Cabrera dresses the sobering frankness of racialist/colonialist ideology in a surprisingly sophisticated system of technical and iconographic practices (see figure I.2).

As with *La mujer barbuda,* the familial tableau is itself a study in the articulation of light and dark, life and death, birth and stillbirth. To the right of the painting a dark (African?) mother stands erect and aloof, maintaining contact with neither her "husband" nor her child. As she is dressed in a midnight-black shawl, her presumed racial distinction is made that much more obvious. She becomes, in fact, a sort of elemental personage, an ideograph. The flowered print of her skirt and the basket of ripe vegetables she carries in her left hand suggest an impersonal fecundity, an ability to give that is embedded less in her will than in her essence. With her right hand she gestures toward the downcast eyes of her child's father. His handsome, immaculately drawn face and his large, light-colored hat rescue him from the emasculation and obscu-

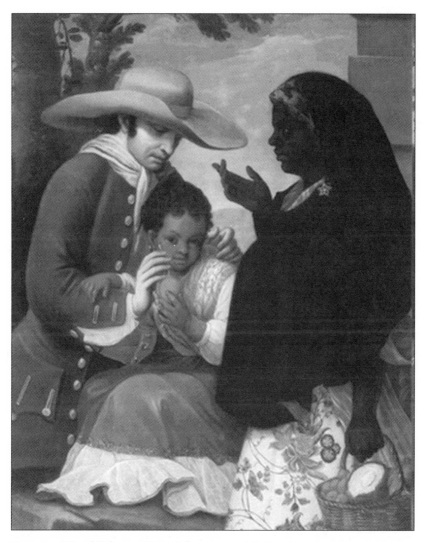

Figure I.2. Miguel Cabrera, *De español y negra, mulata* (1763).

rity that we saw with Maddalena Ventura's spouse, while shielding both himself and his child from the menacing threat of the mother's imposing Africanity. At the same time, the hat's large red ribbon reminds the viewer of both the blood that has been spilled in order to establish the luxuriant order of the painting and the revivification of masculine prerogative that the Spanish colonialist adventure in the Americas allows. The unchecked power of *La mujer barbuda* has been domesticated. The (American) child whom we find in the work of both Ribera and Cabrera leans heavily on the arm of her white father. Indeed, she is fashioned here as a delectable product, brightly dressed in red, white, blue, and gold. The tightly knotted severity of her mother's hair has given way to an abundance of loose—or at least looser—curls. She will be both productive and reproductive. Though yet a girl, the fullness of a pubescent breast is suggested through the careful placement of what appears to be an orange held in her left hand, a gesture that rearticulates her African mother's act of "freely" giving her fruits (child included) to the white colonialist. The primary action of the painting is the girl's nonchalant offering of her bounty to her covetous father, his right ring finger almost on the verge of making contact with the plant's ripe "nipple," thereby reiterating his claim on his American crop.

I hope it is clear at this point that part of the reason that I have chosen to pair Spain and African America is that both cultural formations are easily recognized as sites of what one might think of as (cultural) promiscuity. I want, that is, to expand radically our understanding of the history of the protocols of race and space that underwrite—and determine—contemporary cultural studies. Stated in a more vulgar manner, the enslavement of millions of Africans produced a profoundly destabilizing cultural and linguistic leveling that reconstructed many distinct national and ethnic traditions as nothing more exotic than "the Black." In the face of this reality, one can hardly criticize the many Africans and descendants of Africans who, when confronted by the panicked and shrill claim that Europeans and the descendants of Europeans somehow continue in their ancient specificities and stand above the hardscrabble facts of world history, counter that though Europe possesses a wealth of cultural diversity, it has been radically restructured by the racialist ideologies it worked so assiduously to create. I turn to Spain not only because it is patently obvious that the country's claims to whiteness are so very thin, but also and more importantly because by attending to the history of Spanish (cultural) unification and expansion in relation to the history of Atlantic slavery and the development of a peculiar African American community, one imagines that we might eventually develop enough critical/ethical subtlety to free all of us from the unrelenting nightmares of racialism and white supremacy.

It is only recently that Spain and the Iberian Peninsula could easily be considered either European or white. Ever visible, Africa is less than ten miles away from the Spanish city of Tarifa. It is widely assumed, moreover, that the Iberians, the people who gave the peninsula its name, arrived from the "dark continent" around 1600 BC. They were followed later by "Asiatic" Phoenicians, hailing from present-day Lebanon, and Celts crossing the Pyrenees around 600 BC.[18] What is certain is that Iberia developed specifically as a dynamic meeting point for traveling peoples coming from Africa, Asia, and Europe. Eventually Romans, "Germans," Visigoths, and North African Arabs would cross either the Pyrenees or the Strait of Gibraltar in large numbers, adding to the cosmopolitan and multiethnic nature of the peninsula. Thus there has never been a singular Spanish people. Instead, nearly four thousand years of Iberian history has been marked by increasingly violent attempts to substitute abstract conceptions of white Western homogeneity and unity (Man) for the intense (human) complexity that the region and its various communities have always demonstrated.

Where this fact is most apparent is in the vexed relationship that Spaniards continue to have with the so-called Arab and Muslim world. By the eighth century AD, Arabs dominated much of the peninsula. Syrian-born Abd-al-Rahman I ruled most of Spain from his capital in present-day Córdoba until his death in 788, establishing close and mutually beneficial economic and cultural connections between Iberia, North Africa, and the Middle East (Pierson, *History of Spain*, 25–26). Moorish emirs subsequently used their considerable wealth and often massive armies to push relentlessly northward, eventually arriving as far as the city of Marseilles. All along the way, however, they were met by the hostile and resistant Christian kingdoms of Castile, Asturias, Aragon, Leon, Navarre, and Catalonia. Indeed, the centuries of war between the "Muslim" south and the "Christian" north provided much of the impetus for an often fragile and contentious process of unification as northern monarchs sought the aid of their Christian counterparts in their struggles against the Arabs. Not until January 2, 1492, were Ferdinand and Isabella able to drive Boabdil from Granada, where he sat enthroned among the handsome buildings and lush grounds of the breathtakingly beautiful Alhambra. Immediately thereafter, relentlessly thorough Isabella had the large community of practicing Jews expelled from Spain while allowing both Jewish—and eventually Muslim—converts, *conversos* and *moriscos*, to remain (Pierson, *History of Spain*, 51–52).

The story that is most well known—and obsessively repeated—about this grandest of the grand "Spanish" queens, however, is that in the very year that she presumably purged Spain of the last of its Muslims and Jews, she contracted with the Genoese adventurer Cristoforo Colombo to search for a direct ocean route to the Indian subcontinent, initiating the journey that resulted in the European "discovery" of the Americas. Under the leadership of Ferdinand and Isabella, Spaniards would become primary architects of what we now know as globalization, eventually colonizing not only much of the Americas, but also the Philippines and Guam. Of course the engine that drove this activity was Atlantic slavery. What most concerns me at this juncture, however, is the fact that though the conquests of Ferdinand and Isabella presumably solidified the peninsula's Christian and "white" bona fides, they were nonetheless established on an unstable set of historical paradoxes that would have far-reaching implications for Spanish and Atlantic culture.

If one considers the major points of the brief history that I have just provided, it becomes possible to see a series of obvious cracks in the ideological structure of the Spanish national mythology. First, Ferdinand and Isabella were not the king and queen of Spain per se, but of Castile and Aragon, kingdoms that remained distinct until the couple's marriage. Second, though the last of the "Moorish" kings was forced from the peninsula and into present-day Morocco, he nonetheless left behind scores of Muslims and Jews, those *conversos* and *moriscos*, whose conversions were so doubtful that the Inquisition was established—at least in part—in order to check the presumed prevarication and heresy that the royal couple suspected were constantly taking place in the very heart of the "Catholic" peninsula. Finally, while the discovery of America and the opening of trade with the Far East worked to establish Spain's Golden Age, it also allowed for the constant movement of individuals, goods, and wealth onto, through, and out of the peninsula. Thus the apogee of Spanish wealth and culture was achieved at the very moment when the spatial, cultural, ethnic, and linguistic limits of the country seemed most porous and uncertain.

As Jeremy Lawrance has noted, after the sale of the first African slaves in Portugal in 1444, the Iberian Peninsula soon had one of the largest black populations in Europe, with an estimated 100,000 slaves living in what we now think of as Spain by the mid-sixteenth century. As early as the late fifteenth century, there were enough black freed persons in Seville, Barcelona, and Valencia to support confraternities.[19] Moreover, by the time of the Seville census of 1565, blacks constituted more than 7 percent of the city's population.[20] The fact that in our contemporary discussions of Spain, particularly its unenviable location at the center of the global financial crisis that began in 2007 as well as the hysteria surrounding unwanted "foreign" migrants to Europe, there is so little consideration of the quite significant presence of Africans on the peninsula before and *after* 1492 is itself evidence of the remarkable structural—and ideological—work that was performed during the Reconquista. The expulsion of Muslims and Jews from the peninsula, the denial of the fleshy truth of the necessary/inevitable/enviable mixing of Christian, Muslim, Jew, African, and European, was never simply a martial exercise but also a largely successful attempt to erase knowledge of the long and extremely complex history of Spain's intimate connection to Africa and Africans and to substitute a tinny conception of so-called white and European identity, an identity that would prove invaluable as Spaniards pursued the conquest and colonization of huge swaths of the planet.[21]

* * *

As will become increasingly obvious as you travel through *Archives of Flesh*, my efforts to bring together the variety of texts, contexts, and methods that structure this work are facilitated by a number of reasonably well considered guesses. One of the most clearly defined of these builds upon the fact that the United States became a self-consciously imperial power after divesting Spain of the last of its most significant colonies during the 1898 Spanish-American War. Moreover, even as Spanish culture was disrupted after the country's quick defeat at the hands of the Americans, many Spanish intellectuals, including Federico

García Lorca, believed that the changes the war brought might "res-cue" the country from its "stifling" traditionalism. Meanwhile, African Americans took great pride in the fact that black soldiers played a decisive role in the conflict. More important still, African American intellectuals, especially Du Bois, Robeson, Hughes, Himes, Wright, and Larsen, recognized in Spain a country whose "awkward" relation-ship to Europe resembled their own relationships with America. Black intellectuals continued to remain deeply interested in Spain from 1898 through the Spanish Civil War and on through the years of the Franco regime. Robeson, Hughes, Larsen, Himes, and Wright traveled there. Himes, Wright, and Hughes wrote extensively about their experiences. Meanwhile, many other African American artists ranging from Romare Bearden and Miles Davis to Lynn Nottage and Bob Kaufman have uti-lized "Spanish themes" in their works. For Spaniards, African American culture represented both the promise and the danger of modernity. Lorca treated black life in Harlem with pronounced concern in his post-humously published collection *Poeta en Nueva York* (*Poet in New York*), largely a chronicle of his 1929–1930 visit to the United States and Cuba. Moreover, Picasso's interest in African or "tribal" sculpture was filtered through a pan-Africanist sensibility that owes a great deal to African American intellectuals and intellectual practices.

Still, I hope not simply to retrace the demonstrably broad and deep connections between African Americans and Spaniards. This book is ultimately an effort to transgress and erase the imagined boundaries that continue to demarcate not only the African, the European, and the American, but more important still, the Man, the human, and the animal. I will attempt throughout to make sense of the continual reap-pearance of Spain in the African American intellectual archive by filter-ing my awareness of this reality through an understanding of the long struggle by black individuals and communities against the lack of full consideration of black life within humanism's main precincts. I have less desire to name something like a "black Spain" than I do to use the Af-rican American consideration of Spain and the Hispanic as a powerful heuristic. In the hands of the intellectuals whom we will examine in this book, Spain becomes a particularly creative means by which to de-liver us all from the choking hold of the racialist, anti-black conceits that structure so much of humanistic inquiry.

In the pages that follow, I will produce a theoretical, historical, and aesthetic treatment of the relation between space, race, ethnicity, humanity, and animality in the works of Langston Hughes, Richard Wright, Chester Himes, Federico García Lorca, Nella Larsen, Lynn Nottage, and Pablo Picasso. As I hope is obvious by now, I will attempt throughout to pay close attention to the ways that slavery, colonization, and military conflict have contributed to the aesthetic practices of American and Spanish intellectuals. Beginning with a treatment of the intimate interrelations between gender, aesthetics, and war making, particularly as these are demonstrated in the participation of African American troops in the Spanish-American War and the Spanish Civil War, I argue that even in the progressive archival practices that attend the memorialization of leftist militancy, we see a stunningly naïve reiteration of the necessity of the "little person," the oppressed—and compressed—human form, within our most cherished procedures of history making and aestheticization. Working in a similar vein, I will strive in the next two chapters to demonstrate how Federico García Lorca and Langston Hughes continued to resist the leveling that is so much a part of the structure of modernity. In Hughes's case, he plays with the matter of light and dark in order to imagine forms of human subjectivity that are not wholly structured by capitalism and white supremacy, in order, that is, to name a subjectivity in which the flesh is not always already rejected. In the process, he returns repeatedly to the figure of the prostitute. Indeed, Hughes utilizes images of women and girls selling sex in order to demonstrate the complex relation of mind to body that so vexes modern intellectuals. Similarly, Lorca's fascination with so-called *duende*, or soul, and the low individuals whom he takes to most represent it (Gypsies, women, and homosexuals) grows out of an awareness that the structures and practices of modernity tend at once to extend and obscure individuality. Thus Lorca is truly equivocal when confronted with "two Spains," one modern, the other traditional. He is both celebratory and fretful in the face of a comforting yet stifling Andalusian domesticity. At the same time, he both courts and rejects the freedom and seeming fungibility of the traveling gypsy and the urban homosexual.

I then examine Chester Himes's and Richard Wright's vexed relationships to Spain, narrating their attempts finally to rationalize Western humanism's many contradictions as they make their peripatetic marches through the peninsula in search of the primitivism and paganism that they assume pervades the whole of Spanish life. In the process, they at once criticize and ratify the very processes of abstraction and compression that so much within the practice of Atlantic slavery was meant to enforce. Indeed, both Himes and Wright make bitter retreats from what they take to be a benighted Spain, treating the country as a sort of ugly, inconvenient memory, a scar capable of reminding the modern black intellectual of a dark, distant, and embarrassing past. Yet in both cases they attempt to extract some form of redemption from the country's marginality, to discern on Spanish ground alternatives to the worst aspects of white supremacy and anti-human violence.

I end with a conclusion in which I read Pablo Picasso's 1937 masterpiece *Guernica* and his fifty-eight-work 1957 series *Las meninas* (named in honor or Velázquez's 1656 portrait of the Infanta Margarita Teresa) against contemporary American playwright Lynn Nottage's tragicomic play of race, desire, and intrigue in the court of Louis XIV, also named *Las Meninas*. Paying careful attention to the economy of repetition that each artist deploys as they rearticulate—and de-articulate—codes of representation made plain by Velázquez, I use my examination of the multiple intertextualities binding Picasso and Nottage in order to argue that the necessary task of reconsidering the conceptual structures of Western humanism might easily devolve into metaphysics if we cannot integrate our understanding of radical disruptions in the history of philosophy with our awareness of similarly radical disruptions in politics and economics. Examining Nottage's relentlessly historicist play alongside Picasso's masterworks, we come to understand that the codes of modern representation cannot be broadly understood in the absence of sustained consideration of the effect of slavery and colonization on even and especially the most central, most celebrated locations in elite European and American culture.

1

War Archive

Some stories are too complicated, too dear to tell with elegance. On the afternoon of June 18, 2006, Chanel Petro-Nixon, a sixteen-year-old eleventh grader at Brooklyn's sprawling Boys and Girls High School, left her home in Bedford-Stuyvesant to apply for a job at a local Applebee's restaurant. Her body was found four days later stuffed into a trash bag and dumped in front of 212 Kingston Avenue in the adjacent neighborhood of Crown Heights. The girl was a casualty of war. She left home a typical Brooklyn teenager, with processed hair and a face full of red and brown possibility, only to be caught in one of the many snares systematically laid for the weak and unwary. Was she murdered for her trainers, her phone, her sex? A broken body left on the side of a busy city street, Chanel's corpse represented a stunningly efficient closure of a key circuit within Atlantic society and culture. Like her lost, nameless, and long-forgotten ancestors, the girl was refuse, a creature whose gender, class, and color established her as "only flesh," an entity indistinguishable from her use value. No one was shocked that she was killed, only that the killing was so uneconomical and messy. To attach blame to something as common and expected as the murder of a black girl would be a far too gummy, much too sentimental procedure. The angel of history turns its bemused face in our direction, stunned by the clumsy vigor with which we mourn the ever-increasing detritus. How strange, how profoundly impotent, to pick through reeking mountains of trash, vainly seeking redemption in hastily discarded relics.

This is an essay about war. It is a necessarily confused meditation on the peculiar ways systematic violence against humans is narrated in the liberal communications industries of the United States and Europe. It is a shocked articulation of the blatantly apparent gender, race, and class biases that attend these narratives. Every day, ships and planes embark from the shores of my country loaded with men and hardware ever ready to release breathtaking violence against real and imagined threats to what we name "our way of life." This, we are told, is war, the sovereign practice of Man. At home the violence is just as omnipresent but never so spectacularly or ostentatiously celebrated. The beatings, shootings, endless identity checks, and mass incarcerations continue apace with no real end in sight. Yet we are reminded daily of the privileges, honors, and responsibilities that are the hallmarks of membership in this grandest of the grand hordes. One must stand in the light of Manhood or risk sinking again into the muck. Domestic space becomes martial space. The female and the black must be attacked, must be systematically exploited in order to maintain the basic, everyday ideological structures that support Man's Pyrrhic victories over his animal self.

This is an essay about archives. It is an attempt to make plain the intimate connection between systematic forms of violence and the methods by which we identify, evaluate, store, catalog, and transmit what we take to be the most precious examples of civilization and tradition. In the process I mean to provoke a radical blurring of the "obvious" distinction between practices of war and intellectual/institutional practices of documentation. I argue that the clumsiness with which the contemporary intellectual is expected to approach the (non)topic of a viciously murdered black girl is itself a continuation of not only a process in which black life is continually sacrificed to the exigencies of white supremacy and capitalism, but also one in which the value of our intellectual practices is often predicated on how far we can remain from any direct engagement with this fact. If one takes seriously the reality that notwithstanding her age, race, gender, and class, Chanel Petro-Nixon was a living/struggling/resistant subject, then it becomes essential that we treat her murder not as the culmination of a process in which the "stillborn" black, the individual who never achieves social status, is inevitably culled, but instead as part of a centuries-long process in which (black female) potentiality has been actively targeted for exploitation. I reject out of hand the liberal conceit that systematic murder and abuse are first and foremost effects of ancient and not yet fully conquered forms of racism and woman hating. Chanel's murder was not an atavistic act. Instead it should be seen as evidence of the absolute modernity (one is wont to say sobriety) of her attackers. It is the quite logical continuation of the basic modes of human intercourse developed in the crucible of colonization and Atlantic slavery. I will state again, therefore, my disappointment with and distrust of those humanistic disciplinary practices that were developed precisely to articulate—and then obscure—the ideology of Man through recourse to modes of aloof scholasticism that sniff at profound forms of violence as unfortunate, but nonetheless not quite possessing enough conceptual weight to unbalance "ancient" modes of study and critique.

I have allowed myself to dwell on this subject, to admit my unseemly fears and frustrations, because there is no way that I can maintain the ethical project that I have launched without paying attention to the reality that the structures and ideologies of war have so indelibly marred the most basic discursive and ideological assemblies of humanism. Of course I mean to maintain focus on the fact that slavery and enslavement were first and foremost martial procedures such that for better or worse, to be the descendant of slaves, to walk with a black/brown/yellow/red face through the crowded streets of New York, is to be read as defeated (and thus hostile and dangerous), while to be the descendants of slavers, one's face glowing with hues of cream and pink, is to be marked as conquering (and therefore slothful and smug). I also mean to state unequivocally that war is by definition a raced, classed, and gendered practice, one in which the name of the game is at once to delimit radically the space available to females, people of color, and working-class persons while also actively and energetically exploiting their productive and reproductive potentialities. Our incessant scripting of war as something that happens "over there" is a means by which not only to service (read discipline, punish, incarcerate, extinguish) the "homeland" but also to attach the most blandly sentimental narrative procedures to the process, to evacuate accounts of war of any sustained and complicated consideration of the constant—and necessary—implication of the domestic and especially the female in broadly organized processes of bloodletting. It is for this reason that I continually note that domestic space is always already war space. Maintaining this stance allows us, among other things, to move past sentimental accounts of slavery and colonization, the belief that these systems were first and foremost non-systematic returns of Man's natural tendency toward racialist antipathy, "fixable" disruptions in the march of humanist ideality, lapses that one might more or less easily address through essentially therapeutic practices of good feeling and liberal kindheartedness. The brittleness of our narratives of war is evidence of how little we have allowed ourselves to imagine what the everyday effects of the martial cultures of slavery and colonization actually are. Part of the reason that it is easy for charges of white supremacy to be so effortlessly batted away is the simple fact that our methods of naming are often so very underdeveloped and parochial. We become obsessed with whether a pink thigh might nestle comfortably against a brown one on the seat of a crowded subway car, because to admit that all of our scurrying to and fro is established by—and in support of—efforts to extract value directly from the flesh of huge swaths of the human population would entail levels of radicalization that would forever disrupt the humdrum comforts of our ever so meticulously undertheorized lives.

I am looking for a rhetorical bridge with which to join my shock and disgust about the death of Chanel Petro-Nixon, the desecration of her flesh, with the presumably noble history of Black American engagements with Spain and Spaniards during both the so-called Spanish-American War and especially the Spanish Civil War. I want to avoid the exultant narratives of black male military advancement that structure so much within the official archives of these events. The gender politics surrounding black men's participation in American military campaigns inevitably turn on the rearticulation of dominant notions of Manhood, notions that insistently repeat models of diminution, compression, and leveling of the human form, which are key aesthetic/ideological manifestations of the Man/human bifurcation that stands at Western humanism's conceptual center. The African American soldier remains infinitely aware that perhaps his most important challenge is to collapse the distinction between the black male and the (black) Man. A significant portion of the black soldier's militancy involves his constant effort to increase his stature, to articulate himself in ever more expansive arenas, particularly the grand theater of (anti)colonialist war.

In this sense, black male militants have simply continued in a minor key the androcentric and deeply homoerotic rhetoric of a masculinity seeking its release from the suffocating limitations of a feminized domesticity. Even Paul Gilroy's extremely clever articulation of the sailing ship as a living "micro-political system in motion" is built upon a set of fantastic images of all-male environments that is in serious need of revision. The image of the ship is so potent precisely because it evokes both confinement *and* expansiveness. The sailor enters into the (in)security of the floating cell in order to achieve his escape. Still, even as I can readily see the complexity and beauty of this image, I recognize that it cannot contain all the possibilities available to us in the fecund pit of Atlantic modernity. Though the ship is a key metaphor for Atlantic culture, it is not *the* key. Throughout *Archives of Flesh* I focus equally on ports, brothels, prisons, camps, and markets, locations at which the complicated workings of gender might be more easily discerned, if only because they are less encumbered by dreams of male exclusivity. I insist that we reevaluate the image of discarded female flesh with which I began this chapter. We must recognize the important work that this ugly picture does as we attempt to define the contours of modern culture and aesthetics. Moreover, as I have argued already, the inability to read this image outside the most deeply sentimental modes is itself evidence of an ideological assembly in which the black and the female are always already dead subjects such that the unceremonial dispersal of their remains is less a travesty than a matter of unremarkable, if unsightly, housekeeping. I will ask, therefore, not so much that we bring the wars home, but instead that we acknowledge that these homes, these sturdy desks, handsome chairs, and pleasant scenes glimpsed through leaded glass are not simply the detritus of war but also the very modes through which the "obvious" need to protect "us" from "them" are advanced.

They Are Called Negritos

Perhaps the most important, most useful conceptual advance in African Diaspora Studies of this generation was Brent Edwards's out-of-hand rejection of teleological notions of pan-Africanist structures of feeling ("I am African because I feel African") in favor of a rigorously materialist—and dynamic—conception of diaspora in which the focus remains on structure and production, the many individuals and institutions articulating and translating African identity between key nodal points in Africa, Europe, and the Americas.[1] What many scholars of the African diaspora either miss or ignore, however, is the fact that in this work, traditional intellectuals were—and are—a distinct minority, one decidedly marginal to the project of articulation that Edwards so ably narrates. African Americans are much more likely to exit the confines of the fifty states as working-class laborers, especially soldiers, than as novelists, painters, dancers, critics, or political activists. I would press this argument even further by returning again to the idea of refuse with which I began this chapter. The black in transit is perhaps most often transported as a thing that has lost value in its "native" location. What is, in fact, being transmitted is an empty cipher, a container into which meaning and value might readily be added. Blackness becomes first and foremost a cultural artifact, an idea, raw material waiting to be processed. Still, I must admit that I am delighted by the way that the word "refuse" allows for a species of undisciplined and obstinate theoretical play. Blackness may be that location ever filled with trash, detritus, and useless ephemera, but it is also a location of repudiation, negation, and critique. One of the few dodges available to the subject who has been discarded and discounted is indeed the ability to refuse, to resist rearticulation into dominant social and ideological structures, to decline to bow (or perhaps to do so with a sort of theatrical hesitancy) before the most sacred totems of "civilized" society. The black face that presents itself too abruptly within the precincts of self-satisfied (white Western) civilization seems always to be saying "No." Certainly one of the reasons that African Americans are so easily read as angry, dangerous, and criminal is that our very presence short-circuits jubilant narratives of American and European exceptionalism. Even a single dark individual in the cheering crowd reminds one that these grand boulevards and regal monuments, those stunning feats of cultural sophistication might easily—and rightly—be read as emblems of bloodthirsty acts of violence, acts made more obscene still by rigorous enforcement of a sort of ungainly and only half-effective cultural amnesia.

To gain deep insight into the mechanics of African American internationalism, one must always consider the evidence of the remarkably consistent ways American and European cultural productions have depended upon slavery, colonization and war as primary vessels for their development. The prosecution of what was dubbed the "Splendid Little War," referring to the relatively easy 1898 victory of the United States over Spain, accomplished between the months of April and August with engagements in Cuba, Puerto Rico, and a remarkable naval victory in Manila, was self-consciously understood by President McKinley and other members of the American political elite as a necessary continuation of the role of the United States as a specifically white

Anglo-American country whose destiny was to dominate presumably backwards "colored" peoples in both the Atlantic and the Pacific.[2] It takes no great stretch of intellect or imagination to understand that with the acquisition of Alaska with its largely aboriginal population in 1867; the consolidation of U.S. influence in Latin America, home to huge communities of blacks, Indians, mulattoes, and mestizos; the annexation of Hawai'i in 1894; the near total domination of the Cuban economy and its foreign policy after the enactment of the Platt Amendment; and the occupation of the Philippines until the country's independence in 1946, American "republicans" had little trouble understanding and announcing themselves as the prophets of white supremacy and colonization.[3]

What gives pause, however, what stuns the less than romantic student of African Diaspora Studies, is the fact that 1898 was also a key moment in not only the articulation of African American internationalism, but also the articulation of what one might think of as "modern blackness," a post-slavery, "New Negro" aesthetic in which black individuals utilized the mechanics of war to proclaim an African American avant-garde. Taking place only two years after the Supreme Court's infamous *Plessy v. Ferguson* decision, which initiated more than five decades of state-sponsored, federally supported racial segregation, the Spanish-American War provided a number of key opportunities for African American soldiers and the communities they represented. As Willard B. Gatewood rightly notes, the war gave many black men their first opportunity to fight for the United States as citizens of the republic. The larger-than-life image of the black in uniform, eager to risk his all in the service of country, would presumably blunt the viciousness of increasingly hostile whites against their black compatriots. Barring that, the "colored" nations of Cuba, Puerto Rico, and the Philippines could provide key outlets for ambitious young blacks eager to advance in business and the professions.[4] "I may visit the United States now and then," wrote African American physician and soldier W. C. Warmsley to the *Washington, D.C., Bee,* "gaze once more upon the monument, . . . visit the Capitol Building and White House, converse with my many friends and acquaintances and again enjoy their proverbial hospitality, but to make the States my home, never!" (quoted in Gatewood, "*Smoked Yankees,*" 231).

For black soldiers, participation in the war involved a set of complex negotiations among competing ideologies of gender, race, and nation.

As Warmsley noted, enlisting in the Ninth Infantry and practicing his trade in the relative comfort of eastern Cuba provided a means of at least partial escape from the racial terror of the United States. What I would add to this commentary, however, is the fact that this form of martial escape was absolutely necessary to the production of the idea of the New Negro. Indeed, the post-slavery African American individual confident in *his* citizenship was a notion self-consciously fashioned in the crucible of war, most specifically the Civil War and, as we will see, the wars of Indian removal and the Spanish-American War. It was an identity built upon a negotiation with (if not exactly a refusal of) the systematic violence practiced at all levels of American society against black people.

As many African American intellectuals—including many of W. C. Warmsley's fellow soldiers—recognized, the U.S. incursions into both Cuba and especially the Philippines were largely motivated by the very rabid white supremacy that stood at the heart of the *Plessy* decision.[5] The route that took the physician from Washington, D.C., to Santiago was one that meandered through some of the stranger peculiarities of American-style racialism. Dr. Warmsley was a member of one of the four all-black "immune units" (the Seventh, Eighth, Ninth, and Tenth Volunteer Infantries), a subset of ten regiments composed of individuals thought to be immune to yellow fever because of previous exposure (the whites) or innate racial "qualities" (the blacks). It was only in these units, built upon the presumed physical peculiarity of the colored animal, that black officers were commissioned. The gate through which the African American soldier had to pass in order to gain his ostensible liberation was one consecrated to the unremitting belief in his biological inferiority (see Gatewood, "Smoked Yankees," 10–11).

At the same time, I want to remain focused on the fact that this process involved the self-conscious manipulation of ideologies of both race *and* gender. If you accept my assertion that the soldiers of the Spanish-American War helped to establish the original template for the so-called New Negro, then it is also important to remember that this newly established self-confident black identity was produced in relation to forms of sociality dependent upon ostentatious retreats from the domestic and the female. The New Negro gained his Manhood "out there," gun in hand, the clumsiness of American-style race and gender norms thrown by the wayside in favor of the modern modes of subjectivity for which the black subject presumably yearned.

In making this point, I would warn against assuming that what was on display in the black immune units was simply the continuation of ancient forms of racial antipathy that originated in slavery. On the contrary, both Dr. Warmsley and his white interlocutors were specifically modern. The segregation that he suffered was much more a product of the twentieth century than the nineteenth. The *Plessy* decision represented the court's attempt to rationalize the hodgepodge of law and custom surrounding race in the United States by settling the matter of where a black began and a white ended through rigorous application of the so-called one-drop rule. Part of what segregation produced for blacks was an ability to disestablish the idea that somehow African Americans were nothing more than bastards of an (interracial) American family. Extremely light-skinned Homer Plessy had the vexing question of his genealogy settled by the Supreme Court. He was no longer a creole existing on a continuum between black and white, but instead a (new) Negro, an individual with the potential to establish alternative accounts of his proper relation to the national. In one fell swoop the court helped to establish the white supremacist protocols that still dominate American society while releasing Negro citizens from having to confront complicated questions of primogeniture and paternity. Black men's military service represented a settling of accounts. The disequilibrium of the phrase "mama's baby, papa's maybe" was jettisoned in favor of the bold articulation of a newly established (and indeed war-hardened) black patriarchy, a subjectivity cleansed of the taint of boundarylessness, the shame of the masters' largesse.

Though many of the African American men who participated in the Spanish-American War were volunteers, a significant portion were black regulars drawn from the four regiments established immediately after the Civil War: the Twenty-Fourth and Twenty-Fifth Infantries and the Ninth and Tenth Cavalries. These men had previously been stationed in the western territories and were utilized heavily in the wars of Indian removal, as prior to 1898, military policy did not permit African American soldiers to carry weapons east of the Mississippi River. Commanded entirely by white officers, these soldiers, especially the cavalrymen collectively known as the Buffalo Soldiers, developed reputations as fiercely effective fighters. What I want to warn against, however, is moving too quickly away from the difficulties inherent when one attempts to hold both the enviable reputation of the soldiers and the assumption that they were ill-prepared to act as officers in the same sentences. Instead I would suggest that the one follows logically from the other. It is the black soldier's modernity, not his primitivism, that establishes him as at once a talented fighter and a disabled intellect. Severed from the pastoralism that defined enslavement, he became something altogether new, a figure not yet become a subject, a living being permanently cut off from its roots and thus unencumbered by profundities of will or complexities of intellect. The usefulness of the freedman, at least once he was dressed in khaki and blue, operated in direct relation to the fact that he had been left over—refused, if you will—thus made that much more available to the expansionist projects of the post–Civil War U.S. government. As a consequence, his ferocity as a soldier stemmed in part from his ability literally to lose himself in the work he was called upon to do. He was dangerous not because he was an angry individual with a gun, but because there was no clear distinction between man and weapon. Smoking metal and human flesh were fused into one entity, producing the very half-man/half-machine cyborg that continues to so confuse and fascinate.[6] Ask an American general why send the blacks to confront the natives, and one imagines his quick, undigested response: "When confronted by a savage, send a monster."

Again, I will have been read incorrectly if my readers assume that what I am describing are forms of racialism that have long since gone out of favor. Instead, linking the specific hostility to black soldiers with anxieties confronted by Americans as they witnessed their country undergo quick modernization, I am trying to establish the primary aesthetic/ideological modes that structure the basic gender and race protocols of Western humanism. The black stands at exactly the location at which the conceptual and ethical difficulties involved in maintaining the distinction between human and Man become most palpable. He is a subject whose lack of connection to his "native" land produces him as a potentially perfect modern, an individual freed from the enervating procedures and rhythms of traditional life. Even his much-maligned skin, the marker of not only his animality and barbarism, but also his lack of deep connection to the United States, operates as both the most disabling of encumbrances and a profoundly fruitful site of possibility. As the dark individual, even the dark individual with a rifle slung across his shoulders, can never represent America per se, he has the ability, the "freedom," to transplant himself, to establish connections where presumably none previously existed.

> We are up here in the mountains, where you can hear or see nothing but wild Caribous, deer and ponies. We eat both the deer and Caribous, but not the ponies; we haven't come to eating horseflesh yet. This is a fine little place. The people up here are different from the other Natives. They are called Negritos. They don't wear any clothes but a gee-string and are strung from head to foot with brass band. They don't understand anything. They carry a knife called a bolo, and are a very mean people. They live on rice and dried fish. They are ruled by a president. They never stay in their huts at night, but go into the mountains, returning about 4 o'clock in the morning. They make fine cigars. You can get about fifty for four clackers, which equals one cent in our money. The government has about 400 working the road between here and San Jose and pay them $1 a week and their chow-chow; and they eat every hour. The soldiers are all doing well. They would have better health if they would let that beno alone. It is a drink that the Filipinos make. Poco Tempo [sic]. Tell my friends that I am just the same as a Filipino. (Quoted in Gatewood, "Smoked Yankees," 276–77)

This outstanding note, written from the Philippines by Edward Brown to *The Recorder* of Indianapolis, suggests a level of ontic flexibility and playfulness that is most often associated with experiments by self-consciously postmodern intellectuals. That Brown encounters his own half-naked, knife-carrying, hardworking, cigar-smoking, and mean-spirited doppelgängers, the Negritos, forces the soldier to reconsider where he stands within the particular chain of being that he describes. The people whom Brown met, properly referred to in the Philippines as Agta, are small, dark-skinned persons who can still be found in isolated communities throughout Southeast Asia. They were given the name Negritos (little blacks) by early Spanish explorers; it is not entirely clear whether they are direct descendants of the earliest humans or the remnants of nomadic African communities. In any case, the discursive structures that Brown utilizes to describe the community that he encounters were wholly overdetermined by the history of slavery and colonization of which his expedition to the Philippines was a part. That Spanish explorers and colonists assumed that the Agta were recently arrived Africans spoke to the breadth and complexity of the colonialist project. The presence of the Negritos reinforced the aesthetic practices that we saw with painters like Ribera and Cabrera. The fascination in Golden Age Spain with depictions of midgets, dwarves, *bufones*, *and* Negroes represented not only the fact that the "little people" were key to the support and functioning of the Spanish courts, but also that the shrinking and compartmentalization of their human potential were necessary aspects of the production of global systems of human domination, including capitalism. A Spanish explorer encountering Negritos in the Philippines was confirmed in the assumptions of human fungibility that lie at the center of colonialism. The little blacks of the Philippines, the little blacks of Africa, the little blacks of the Americas are all one and the same.

This begs the question of the African American solider, ostensible agent of American modernity, as he is invited to regard with amusement and disdain people who are snarlingly referred to as "little blacks." I would remind you of the brief military history that I sketched earlier. Brown was a member of the regular army, the Twenty-Fourth Infantry, a regiment that, stationed in the American West, regularly engaged native peoples in combat before they were deployed to fight in Cuba in 1898. The following year they were called upon to fight against insurrectionists in the Philippines. Tellingly, the Agta were not widely represented as fighters in the Filipino struggle for national independence. For American soldiers, the presence of these people represented a strange and comical exception to the complexities of geopolitics and statecraft of which they were a part. "The people up here are different from the other Natives," Brown writes. Their food, their dress, their conceptions of time all mark the Agta as aloof individuals living a presumably archaic existence not unlike the aboriginal people of the western plains. As such they became (much like the African American community) a sort of perfect resource, providing nearly free supplies of cigars and labor remunerated only by one dollar a week and regular "chow-chow." When Brown announces that he is "just the same as a Filipino," one must ask, "Which Filipino?" Is he a "Negrito," a primitive subject only vaguely aware of the complex negotiations of power taking place all around him, or is he just as sophisticated as the insurgents who have developed gorgeously effective methods by which to rob him of his life? In a sense, Brown's shock and amusement upon encountering the Agta were based in the fact that though defeated, these people could not be said to be "compromised." Their reactions to Spanish and American colonialism did not involve taking up "the master's tools," those guns attached to mahogany-colored, khaki-covered shoulders. Unlike their Negro American counterparts, they could hardly be understood to be modern or new. Brown names no clearly discernible individual among the Agta. Instead, the Negritos remain as one indistinguishable mass. They are (human) beings not yet become Men. Ostentatious in their nakedness, they lack not only class, race, and gender, but also the protocols of violence that underwrite the structures of so-called Western modernity.

The reactions of black soldiers to their experiences in the Spanish-American War are clear examples of the "camp thinking" about which Paul Gilroy warns us in his 2002 work, *Against Race*.[7] Of the many significant claims made by Gilroy, one of the most important is the idea that the public sphere is deeply marred by our overreliance on martial models of sociality in which various "racial" communities, "camps," are inevitably figured as ancient and bitter rivals. While I find this idea wholly convincing, I would push against Gilroy's tendency in *Against Race* to overvalue narratives of fascism and what he names "raciology" that take the Second World War and its aftermath as not simply key, but in a sense, elemental. Camp thinking has an extremely complex history in the United States, Spain, Cuba, Puerto Rico, and the Philippines that predates the struggle against the Axis powers. Thus I resist deployment of the term "fascism," to the extent that it presupposes a distinction, clear or otherwise, between slavery, colonization, forced migration, and the atrocities committed by Germany, Italy, Japan, and their allies. There is no way to dismantle racial peculiarity that does not involve careful attention to the specificities of the manner in which racialism and nationalist militancy have become intertwined in our most precious notions of national culture. Hastily produced propaganda notwithstanding, the African American soldiers fighting in the theaters of Cuba, Puerto Rico, and the Philippines could not be said to be generic "Americans." No such creature exists. Instead, their very presence forced a re-modulation of what we might think of as hegemonic camp mentality. Our critique must involve, then, not only a return to—and expansion of—local archives, but also a recommitment to nuanced analyses that eschew overreliance on rhetorics of sophistication and cosmopolitanism that all too often remain unself-consciously enmeshed in Anglo-American parochialism.

What the African American soldiers, both regulars and volunteers, most readily confronted as they set sail for Cuba, Puerto Rico, and the Philippines was the starkness of the ontological choices they were offered. One must leave America as either Negrito or Negro, establish oneself as a Man willing to carry a gun and use it or an unwitting target viewed through a rifle's scope. We begin to see the contours of a fascination on the part of many African American intellectuals with the ways that Spanish aesthetic practices resonate so profoundly with just this dilemma, with these intensely difficult questions concerning the nature of human subjectivity. In our nobility, vulnerable as the caribou, we were half-naked and ignorant, eating rice, dried fish, and the occasional deer. We wanted nothing more than our knives and cigars. The sour-visaged angels had not yet turned their faces in our direction. In our maturity we are dressed in the raiment of militants, the guns in our hands intricately notched, detailing the unrelieved spilling of ancestral blood. The Spaniards remind us of us. The staccato rhythms of their singing, the uneven proportions of their art reveal a people used to speaking multiple languages at once. It was inevitable that some of us would find our way to the peninsula. Whether our hands were empty or loaded with deadly metal, we had scores to settle.

Toward a Wider Horizon

On December 30, 1938, the *Daily Worker* announced a call by "Eight Outstanding Negroes" for a conference to be held the following January in Washington, D.C., in order to discuss "Spain and the Fascist Menace."[8] Signed by Max Yergan, executive secretary of the International Committee on African Affairs; A. Philip Randolph, president of the Brotherhood of Sleeping Car Porters; William Pickens of the National Association for the Advancement of Colored People; Marion Cuthbert, member of the National Board of the YMCA; the Reverend William Lloyd Imes of the famed St. James Presbyterian Church; Mary McLeod Bethune, president of Bethune-Cookman College; Dr. Julian Lewis of the Department of Pathology of Chicago University; and Channing Tobias of the National Council of the YMCA, the call was intended to present a unified front of black progressive thought. Whether they were aligned with social liberals like Bethune or labor radicals like Randolph, many African Americans, particularly those of the intellectual class, saw the Spanish Civil War as nothing less than the continuation of particularly virulent forms of anti-African, anti-black aggression by governments in both Europe and the United States. The violence in Spain and the gory methods used by white colonialists in Africa and the United States were part of one inglorious whole. The Italian invasion of Ethiopia in 1935 and the subsequent support of the Spanish rebels by both Mussolini and Hitler demonstrated conclusively that so-called European fascism was but the return home of the methods and ideologies that had long structured white supremacist projects of colonization and enslavement.

> The conference will discuss the Italian invasion of Ethiopia and the present Italian aggression in Spain: Czechoslovakia and the current demand of Germany for African colonies; Hitler's penetration of South America and the Caribbean and its significance to the civil rights of Negroes in those countries. Out of these deliberations are expected resolutions against the United States' recognition of the Italian conquest of Ethiopia and for the lifting of the embargo against Loyalist Spain. ("Negro Leaders Call Conference on Spain and Fascist Menace")

Ethiopia = Spain = Czechoslovakia = the Caribbean = the United States. There was nothing particularly new about either the ideologies or the methods being used by Franco and the Spanish rebels. They were, in fact, exactly those that had been utilized to great effect by generations of slavers and colonialists. The left propaganda produced to encourage the support of African Americans for Republican Spain made no bones about the essential connection between capitalism and white supremacy in the United States, colonialism on the African continent, and the fascist rebellion in Spain. Those black militants who traveled to Spain to fight as part of the international brigades (*brigadas internacionales*), particularly the all-American Abraham Lincoln Battalion, were quick to narrate the war as an extension of the generations of struggle against slavery and white supremacy of which they were intimately familiar.[9] Speaking of a monastery where he was housed with other recruits sneaking across the Pyrenees in order to fight on the part of the Republicans, James Yates observed, "this monastery was much like the places used by the abolitionists who temporarily housed slaves escaping from the plantations of the South in America."[10] The journey to Spain represented for black militants both an escape and a return. If capitalism, fascism, colonialism, and white supremacy could be said to have achieved anything, then it was a diminution of space between peoples and cultures. The narratives of assault, exploitation, escape, and resistance that Yates first heard as a boy growing up in Mississippi proved to be perfectly workable as he attempted to make sense of the situation in which he found himself after he entered the not so civil Spanish Civil War.

I am surprised by the amount of clarity that one finds in the materials surrounding African American participation in the Spanish Civil War. In an intellectual tradition haunted by the belief that our histories have been lost, our noble past stolen from us, one encounters in the well-preserved and well-organized collections of materials associated with the war meticulous attention given to the task of naming (as individuals) approximately 90 African American soldiers among the 2,800 or so persons who left the United States to become part of the Abraham Lincoln Battalion.[11] This reality is made that much stranger by the fact that we are not telling the stories of victorious heroes. Spain did, in fact, fall to the fascists. In the face of the impassioned cry that the rebels would not take the Republican city of Madrid (¡No pasarán!), Franco and the Spanish fascist party, the Falange, did come to power, killing nearly a third of the Lincoln Brigade and setting up a government atop the corpses of hundreds of thousands of Spaniards.

What one encounters while wading through the resources of the Abraham Lincoln Brigade Archive (ALBA), housed in the Tamiment Library and Robert F. Wagner Labor Archives of New York University, is evidence of a striking self-consciousness on the part of leftist—and often Communist—militants about not only the need to disrupt the political lethargy and ethical clumsiness of an American public still deep in the throes of the Great Depression, but also the necessity of rescripting the

many rigid articulations of race that developed out of formal segregation in the United States and the country's colonialist projects in Puerto
Rico, the Philippines, Guam, and Hawai'i. As with those eight Negro
leaders calling in late 1938 for a conference on Spain and the "fascist
menace," the propagandists working to build support for Republican
Spain were wholly aware of the fact that at the core of notions of American exceptionalism was the widespread assumption that though the vicious exploitation of the African American people was unfortunate, it
was in no way related to the colonialist projects of Europeans. African
Americans—little Negroes, if you will—are very much understood as a
people in constant need of development. Our many fetters are not forms
of persecution per se, but instead the detritus of an essentially pedagogical apparatus designed to provoke our maturation. Moreover, this
particularly self-serving version of white paternalism has been carefully
packaged and relentlessly applied to subject populations in many parts
of the globe. Americans do not exploit; we develop. We do not colonize;
we assist.

In the face of this reality, the modern and progressive African American subject had to be represented as at once militant and deeply committed to internationalism. He had to demonstrate with vigor and precision
that the "plantation Negro" with his unwavering allegiance to his white
masters was long dead. The African American had to refuse. He had
to resist the contorted idea that he represented nothing more than the
flesh into which essentially mechanical structures of (white) modernity
might be placed. The representation of individual black soldiers in the
archives that developed around their involvement in the Spanish Civil
War was itself evidence of a will to negate the namelessness and amor-
phousness of an always already only half-formed black "subject." In his
place stood a broad-shouldered "New Negro," radicalized by both the
liberation of urbanization and the insult of segregation. Though only
ninety African Americans served in the Abraham Lincoln Brigade, they
were extremely effective emblems of the leftist propaganda machine that
developed around the war because their stories fit so neatly the ideological requirements of early twentieth-century radical internationalism. "I
had read Hitler's book, knew about the Nuremberg laws," remembered
Harlemite Vaughn Love, "and I knew if the Jews weren't going to be allowed to live, then certainly I knew the Negroes would not escape and

that we would be at the top of the list." "I saw in the invaders of Spain the same people I've been fighting all my life," said Mississippian Eluard Luchelle McDaniels. "I've seen lynching and starvation, and I know my people's enemies" (quoted in Carroll, *Odyssey of the Abraham Lincoln Brigade*, 12).

The articulation of just these types of black commitments to anti-fascism and Spanish Republicanism continued unabated throughout the war. Tellingly, however, the expression of African American support for the loyalists was always understood as peculiar, a thing emanating from an essentially domestic experience of unambiguously African American culture. The New Negro would become a solidly established subject, a creature separated from his spectral past, exactly to the extent that he was able to define the contours of black specificity, racial and cultural difference that placed him on a parallel and sometimes overlapping yet nonetheless distinct path of modernization.

In an April 26, 1938, article entitled "International Letter from Paul Robeson, Jr.," the *Daily Worker* published an extremely odd note, presumably written from Moscow by the ten-year-old son of the famed singer, actor, and activist Paul Robeson. The piece titillates its readers by catering to a desire to see an articulation of Negro internationalism that though radical nonetheless continues familiar tropes of race, gender, and domesticity. "Dear Friends," he begins, "How am I ever going to answer the hundreds of letters I have received from you? . . . Oh, I know—I'll answer them collectively. And each of you must take this collective letter as your own: that is why I am saying 'Dear Friends.'"[12] What follows is a (black) child's-eye view of the major conceits and concerns of the internationalist left. Robeson tells us that his parents brought him to be educated in Moscow because "there is no race prejudice" in the Soviet Union and because he is being taught "kindness and cooperation." His grandmother, with whom he lives in the city, tells him that the religion of the country is brotherly love. Even more to the point, the boy's note carefully sentimentalizes both the war in Spain and the second Sino-Japanese War, appealing to his readers' sense of moral indignation more than their shared political commitments:

While my Dad and Mummy were in Spain, I could not help thinking of all the Spanish children and the Chinese children whose fathers and

mothers wouldn't come back and also of the thousands of children themselves being murdered by fascist bombs. And there are the children, also
of the Japanese, Italians, and Germans; they have fathers and mothers too.

What a terrible thing war is: can't we children do something about it?
We can ask our parents to work, vote and talk against it. ("International
Letter from Paul Robeson, Jr.")

Strangely, we see deployed in the pages of the *Daily Worker*, chief propaganda organ of the Communist Party of the United States, the very
rhetorical tricks long deployed by liberals. The political argument being
advanced here, the belief that progressive Americans had a pressing
need to support besieged peoples in both Spain and China, is made as
if it is no argument at all. Instead, it is but the musing of a child innocently speaking a child's sense of reality. That even a reader inclined
to agree with the logic of the piece might seriously doubt that it was
actually written by Paul Robeson Jr. is beside the point. What one sees
is a tremendously interesting experiment with propaganda. Though the
boy is in many ways an anomaly (black, upper-class, highly cultured,
expatriated), he is represented as typical. His concerns for his parents,
his language (Mummy, Dad, cheerio), and his youthful interest in sport
and games mark him as any boy anywhere minus the fact that he is
black, American, and the only child of Paul Robeson. Again, what we
see is the awkward process of aggression and conciliation that structures
New Negro identity. The highly sentimentalized rhetoric of this article
notwithstanding, it is clear that the wars of Europe, America, Africa,
and Asia take place not simply at the edges of human habitation but
also within domestic space itself. The brilliant child of Paul Robeson has
been called upon to enter the fray, the difficult contortions to which he
submits himself in the process be damned.

The game for the editors of the *Daily Worker* was one in which they
attempted to create a language capable of making plain the connections
between fascist aggression abroad and segregation in the United States,
to state without blushing the indistinction of war in its foreign and domestic iterations. We have seen already that central to this enterprise
were Paul Robeson and his family. What Robeson brought to the effort
was nothing less than the disruption of the distinction between Man
and human. His physiognomy (dark skin, broad features, kinky hair,

large stature) marked him as an animal, a creature with his ancestors' experience of enslavement written across his face; while his talent, poise, cosmopolitanism, and militancy demonstrated him as equal to any Man. He represented the ideological compromise worked out between black freed persons with the rest of American society, the very compromise cynically warped and rearticulated by the Supreme Court in the *Plessy* decision. Blacks might be accepted as moderns—and perhaps even cit-izens—in the contemporary United States, but only if they were able to continually announce and maintain an essentially unbreachable racial difference. Thus part of what the image of Robeson gives us is the ability to understand that war is in fact a place where a highly formalized set of ideological and aesthetic practices take place. Robeson was a Man, perhaps even a great Man, but one whose presence was always contained within the limiting/leveling confines of race. The Spanish theater of war was then just that, a theater. Robeson, the actor and ideologue, uses the stage provided him by Spain to rehearse a new character, a New Negro, as a mode of being in the world that had previously been unavailable to most of his audience.

In an interview with Robeson by the Cuban poet Nicolás Guillén, first published in 1938 in the Marxist journal *Mediodía*, then translated and reprinted in 1976 in the *World*, we find a surprisingly clear articu-lation of a developing ideology in which the tables seem to have been turned on white supremacists such that a black subject like Robeson is imagined as not simply human, but also the very quintessence of what modern Man could be. There is little evidence, however, that Guillén ever made his way to what one might think of as "post-racialism." In-stead, Manhood is imagined as a state one might achieve only after fully inhabiting the best traits of one's race and ethnicity:

> At the side of democracy in Spain, and on every front of struggle for its triumph, there are men of the most diverse races, from the most diverse places in the world. Silent Chinese who fire their rifles at Italians and Germans, confident that it is the same as their fight against the Japanese who profane Nanking, and Hindus who traded the dirty banks of the Ganges for the narrow waters of the Jarama; Blacks born in the Yankee south, in Cuba, in Jamaica, in Brazil.[13]

For Guillén there is no need to make a distinction, fine or otherwise, between struggles for national liberation and the march toward international socialism. At the heart of internationalism is both nationalism *and* racialism. "The Negro's position as outcast is his most powerful human driving force," Guillén argues, "a force which hurls him forward towards a wider horizon that is more universal, more just, towards a horizon for which all honorable men are struggling today."[14] The value of the African American in the Spanish Civil War was altogether caught up with the matter of his blackness, with the ways his anomalous presence in the midst of a conflict ostensibly taking place between white Europeans portended other horizons, to borrow Guillén's language, locations at which the most burdensome structures of capitalism and white supremacy might collapse in upon themselves. As a consequence, Guillén spends no time at all attempting to dismiss the fact of Robeson's racial "difference," but instead presses heavily on the correspondences between black and Spanish culture. "I belong to an oppressed race, discriminated against, one that could not live if fascism triumphed in the world," Robeson tells Guillén in response to a question about his motivations for taking up the cause of Republican Spain. "My father was a slave, and I do not want my children to become slaves" ("Spain, 1938: Guillen and Robeson Meet").

I have noted already that much of what motivated the adoration that Robeson evoked was his athleticism. His heavily muscled body represented a newly assertive and active Negro presence, the very presence on display in images of black soldiers wallowing through muddy trenches in Spain. The aesthetics of the conflict were played out between poles of good and bad, black and white, strength and weakness that were only further solidified as the fight continued. Of course what was announced and celebrated in the iconography that developed in and around the Spanish Civil War was a spectacular idea of a muscular and self-confident masculinity, the very idea carried about so ably on Paul Robeson's handsome frame. What immediately strikes one, however, is how fragile these images of male virility appear upon close examination. The fuller and bolder the drawing, the more it seems prone to cracking. Moreover, it is striking how much gender segregation is actually celebrated in war iconography. Whether one encounters the female form crumpled by the side of the road or not, her place is always and ever imagined as distinct from that of the combatants. Even when the sanctity of the domestic sphere is shattered, war is imagined to take place at a masculinist conceptual and spatial remove.

One of the reasons that the Spanish Civil War continues to be so fascinating is the fact that in an era of widespread illiteracy, the Republicans were particularly successful at using modernist innovations in graphic design to advance their arguments about the necessity of defeating fascism. They produced hundreds of posters demonstrating the ideological parameters of the threat they perceived. What is most interesting when we look at these images today is not simply that they reproduce a set of decidedly old-fashioned gender ideologies, but also that they are dripping with both homoerotic desire and profoundly complicated articulations of race. The Confederación Nacional del Trabajo (National Confederation of Labor, or CNT) is a Spanish confederation of mainly anarchist labor unions often affiliated with the Asociación Internacional de los Trabajadores (International Association of Workers, or AIT). Founded in 1910 in Barcelona, the CNT was largely responsible for expanding the role of anarchism in Spain and played a very significant role in the articulation of leftist ideology during the war, particularly through its production of posters (see figure 1.1).

What arrests one's attention when first encountering this particularly fine example of the graphic arts practiced during the Spanish Civil War is the seeming effortlessness of the work's iconography. A naked, visceral masculinity stands alone against the beast of fascism. His prepossessing form is nearly overwhelmed by the impressiveness of his musculature, making his body seem almost an experiment in modernist technique, a collection of discrete parts struggling one against the other to form an organic whole. His skin is dark, nose large, lips thick, hair close-cropped. The effect is particularly "Iberian," suggesting to the viewer that "the Spaniard" is but a nodal point in a much longer history of racial and cultural mixing. The plainly drawn phallic symbols, the hammer and the snake, remind us of what the battle is truly about. The threat of *fascismo* is the threat of penetration, the threat of the snake's tail caressing even the firmest of buttocks. Paul Robeson himself might have stood as the model for this poster. He traveled to Spain during the war and worked

Figure 1.1. Poster produced by the Comité Nacional of the CNT/AIT Spanish labor union. Held by the Biblioteca Nacional in Madrid. Used under CC BY NC SA (Creative Commons).

tirelessly in support of the Republican cause. His image appeared on the front cover of the special January 1936 issue of the leftist journal *Nueva Cultura* entitled "Hallo América." Featuring pieces by Rafael Alberti and María Teresa León as well as an article on the young poet Langston Hughes by Miguel Alejandro, *Nueva Cultura* stressed modernism, internationalism, and experimentation while demonstrating a decided emphasis on naming, if not exactly breaking down, boundaries of nation, race, and gender. As with the New Negro, the new Spaniard is a creature that has broken free of the confusion and viscosity of human animality. He has become an independent and fully formed modern. Yet the vulgar reproductive protocols of his ancestors still lurk.

Once we recognize this, it becomes that much simpler to understand why in their efforts to lampoon Falangistas and other conservative elements in Spanish society, left propagandists so often developed images of effete and enfeebled survivors of a set of social and cultural tendencies that had long since outlived their usefulness. The fascists' retreat into rebellion and disloyalty to *patria* was simply evidence of the fact that turpitude and viciousness were the only things they had left to offer. No one was more available for such critique than King Alfonso XIII (see figure 1.2). Born in 1886 shortly after the death of his father, Alfonso XII, the king came of age just after the country lost its most important colonies in the Spanish-American War. Eager to return the country to what he took to be its previous glory, Alfonso supported the leader of a 1923 coup, Don Miguel Primo de Rivera, eventually appointing him prime minister and allowing him to suspend the constitution and establish martial law. After Primo de Rivera's resignation in 1930, Alfonso's hold on the throne became increasingly tenuous. With the founding of the Second Spanish Republic (which Franco would eventually overthrow in 1939), Alfonso was forced into exile in Italy. Having never renounced his throne, he returned to Spain after the war, eventually relinquishing his title in favor of his son, Juan Carlos de Borbón. Juan Carlos would never, however, become king, having had his own access to the throne blocked by Franco in favor of Alfonso's grandson, Juan Carlos I, father of Felipe VI, the current king of Spain.

What becomes clear is that the figure of Alfonso was synonymous in the minds of many Spaniards with the greed, vulgarity, and licentiousness of the monarchy and also the profound decline in stature of the

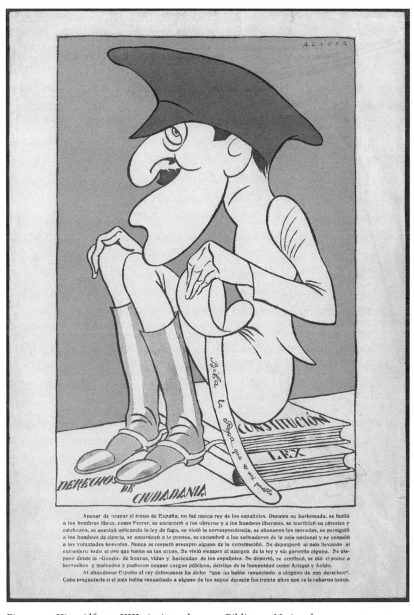

Figure 1.2. King Alfonso XIII. Artist unknown. Biblioteca National.

country following the disastrous war with America. That is to say, Alfonso was not a Man. Unlike the impressively athletic militant fighting against the serpentine threat of fascism, Alfonso is effete and comical. Seated atop the law and the constitution, his sword a flaccid and comically ineffective toy, he tramples the rights of the citizenry (*derechos de ciudadanía*) as mindlessly as an impudent child trampling roses in the family garden. Even the colors that frame him, the bright orange of the background and the royal purple of the oversized cap he wears, suggest a cartoonish figure to be pitied and dismissed. The effect is to separate Alfonso's own stature from that of the Spanish throne. The presumed weakness of Alfonso's masculinity disrupts his claims to the most regal forms of Manhood. This allows us to get a bit nearer to understanding the bitterness of the long explanatory text that accompanies Alfonso's image:

> A pesar de ocupar el trono de España, no fue nunca rey de los españoles. Durante su borbonada, se fusiló a los hombres libres, como Ferrer, se encarceló a los obreros y a los hombres liberales, se martirizó en cárceles y calabozos, se asesinó aplicando la ley de fuga, se violó la correspondencia, se allanaron las moradas, se persiguió a los hombres de ciencia, se amordazó a la prensa, se encumbró a los salteadores de la caja nacional y se aniquiló a las voluntades honestas. Nunca se respetó precepto alguno de la constitución. Se depauperó al país llevando al extranjero todo el oro que había en las arcas. . . . Al abandonar España el rey delincuente ha dicho "que no había renunciado a ninguno de sus derechos." Cabe preguntarle si el país había renunciado a alguno de los suyos durante los treinta años que se le robaron todos.

> (Despite occupying the throne of Spain, he was never king of the Spaniards. During his "Borbonada,"[15] free men like Ferrer were shot; workers and liberal men were jailed, martyred in prisons and dungeons, killed by application of the excuse of escape [*ley de fuga*]; correspondence was violated; homes were raided; men of science were persecuted; the press was muzzled; highwaymen were raised to the national bank; and honest intentions were annihilated. Never was any provision of the constitution respected. The country was impoverished by having all of the gold that was in the coffers carried abroad. . . . Upon abandoning Spain, the delinquent king said "that he had not renounced any of his rights." It is fitting

to ask whether the country had renounced some of its rights during the thirty years that everyone was robbed.)

There are a number of competing goals in this passage that make it particularly complex—and somewhat confusing—syntactically. On the one hand, Alfonso is described as not only profligate but also vicious. Men were shot, killed, martyred, and jailed. Homes were raided, the press muzzled; estates were confiscated and patriots deported. Still, the sober response to these claims is that though these actions were heinous and perhaps criminal, they were certainly not outside the prerogatives of a king. As Giorgio Agamben reminds us, sovereignty is established at the location at which an individual, an institution, or a state gains—or at least claims—absolute dominion over life and death.[16] What the anonymous authors of this text imply is that though Alfonso held the throne, he was never king, because to be a king one has first to be a Man. The graphic depiction of an effete, buffoonish, and flaccid Alfonso works to denigrate him while also reiterating the idea that royal sovereignty is but an extension of the presumably natural dominance of strong men over the rest of human society. The king was far too womanish. He is not faulted so much for being vicious as for being too inwardly focused, for directing his greed and rage toward the domestic sphere. It is telling in this respect that this piece mentions not a word about Spain's colonialist atrocities in North Africa.[17] Instead it is only the Spaniards who can be recognized as having suffered Alfonso's insults. They represent living beings whose Manhood has been denied and attacked.

The many crimes of which the king had been charged were described as events that happened *in spite* of him. Even though this criticism of the "sovereign" was not written in the passive voice per se, all action is directed outwards. Through the continuous use of the impersonal pronoun *se* (one) rather than the personal pronoun *él* (he), the propagandists who produced the poster cleverly critiqued the king while refusing him the dignity of remarking his agency. *Se fusiló a los hombres libres.* (One shot free men./Free men were shot.) *Se encarceló a los obreros y los hombres liberales.* (One jailed workers and liberal men./Workers and liberal men were jailed.) Even and especially in war, even and especially as Spanish radicals groped toward new languages with which to name and describe the dynamism of their social and cultural lives, they nonetheless found themselves hobbled by old-fashioned bias. As a consequence, the discursive structures with which they described their beliefs were at times stiff and thin, incapable of conveying the complexity of the social, ideological, political, and aesthetic worlds they were intended to describe.

A (Negro) American Nurse

I turn now toward the rather remarkable figure of Salaria Kea, the only black female member of the Abraham Lincoln Brigade (see figure 1.3). As with Chanel Petro-Nixon, I will ask what happens when female actors resist dominant ideological narratives? What entails a feminist, woman-centered articulation of the war archive? Given the masculinist iconography we have just encountered, how might we talk about war without also collapsing the female and the feminine into anthropophorous animality? These questions were made more pressing still by the fact that Kea's presence in the conflict was almost immediately recognized as an incredible boon for propagandists eager to link Republican efforts in Spain with the more general struggle against fascist aggression against blacks in the United States. At the same time, her anomalous position as a black woman struggling against fascist aggression in Republican Spain triggered the deployment of a set of reactionary disciplinary practices designed to corral the serious disruptions to hegemonic notions of race and gender that her presence provoked.

Years after returning from Spain, Kea again volunteered her services as a member of the Army Nurse Corp. In her January 25, 1945, application to the service, Kea, using her married name, Salaria Kea O'Reilly, recorded herself as a Spanish-speaking, female, Negro American citizen of the United States. Born on January 13, 1913, the thirty-two-year-old was a broadly experienced member of the American Nurses Association living with her husband, Joseph O'Reilly, at 261 Livingston Place in Akron, Ohio. Between 1934 and 1943 she had worked as a staff nurse, head nurse, chief nurse, and instructor at Harlem Hospital, Seaview Hospital in Staten Island, the New York City Department of Hospitals, and at field hospitals erected by the international brigades in Spain. She was childless, stood five feet, five inches tall, and weighed 105 pounds.[18]

Her unique story was first brought to the attention of the general public in a handsome pamphlet, *Salaria Kee: A Negro Nurse in Repub-*

Figure 1.3. Salaria Kea. Photograph in Abraham Lincoln Brigade
Archive, New York University.

lican Spain, published by the Negro Committee to Aid Spain and the
Medical Bureau and North American Committee to Aid Spanish Democracy. It was republished in 1977 by the Bay Area Post of the Veterans
of the Abraham Lincoln Brigade.[19] It was this pamphlet that solidified
the mythographic structures that would come to define Kea's remarkable contributions. Her "life began much as the life [*sic*] of millions of
other Negro girls in this country" (*A Negro Nurse*). When Salaria was

six months old, her father was stabbed to death by a patient at the Ohio State Hospital for the Insane, where he worked as an attendant. Facing ruin, Salaria's mother moved with her four children to Akron, Ohio, to seek the assistance of family friends. Two years later, Mrs. Kea returned to her childhood home in Georgia, eventually marrying a man she had known from her youth but never again taking her children to live with her. Salaria and her brothers were placed in the home of a black Akron family, but the added strain on the household quickly forced Salaria's brothers, George and Arthur, to leave school to support themselves and their sister. After completing high school, Salaria briefly worked in the office of a local black physician, Bedford Riddle. Originally interested in pursuing accreditation as a physical education teacher, the athletic young woman was thwarted in her efforts by the fact that the local universities to which she applied refused to allow black students to swim in their pools. Though she might enter the training course, she would never be able to complete it as she would not be allowed to pass the swimming requirement. Following the advice of Dr. Riddle, Salaria decided to pursue a nursing degree. Again refused entry to the state's programs because of her race, she eventually entered the nurse's training program of Harlem Hospital.

As a young single woman in New York, Kea prospered both socially and academically. Becoming increasingly impatient with the most obviously vulgar aspects of everyday racism, she chafed under the rigid racial hierarchy of Harlem Hospital, eventually leading a successful student protest against the segregation of the nurses' cafeteria that resulted in the integration of the facility and the hiring of a black dietician. Graduating in 1934 with a refreshed sense of her own abilities and the capacity of aggrieved persons to work together for positive change, Kea briefly worked in the tuberculosis ward of Seaview Hospital and then returned to Harlem Hospital for a job in the obstetrics ward. Along with a group of other progressive nurses, Kea began attending lectures and discussions of key social issues, particularly international politics. This led to her active participation in efforts to finance and outfit a seventy-five-bed field hospital for Ethiopians struggling against the 1935 Italian invasion. When Mussolini turned his focus from Africa to Spain, Kea immediately understood that the struggles in the two countries were one and the same. On March 27, 1937, she sailed from New York as an international volunteer for the defense of Spanish Republicanism. She arrived on April 3 and was quickly removed to Villa Paz, a former residence of Alfonso XIII outside Madrid, where she helped to erect and staff a large and extremely active field hospital.

The unlikely presence of a small, young African American woman among the other personnel at Villa Paz immediately caught the attention of the political and ideological leaders in the international brigades. Kea would eventually become a singularly effective tool in the leftist propaganda arsenal that had been established to support Republican Spain. Not only did she appear in two films about the conflict (*Heart of Spain* and *Return to Life*), but her marriage to a white Irish brigadier served as a living example of the type of interracial harmony that the socialism being defended in Spain would encourage and defend. The rhetoric of *A Negro Nurse* was strongly tilted toward the assumption that Kea's story was indicative of the shared motivations of the progressive militants drawn to fight in Spain, militants who did not so much relinquish modern forms of racialism as flatten them out.

> Ethiopians from Djibouti, seeking to recoup Ethiopia's freedom by strangling Mussolini's forces . . . in Spain. Cubans, Mexicans, Russians, Japanese, unsympathetic with Japan's invasion of China and the Rome-Berlin-Tokyo axis. There were poor whites and Negroes from the Southern States of the United States. These divisions of race and creed and religion and nationality lost significance when they met in Spain in a united effort to make Spain the tomb of Fascism. The outcome of the struggle in Spain implies the death or the realization of the hopes of the minorities of the world.
>
> Salaria saw that her fate, the fate of the Negro race, was inseparably tied up with their fate; that the Negro's efforts must be allied with those of other minorities as the only insurance against an uncertain future. (*A Negro Nurse*)

Kea became a figure for whom meaning trumped presence. Her literally lifesaving work as a nurse was never rendered as more significant than the model of post-racialist cosmopolitanism that her form represented. As with all subjects of propaganda, she is at once stunningly thin and shockingly broad. With the image of a single black woman one might see Spain, Ethiopia, Cuba, Mexico, Russia, Japan, China, Italy, and the United States as "inseparably tied" entities. In the process, Kea is converted into a spectacular creature, one capable of convening the most outlandishly optimistic conceptions of what the struggle in Spain represented. The presence of a single black woman, a figure overdetermined by the specter of a sullied—and sullying—American domesticity, would either help solidify progressive internationalism or throw it into disarray. Kea's small body became the marker of both the promise and the threat of the flesh, that place at which possibility is at once celebrated and extinguished.

Injured in a bombing raid on her hospital, Kea returned to the United States after thirteen months in Spain. The leaders of the CPUSA and the editors of the *Daily Worker* wasted little time in utilizing her story to reiterate the poetics of internationalism underwriting the activities of the Spanish brigadiers. "In spite of the lack of aid from the democratic countries, . . . the morale of the people is really splendid," Kea reported in a May 18, 1938, article in the *Daily Worker*. "With every advance of the fascists, the people responded even more courageously. Franco will never rule a fascist Spain."[20] A little more than a year after Kea's return from Spain, however, the international brigades would leave and Franco would begin a nearly forty-year dictatorship that did not end until his death in 1975. It was at this juncture that the structure of the propaganda apparatus that had been constructed around the image of Kea became most apparent. Not only did the young woman continue to use her image in order to encourage support for the Republicans, but also the debate over the question of what the "(New) Negro nurse" represented in the ideological structures supporting socialist internationalism would be hotly deliberated throughout the rest of her life.

As an older woman, Kea penned "While Passing Through," a sketch meant to be the basis for a longer autobiography. Borrowing heavily from *A Negro Nurse in Republican Spain*, Kea's outline differed from the earlier text primarily in that she clearly intended to reassert her own individuality. To that end, she inserted an unapologetically gallant scene into the story that worked to reestablish both its narrative specificity and her own heroic stature. Her field hospital coming under heavy attack, Kea was separated from her unit and forced to hitchhike on her own toward Barcelona. Passing though the Catalan city of Lérida, she saw a car approaching. Realizing too late that it was carrying armed Nazi soldiers, she ran into a nearby ravine but proved too slow for the pursuing men, one of whom came upon her, weapon at the ready as she lay trembling on the ground.

> "Get up you savage!" he yelled in English.
> My body quivered as I said, "Shoot you coward!"
> He pushed the butt of his gun under my body and flipped me over as if I was a coin. With the gun pointing at my stomach, he asked, "Who are you?"
> I licked my lips,
> "I am an American nurse," I said.[21]

After her capture, Kea was blindfolded and loaded into the car, then taken to a building, marched down four flights of stairs, and locked into a room, where she was left for the night. The following morning she was escorted by a guard three flights up to a smaller room, where she was ordered to look out a window as Republican soldiers were executed.

> "That is how we destroy our enemies, poof!" . . .
> "One day I hope soon your enemies will destroy you," I said.
> He slapped me across the face and said,
> "I alone will kill you, not fast but slow," and then stomped out of the room. ("While Passing Through," 40)

Kea was eventually rescued by brigadiers from a British battalion, who ran with her toward a refugee train packed with hundreds of people. There she assisted with the wounded until the train came under attack from enemy bombers, forcing its passengers to flee once again until the attack was over and the company could continue its journey to Barcelona.

Of the many remarkable things about this story—Kea's promotion from "Negro nurse" to "American nurse"; the ease with which three languages, English, Spanish, and German, are negotiated; the heroine's bravery in the face of near-certain death; the spectacularly cinematographic murder of the Republicans; and Kea's escape and quick return to duty aboard the refugee train—none is more extraordinary than the extreme dissonance between this version of the "facts" of her time in Spain and those put forward in *A Negro Nurse*. In the earlier narrative of the events surrounding Kea's separation from her medical colleagues, the heavy melodrama of her self-penned sketch is nowhere in evidence.

> Salaria was lost from her unit. She hitchhiked and by slow stages rejoined the American medical unit near Barcelona. Here they set up a 4000 bed hospital. They were pitifully short of the most commonplace supplies. Many seriously wounded patients had to go with bandages unchanged for days because there were no surgical dressings. Patients who were able to sit up washed their soiled dressings in the early morning and had them waiting for the doctors and nurses when they came to redress them. (*A Negro Nurse*)

When we read these two versions against one another, it becomes clear that the distinction between the two, the very distinction represented in the not-so-subtle difference remarked in the juxtaposition of the pamphlet's Negro nurse with Kea's American nurse, is remarkably resonant with Sylvia Wynter's gloss on the Foucauldian articulation of the history of "Man" and humanism.

If one grants Foucault's claim that the modern period has been established upon a conception of a broken relation between sign and object such that the pairing of names and things is always a random occurrence, one that gives rise to the hypervaluation of grammar and rhetoric and a diminution of the focus on "pure" substance, then it follows that, notwithstanding all the handwringing about the need to tell the truth of the Abraham Lincoln Brigade's story, the real action of the archival and memorialization processes surrounding the brigadiers takes place at the level of the rhetorical and the stylistic. Foucault writes,

> Having become a dense and consistent historical reality, language forms the locus of tradition, of the unspoken habits of thought, of what lies hidden in a people's mind; it accumulates an ineluctable memory which does not even know itself as memory. Expressing their thoughts in words of which they are not the masters, enclosing them in verbal forms whose historical dimensions they are unaware of, men believe that their speech

is their servant and do not realize that they are submitting themselves to its demands.[22]

To turn again to the question of which narrative of Salaria Kea's time in Spain ought to be more valued, I would point out that in both instances, though the presumed engine driving the two forms of articulation is a pure desire to tell the simple truth, there exists nonetheless a rather obvious struggle surrounding which rhetorical strategies might most efficiently accomplish this work. In both narratives we can be certain that Kea was briefly separated from her unit. In the version of the story in *A Negro Nurse in Republican Spain*, however, the young African American woman seemingly ceases to exist as a fully formed subject once her vital connection to the rest of the brigade has been severed. In the single paragraph devoted to this episode, Kea's name is mentioned only once. Instead, the focus turns rather quickly to the problem of clean bandages that she met upon her return. Though as a Negro nurse, Kea was imagined as representative of "other minorities," once that procedure had been accomplished, it seems that there was nothing more to say. In contrast, in Kea's own rescripting of this incident, she is especially careful to remark the fact of a distinct individual whose particularities support the noble actions of the paper-thin heroine described in the pamphlet. The continual repetition of "I" and "me" in Kea's narrative reiterates the reality that a knowable individual, a creature whole and self-possessed, was present in Spain. The Nazi soldier who strikes her is named: Karl. She walks down *four* flights of stairs and up *three*. The passage evokes not simply the expansiveness of her experience, but also the reality that this story, *her* story, gains its potency from the ways it is viscerally connected to the whole of the spectacular complexity established beneath the sign of the Spanish Civil War.

What I have most clearly in my sights are the practices and procedures of an ideological structure that I have named the war archive. The violation and destruction of human beings are far too easily understood—at least for many U.S. audiences—as an exotic procedure, one inextricably tied to the "escape" of men from domestic norms. If and when females are present, they are assumed to exist within bracketed realities, or in Kea's case, contained within the wilted grandeur of Villa

Paz. Their presence can be understood and announced only as evidence of a fundamental distinction between the domestic and the martial. As a consequence, Kea's unscripted wandering represented a profound conceptual/ideological tear, a site of vexed contestation.

In a 1975 appreciation of Kea and her husband, John O'Reilly, originally published in *Cleveland Magazine*, Kea is said to have reported a scene that took place during the trip to Spain that was extremely difficult for other veterans of the conflict to either believe or countenance:

> The Spanish adventure started badly for Salaria Kea. At her first meal on the French ocean liner taking the medical team overseas, the medical officer in charge announced, "I've never eaten with niggers and I'm not going to start now." The ship's officers responded immediately with European courtliness and the rest of the trip, she recalls with amusement, she was the special guest at the captain's table.[23]

The first thing likely to strike contemporary audiences when encountering this passage is just how very mundane it is. A single black woman huddled with white passengers on a 1937 Europe-bound ocean liner might be lucky to get off with just being called a nigger when the dinner bell rang. The problem, however, was that this was not just any black woman. Nor were her shipmates just any white travelers. The very fact of their journey, the dream their isolation in the staterooms of a liner slipping across the Atlantic was designed to evoke, was one in which the pettiness of white racism would become not simply ridiculous, but impossible; all their progressive rhetoric notwithstanding, it was extremely difficult for the travelers to fully embrace the fact that the war "over there" was in no way distinct from the (race, class, gender) war at home. Even more to the point, Kea's repetition of these ugly scenes seriously challenged the most cherished conceits of a self-consciously constructed archive of American radicalism, an archive centered upon the heroism of the Abraham Lincoln Brigade. Could leftist partisans be as foolishly racist as the rest of white America? And even more significant for our concerns here, could Kea's story be so warped by the facts of race and sex that her meticulously groomed image might begin to unravel, to transform itself into something no longer available for the acts of celebration and memorialization so desperately needed by

American progressives stranded in their forgetful and militantly capitalist nation? These questions are hardly rhetorical. Better put, rhetoric is hardly ever simple and never inert. The matter of how Kea's story might be represented stood at that uncomfortable cultural node at which rhetorics of race, gender, American identity, and progressive internationalism violently clashed, threatening to disrupt sacrosanct ideologies of racial liberalism in the process.

My ability to make these claims is largely dependent upon the often remarkable archival work accomplished by intellectuals who were absolutely committed to preserving the history of the American participation in the Spanish Civil War. To their very high credit, these individuals were especially keen to represent the particular struggle of African Americans in these efforts. One such person was Frances Patai. Born in New York in 1930, Patai took bachelor's and master's degrees from the City College of New York, then committed the remainder of her life to teaching and struggling for human and civil rights. She dedicated the last decade of her life to writing a book on American female personnel in the medical units attached to the Abraham Lincoln Brigade. Though she did not complete the book before her death in 1998, her collection of research materials now constitutes a key element in the Abraham Lincoln Brigade Archives at New York University's Tamiment Library. In particular, Patai did perhaps the best archival work on Salaria Kea ever accomplished. It is questionable, however, whether at the end of her efforts she could be said to have liked her subject.

What the archive leaves us of both Kea and Patai are not simply the unedited representations of the two women that one might find in the letters between Patai and her correspondents, but also an unusually frank, splendidly innocent articulation of the ideological stakes that Patai unearthed and announced as she made her way through Kea's sometimes less than salutary discussions of the conduct of her fellow brigadiers. In a December 7, 1990, letter Patai received from Martin Balter, the key issue between the two correspondents was the matter of Kea's claims about having confronted racism during her journey to Spain, a claim that proved severely unnerving to the archivist:

Bill Sussman phoned me two weeks ago to ask whether I knew Salaria Kee and any confirmation or rebuttal of her allegations about the racist slurs by Dr. Pitts, and about the commotion in the ship's dining room. Salaria had also alleged that a "Mrs. Cunard" had then invited her to dine with her for the rest of the voyage in the first-class dining room. I replied to Bill that no such incident had occurred, that we had eaten and socialized as a distinct group throughout our travel en route to Villa Paz. I pointed out a major discrepancy: "Mrs. Cunard" of the Cunard Line family—a British steamship company would not have been travelling on the S.S. Paris—A French line which was *our* ship.

You had mentioned these stories to me previously but I hadn't realized how damaging they could be until Bill Sussman informed me of the forthcoming volume of Black participation in the S.C.W.

I sent a formal statement of my knowledge concerning the period I knew and worked with Salaria to VALB.[24]

Patai answered Balter immediately, assuring him that she shared his suspicions of Kea's claims of racist attack:

And, your thoughts to Bill Sussman re Salaria Kea mirror mine (and, of course, *you were there*). It's all a figment of her imagination, as is her story of being captured and then escaping from the Germans. It's totally absurd that Pitts (who may have been a not-good person and a sexist) would make such an outlandish rasist [sic] insult. Had he done so the AMB personnel and the Lincoln volunteers on the boat would have been up in arms. It just didn't happen. I told Sussman that even before I got your letter. . . . So the whole incident will not appear in my book, not I think, anywhere in the history of the African Americans who served the Republic project ALBS is working on. All this is good, because none of us want such an untrue lie to dim the glory of the U.S. volunteers.

However, the fact that Salaria may have confused fact with fiction does not in any way diminish her bravery, courage, nobility in volunteering. Nor does it lessen at all her truly radical political actions in integrating the dining room and staff at Harlem Hospital—at considerable risk to her well being and future.[25]

It is best that I pause for a moment, that I attempt to rein in my irritation a bit, demote my critique from blistering to serious. While I am wholly sympathetic to the historian's need to maintain healthy skepticism in relation to her subjects, I am surprised that Patai seems so very incapable of countenancing Kea's actually quite plausible claim of having been the victim of racist harassment. Regardless of the available evidence, Patai will not allow any narrative ripple to "dim the glory of the U.S. volunteers." Part of what is on display here is, in fact, a dramatic fretfulness about the status of that glory. A single incident from one (obviously sexist but surprisingly nonracist) doctor aboard the S.S. *Paris* would throw the entire logic underwriting the heroism of the Lincoln brigadiers into disarray. As a consequence, Salaria Kea must become an almost spectral figure in these letters. Bill Sussman has contacted Martin Balter, who wrote to Frances Patai and received his response in turn; the problematic subject dripping from the ends of their pens, Salaria Kea. Her narrative is treated as an absurd and confused figure of the imagination. For reasons that remain unclear, Kea's memory of a specific incident is trumped by Balter's generalized recollections of the brigadiers' having "eaten and socialized as a distinct group." And lest any question remain as to where the weight of the evidence lies, the very letters exchanged between these interlocutors, their conversations, and the supporting "evidence" sent by Balter to the Veterans of the Abraham Lincoln Brigade produce a rhetorical depth (a paper trail, if you will) that trumps Kea's obviously hysterical notions. The entire process is sealed by the deployment of Patai's wholly dismissive postscript in which she covers Kea's embarrassing "confusion" in a cloak of long since established bravery, courage, and nobility. At the risk of being overly repetitive, I will point out that what the archive reveals in this instance is indeed a process of rebirthing. As with the Christian ritual of baptism, the sinful, untamed human animal is immersed in the muck, suffocated, and destroyed only to be reborn, finding life in death, a glistening purchase on Manhood suiting the newly formed individual for a comfortable and secure place in the dominant social order. Kea the absurd, outlandish, confused living subject is translated into a usefully dead anthropophorous being dressed up in pretty robes of bravery, courage, and nobility.

This will perhaps help you to understand why I continue to remain distracted by the ideological distinctions articulated by the labels "Negro nurse" and "American nurse." In both instances, Kea's status as a woman of education and skill is clearly represented. Where the two labels are dissimilar, however, is the relative straightforwardness with which they acknowledge the ways white supremacy distorts the basic structures and practices of many professions, including nursing; the ways basic social intercourse is dependent upon careful negotiation of the most vulgar racial protocols. Founded in 1896, the Nurses Associated Alumnae of the United States and Canada transformed itself in 1911 into the American Nurses Association (ANA). The ANA was an emblem of the professionalization of the nursing profession in early twentieth-century America, a process that was greatly aided by the extreme need for nurses during the First and Second World Wars. While the ANA was never explicitly segregated, the fact that its membership was exclusively drawn from nursing schools that largely refused entry to African American women worked to produce the organization as an overwhelmingly white institution until well into the twentieth century. The point here is not to make the extremely simple move of pointing at well-established American bodies in order to demonstrate the tastelessness of the racist practices that helped to produce them. Instead, I want to argue that modernization and professionalization are hardly antidotes to white supremacy. As I have argued already, the *Plessy* decision, a decision taken in the same year as the founding of the Nurses Associated Alumnae of the United States and Canada, was itself an attempt to modernize the country's racialist and white supremacist structures, an attempt, that is, to produce a new Negro. Both the women who founded what would become the American Nurses Association and the justices who adjudicated the *Plessy* case operated in a context in which the quick movement of the country into the contemporary era was driven by changes brought about by the Civil War. Scores of women worked as nurses during the conflict, while the victory of the Union made the country's rapid industrialization inevitable.

The professions were established at those locations where the Negro was not so much disallowed as veiled. Negro nurses—indeed, all so-called New Negroes—were forced to contort themselves into monstrous caricatures of black identity. They had to revert to the very anti-black segregationist ideology that so disabled them in order to gain access to even the barest semblance of professional life. The Negro nurse entered into the public sphere as an already shrouded being. In the quickly multiplying segregationist practices of the early twentieth century, Negro professionals were absolutely necessary. Black and brown hands were needed to service and control black and brown bodies. At the same time, if the Negro professional should put on her nurse's cap and approach her work with the same innocent rigor as her white counterparts, she would seriously disrupt the hard-won respect of the profession. There were reasons that nurses' dining tables at the Harlem Hospital were segregated. It is doubtful, however, that any of the women participating in this particularly vulgar piece of theater seriously thought that the mixing of white and black individuals at lunch was so noxious as to be insupportable. Instead, the point of the practice was wholly pedagogical. White nurses might enter into "the" profession, while Negro nurses might enter only into a realm specifically—and begrudgingly—created in order to corral and further exploit black potential.[26] This reality was met, however, by the functional challenges of work, the insistent interventions and interruptions of the flesh. The everyday articulation of white supremacy was—and is—enacted as a means by which to rebalance a set of unstable equations, to support the (white supremacist) structures of liberal humanist discourse while attending to dirty bandages and overfull bedpans.

* * *

I continue to struggle with my outrage that a young black girl could be killed a mere whisper from her home with only the slightest tremble of disapproval or regret. I struggle with my bewilderment that this type of violence is so remarkably common yet ultimately so "unknowable." The physical death of an already socially dead figure holds no weight in the discursive and ideological apparatuses that comprise humanism. My awareness of this fact is what fuels this work's disloyalty and discontent, what leads me to avoid pretty eloquence. I mean to judge my success or failure by whether or not I am able to integrate the vulgarity of Chanel Petro-Nixon's assault into my arguments about Spain, African America, and Western humanism. I am trying to make good on my claim of moving past the inwardly focused, academic, costly, and ineffectual nature of so much within humanistic discourse. The murder of Chanel Petro-Nixon, her sacrifice, has become for me not only an emblem of constant and systematic violence against black women and girls, but also a sign of the obscene silence that accompanies and supports that violence. In truth, I do not believe that the girl was killed because she appeared too weak, but on the contrary, too strong. Her murder was an attempt to access her amazing potential. Her death was a misbegotten attempt at rebirthing; a living girl left her home in Bedford-Stuyvesant only to be transmogrified into a dead anthropophorous animal a few blocks away in Crown Heights. The abuse of her body, that bag, those twisted limbs, the ugly stain left on the memory of an otherwise radiant day, seem to me apt metaphors for the ways African American life and culture have been handled in the main precincts of U.S. cultural criticism.

The modern black subject is always an awkward mix of individual subjectivity and the protocols of white supremacy. The black soldier and the brown nurse represent an inevitable tension within systems of colonization and white supremacy. Though they may be exceptional, they can never be *exceptions*, beings not fully captured by the common sense of race and class. As a consequence, they are always suspect. Venture too far afield from locations where they are known, where normative narratives of identity seem to conform to the local common sense, and they become disruptive, potentially dangerous "living" entities in need of discipline and normalization. Chanel was in transit. In the hours before her death, she ambled through a Brooklyn neighborhood largely constructed between the period of the Spanish-American War and the Spanish Civil War. The long transition of the neighborhood from a place thought to be "white" to a thing assumed to be "black" is itself a sign of the remarkable restructuring of American social life—war, if you will—wrought by the reality of American colonialist and imperialist projects, projects brought into sharp focus by the victories of 1898. As with African American soldiers in Cuba, Puerto Rico, and the Philippines, Salaria Kea was also a subject in mid-stride between here and there. Her self-consciousness about this fact, her awareness that both her movements, first to New York and then to Spain, represented breaks with notions of the "natural" stability of the Negro and the female, created her as an unruly and irregular subject. The homeless, restless, unsatisfied black has always already broken a key element of the racialist social contract that allows the extremely uneasy peace to which we have become accustomed in the United States. To step off the path, to wander, to court the simple joy of being lost is to resist the constructions of (racial) figuration negotiated at the turn of the twentieth century as the country made its wrenching transition from an agricultural slave society to an urban "free" one. As with Chanel Petro-Nixon, Salaria Kea's remains have been roughly handled. They have been broken and shifted to suit a narrative that compliments individuals whom Kea understood to be hostile and racist. One wonders if in the memorialization process that surrounds the Abraham Lincoln Battalion any (black) narrative can be allowed that does not breathlessly celebrate liberal projects of reclamation in which the black always exists as an adjunct, a creature created and maintained in order to reflect and reiterate dominant conceits.

The presence of international brigadiers in Spain was testament to the fact that the ideological fissures that gave rise to the war were bunched around incredible uncertainty about what constituted the country's geographic and cultural boundaries. Ninety African American soldiers fought on behalf of the Republicans in white European Spain. Thousands of African soldiers fought with the rebels.[27] In all cases, however, the unchecked movement of peoples (whether that movement takes place in the heart of Brooklyn or the heart of Spain) is always read as either a stunningly potent resource or a profound threat. In hearing that Kea was absurd and confused, I am less struck by the obvious slurs being pointed in her direction than by the fact that the language her critics deploy is so very imprecise and reedy. We see among the chroniclers of Kea's remarkable journey a self-conscious will to resist the messiness unleashed by her own version of events. They attempt to order the archive, to create it as a location of coercion and discipline without ever seeming to have done so. In the process, a highly sanitized image of Salaria Kea was produced and disseminated, while that which proved useless, clumsy, unspeakable, refused, refusing, and human was unceremoniously tied up and discarded with the morning trash.

2

Lorca's Deathly Poetics

There were a thousand Federico García Lorcas, stretched out forever in the attic of time and in the storehouse of the future; I contemplated another thousand Federico García Lorcas, very tightly pressed, one on top of the other, waiting to be filled with gas in order to fly off without direction. This moment was a terribly fearful moment, my mother Lady Death had given me the key of time and for a second I understood everything. I'm living on borrowed time, what I have within is not mine; let's see if I'm going to be born.
—Federico García Lorca

WHEN THE POET PROTESTS THE
DEATH HE SEES AROUND
HIM,
THE DEAD WANT HIM SILENCED.
HE DIES LIKE LORCA DID,
YET LORCA SURVIVES IN HIS
POEM, WOVEN INTO THE DEEPS
OF LIFE. THE POET SHOCKS THOSE
AROUND HIM. HE SPEAKS OPENLY
OF WHAT AUTHORITY HAS DEEMED
UNSPEAKABLE, HE BECOMES THE
ENEMY OF AUTHORITY. WHILE THE
POET LIVES, AUTHORITY
DIES. HIS POEM IS
FOREVER.
—Bob Kaufman

And indeed the advent of this anthill society began with the masses, who were the first to be subjected to the framework of leveling rationality.
—Michel de Certeau

To immerse oneself in the work left us by the exquisitely talented poet and dramatist Federico García Lorca (1898–1936), to begin the arduous, if infinitely beguiling, task of familiarizing oneself with Lorca's poems, plays, essays, letters, and drawings, not to mention his "drama"—the endless sessions of self-promotion and self-parody, the theatricality and fits of paranoia, all presented to great effect in the cafés and salons, homes and recital halls of Granada, Madrid, Barcelona, New York, Havana, and Buenos Aires—is to remind oneself of the art of reiteration by which Lorca himself was so fascinated and bothered. Yes, there were—and are—a thousand Federico García Lorcas. Yes, they existed—and exist—in uneasy proximity one to the other, frighteningly similar yet each with its own subtle marks of distinction, much like identical twins finishing each other's sentences, heedless of the bemused/confused reactions of neighbors and friends.

One might rightly argue that it is no longer possible to address Lorca's poetics without taking into account the "fact of *lorquismo*," the reality that he, like the Black Americans with whom I frame him, is a figure who cannot be properly separated from the many overdeterminations that bunch around his name.[1] Part of what one begins to understand when examining a (European) artist with the talents and sensitivity of Lorca is that the so-called double consciousness that presumably underwrites everything in Black American culture is best understood not as a phenomenon specific to blacks, Africans, or Americans for that matter, but instead as a sort of shorthand for the social, ideological, and aesthetic procedures established by and within modernity. It becomes increasingly difficult to locate the "I" in one's sentences once you recognize that all media (the pens and paper, books, drawings, and charts that litter these rooms) are themselves the residue of (African) bodies pressed together, "one on top of the other," and transported presumably without name, history, kin, or culture below deck on the *Brooks* and the *Amistad*, the *Brownlow* and the *African*, only to be reanimated, "filled with gas," for the sole purpose of becoming perfectly constructed human automatons, the "slaves" or "Man bearers" so very necessary to the production and reproduction of capital and culture.

My work, then, is to read Federico García Lorca as one of us. I will treat his life and art, including his murder at the hands of fascists early in

Spain's civil war, as a continuation of the violent articulation of humanism of which slavery, forced emigration, and colonization are both cata-
lysts and effects. The procedures of effacement and compression that
we saw so dully practiced in relation to a figure like Salaria Kea are of
central concern to Lorca. With particular emphasis on his poetry, I will
demonstrate that the great difficulty that this "once and future" scion of
a "profoundly Iberian," "specifically Spanish," "peculiarly Andalusian"
culture faced was that he came to understand, sometimes more, other
times less, that the "particular" voice and "peculiar" individuality for
which he often longed were anachronistic notions that were especially
difficult to sustain in the face of ever *de*-individuating, *de*-humanizing
processes of global modernization, whose economic infrastructures
and aesthetic/ideological superstructures were produced out of long-
established, well-articulated practices of enslavement and colonization.
I mean, therefore, to demonstrate Lorca's aesthetic experiments against
and within the self-conscious attempts by African slaves and their descendants to name and counter the ideological structures underwriting
slavery, colonization, racism, and white supremacy. I will also read Lorca
as an *Atlantic* writer, one with an uncanny sensitivity to the intimate relation between the "mastery" of human beings and the "mastery" of art.

   Much of this chapter's rhetorical force turns on reiterating Henri Lefebvre's call for the production of a revolutionized "new space," a place in
which the norms of language, culture, the built environment, and daily
life are self-consciously reconceptualized in order to acknowledge and
address the profound disruptions of the common sense attending modernity and Western humanism.[2] In Lorca's case, I intend to unsettle the
often narrow critical procedures that bunch around his work. I struggle
against the leveling that he found so distressing by pushing back against
his own tendencies toward primitivism when addressing Africans and
African Americans. I refuse to accept Lorca as a talisman, an empty cipher full of possibility and desire. Instead, I recognize him as a clearly
articulated co-conspirator in the effort to dramatize the complexly intimate interrelation between our most basic social and aesthetic arrangements. My job is to make plain what one might think of as the dialogical
ethics that bind Lorca to his African American peers. The revolutionary
space that I am attempting to articulate can be discerned only through a
process of critical interlocution in which it may not be possible to refuse

that flattening and leveling that de Certeau announces, but which none-theless may offer us access to the ways Lorca and the African American intellectuals with whom he is in dialogue might begin to access alter-native, indeed post-humanist, responses to the processes of modernity encompassed within the Atlantic imaginary.

In making these interventions, we must become ever more alert to the forms and structures of the often creative, if not always exactly re-sistant, ways that our inevitable immersions and implications within capitalist society are filtered through ritual and representation, allowing us to establish "counter-logics" within this "anthill society" that oper-ate as cystic ellipses, places where individual subjectivity is *not* canceled or blotted out by capitalism's "leveling rationalities."[3] Moreover, as my central concern is how one might discern the counter-logics produced by enslaved persons, I will remind you that even in the most acutely repressive situations, human beings, including enslaved human beings, have studied with great rigor both their oppressors *and* their oppressors' tools. While traders in human flesh busied themselves attempting to perfect methods by which to read—or perhaps better put, to break—the artifice of slaves at market, they were themselves constantly being evalu-ated by slaves intent upon manipulating, if not exactly beating, the odds within this most repressive of situations. As Walter Johnson has noted regarding antebellum American slave markets,

> Although one of the conceits of the southern ruling class seems to have been the idea that slaveholders were invisible, and that therefore they could parade around naked, drink too much, argue, and discuss the most intimate affairs of their business and personal lives without making them-selves vulnerable to on-looking slaves—they were not. When the buyers came into the pen they were subjected to careful scrutiny.[4]

In their attempts to secure their survival and better their conditions, American slaves were relentless in their efforts to decipher the aesthetic and ideological codes of their society. They did so, moreover, in order to support *and* circumvent the practices of the leveling named by Lorca and de Certeau. Or to return to Johnson's example, while the slave at market had to reiterate the assumption that an impenetrable veil divided the slaver from the enslaved, he nonetheless paid careful attention to what was transpiring "on the other side." Whether the slavers allowed themselves to admit it or not, the enslaved were not only able to see and respond, but also to judge and improvise. Disregarding the assumption of what one might think of as a blank whiteness, they became connoisseurs of the often subtle nuances of self-presentation and demeanor that might distinguish the "good" owner from the bad. They exploited the contradictions of those humanist protocols that rendered them socially dead (non)subjects. Moreover, even while their actions did not always produce radical change (slavery did not immediately end), they nonetheless provoked any number of generative ruptures in the ideological structures undergirding Western humanism, thereby allowing space for the resistant and corrosive counter-logics that have given rise to insurgent post-disciplinary fields such as Black Studies.

Again, however, I do not mean to obscure the fact that the methods utilized by enslaved persons were quite necessarily limited and subtle. Instead, I argue that part of what confronts the scholar of the humdrum modalities utilized by those many communities and individuals who continuously struggled to survive—and to prosper—in societies whose most advanced procedures seemed designed first and foremost to lock the unwashed masses into chains and to turn them out into the fields, is the simple fact that these modes were at once commonplace and ephemeral. They were mumbled, shuffled, carried out behind the back. Following the work of political scientist James Scott, we know that the efficacy of so-called weapons of the weak often turns on the occult manner in which these weapons are utilized.[5] The worker who dawdles, the captive who dissimulates, the slave who acts the fool do not necessarily openly challenge their bondage and presumed defeat. Instead, they translate and rearticulate the logics underwriting these realities. In the process, they often become their captors' most intimate interlocutors: living, thinking tools capable of reflecting their masters' invisible nakedness, (un)reported rage, and (un)heralded desire while remaining careful never to reveal their own efforts to bend those reflections. Given this, what the contemporary critic must guard against as he attempts to launch progressive critique is the rehearsal of pedantic forms of inquiry that are *necessarily* deaf to the modes of (embodied) resistance utilized by those many individuals and communities who find themselves on the less glamorous side of the Man/human divide.

Understanding this helps to soothe my embarrassment that my turn toward García Lorca begins with nothing more than a guess. I sense that there might be something one might discern about what I will call, with only a bit of winking, the "dark arts" by reading the great artist's writing from the wrong way round. Specifically, I reiterate and extend my earlier arguments by again refusing the nationalist(ic)—and linguistic— conceits that underwrote the ideologies supporting the Atlantic slave trade. As I argued in the introduction, the ability of competing European and American nations to imagine captive Africans as stateless/nationless/cultureless persons and fungible objects was essential not only to the practice of Atlantic slavery, but also to the entire ideological and institutional apparatus of humanism. In 1839, when slaves on board the schooner *Amistad*, traveling along the coast of Cuba, rebelled, eventually steering the ship to Long Island, where they were retaken by Americans, the key question in the trial and ensuing public debate was whether the rebels had been illegally captured off the coast of Africa or whether the very fact that they had already been transported to Spanish territory superseded these claims, making them (black) wards of the Spanish state, which might do with them as it pleased. Don Angel Calderón de la Barca, Spanish minister to the United States, made exactly this point when he wrote to U.S. Secretary of State John Forsyth that

> the crime in question is one of those which, if permitted to pass unpunished, would endanger the internal tranquility and safety of the island of Cuba, where the citizens of the United States not only carry on a considerable trade, but where they possess territorial properties which they cultivate with the labor of African slaves.[6]

Calderón de la Barca was attempting to produce a sort of racialist/ transnationalist sleight of hand whereby the *only* figures imagined to be provincial, to lack the ability to throw their voices across the Atlantic from the United States through Cuba on to Spain and then back again, were the slaves themselves. He was reminding his interlocutors of just how humanism's binding logics (dead slave/living Man) actually operated.

This gets you closer to understanding the structure of that guess that I have just admitted making. For if de Certeau is correct that the forms of articulation by which repressed subjects express their understanding of and resistance to dehumanizing power structures are always ritualistic and quotidian, then the progressive critic must necessarily remain attuned to what one might think of as subterranean discursive structures that are effaced at the very moment of their production. Apologists for slavery and colonization like Calderón de la Barca are all too willing to suppress supposedly universalist ideals of fairness when it suits their purposes. Thus enslaved and colonized people must remain particularly attentive to the art of dissimulation, the art produced from within the lie of an always already deadened human subjectivity. This is why I find it so infinitely telling that even as Lorca attempted to create work that took the human as its touchstone, he ran headfirst into the simple reality that all forms of modern human iteration, including the deep song or *cante jondo* that he so valued, are overdetermined by transatlantic structures of not only aesthetics, but also capital accumulation, repression, reiteration, and violence.

If I were to be a bit more fastidious, I might even venture to argue that a close examination of Lorca's poetry suggests an artist who often does away with etymological distinction between these terms, such that to violate a subject becomes indistinct from "stretching him out." A thousand live Federico García Lorcas hold exactly the same phenomenological weight as one dead one. Moreover, it seems that what we often take to be the most solidly fixed aspects of human differentiation—gender, race, sexuality, nationality, and language—are also reduced, leveled, and duplicated within the processes of packaging, compression, and repetition that Lorca laments in the epigraph that begins this chapter. It is clear, therefore, that García Lorca understood as well as anyone that so-called ancient norms are not only structured by but also policed and enforced within the social/ideological apparatuses of Spain, Europe, and the Americas. Thus violence, in both its hard and soft versions, is the name of the (modern) game for Lorca. The intolerance of Catholicism, the sequestration of women, the oppression and "naming" of homosexuals, the vulgarity of capitalism, the bloodletting of the Spanish Guardia Civil, and importantly the denaturing of the artist's talents, the clipping of his wings, were for the martyred writer not only the social realities in which one might find oneself enmeshed, but also the defining configurations of modern intellectual and artistic practice.

"Let's See If I'm Going to Be Born"

It is somewhat difficult to decide, when examining García Lorca's life and work, whether or not he demonstrated a childlike carelessness or a hardheaded sense of mastery in relation to the dates affixed to his poetry, plays, and correspondence. His letters were only haphazardly dated. He might work and rework a poem, play, or essay over many months and sometimes years, often performing pieces long before they were actually published. He also helped to foster considerable confusion in relation to the date of his own birth. Following his two most significant contemporary biographers, Ian Gibson and Leslie Stainton, we can be certain that Federico del Sagrado Corazón de Jesús García Lorca was born on June 5, 1898. Lorca regularly told friends and interviewers, however, that he had been born in either 1899 or 1900.[7] Adding heft to these acts of dissemblance, he also often remarked that he dated his own loss of childhood innocence as 1909 or 1910, when, as a ten-year-old (he was actually closer to twelve), he moved with his family from the village of Fuente Vaqueros to the much larger and more active Andalusian city of Granada.[8] He even went so far as to immortalize the notion of ten as the age when children must confront the complexities and disappointments of adult life in the poem "El niño Stanton" ("Little Stanton"), published in his posthumously released collection *Poeta en Nueva York* (*Poet in New York*).

> Cuando me quedo solo
> me quedan todavía tus diez años,
> los tres caballos ciegos,
> tus quince rostros con el rostro de la pedrada
> y las fiebres pequeñas heladas sobre las hojas del maíz
> Stanton. Hijo mío. Stanton.
> A las doce de la noche el cáncer salía por los pasillos
> y hablaba con los caracoles vacíos de los documentos.
> El vivísimo cáncer lleno de nubes y termómetros
> con su casto afán de manzana para que lo piquen los ruiseñores.
>
> (When I'm by myself
> your ten years stay with me.

> So do the three blind horses,
> your fifteen faces with the face after the stoning
> and tiny frozen fevers on leaves of corn.
> Stanton, my boy, Stanton.
> At twelve midnight, cancer wandered through the corridors
> and spoke with the documents' empty snails,
> cancer springing to life, full of clouds and thermometers,
> with an apple's chaste longing to be pecked by nightingales.)[9]

Especially in a poem like this one, in which Lorca's on-again, off-again fascination with the "unconscious" and "illogical" imagery that many take to be the hallmark of the surrealist style (which very much interested though never fully captured him) is apparent, he remains relentless in his insistence that the process of coming to understand one's self in relation to the rest of the world is indistinguishable from the recognition of the ways that death haunts our most intimate, most "alive" experience. Thus to be a ten-year-old verging on adolescence is to exist in a world of blind horses, leaves of corn, empty snails, apples, and nightingales, all of which are brought into relief by the stalking threat of cancer as it wanders through the corridors (*salía por los pasillos*) at midnight. Indeed, it is cancer itself that is most alive and vibrant (*vivísimo*), "springing" in this translation by Greg Simon and Steven White, suggesting again Lorca's understanding of death as not only inevitable, but also formative and foundational, the mother who urges and assures the child's presence.

What I am attempting to do is to broaden the pathbreaking efforts of Orlando Patterson in his 1985 work *Slavery and Social Death*, by pointing out the obvious fact that one of the legacies of Atlantic slavery is the continual production and reproduction of a catastrophic subjectivity, a state of being in which one must necessarily trade upon the vertiginous state of being physically alive and socially dead.[10] When I speak of broadening Patterson's thinking, however, I mean to resist the segregationist procedures that operate at the heart of both the humanities and the human sciences. By slave culture I do not mean simply black culture or American culture, but instead the entire discursive/ideological/social nexus that binds Africa, America, and Europe.

While I find many of Patterson's arguments compelling, I am resistant to two-dimensional, inert, and wholly defeated images of slaves.

Instead, I seek modes of resistance that cannot be recognized within the more rigidly collegiate forms of sociology. As with the slaves at market whom Walter Johnson examines, "resistance" can never be adequately quantified or graphed. What attracts me to Lorca, what I will call his genius, is not only that he demonstrates so ably the life-in-death aesthetic that attends both the worst aspects of slavery, colonization, and white supremacy and the "best" aspects of modern aesthetics, but also that he stretches himself beyond this recognition, brilliantly describing the many counternarratives to those of leveling, repetition, and fungibility that dominate so much within humanist discourse. In making these arguments, I will attempt to place Lorca's fascination with death, the deadly, and the deathly in their historical contexts. Returning to the matter of Lorca's having consistently fudged the date of his birth, it is important to move past the too easy assumption that the poet was simply engaging in an old-fashioned exercise in vanity. Instead, I would counter that it is obvious that part of what Lorca hoped to achieve by associating his birth with 1899 or 1900 was to place himself in intimate dialogue with the freshness and promise of the new century. He wanted, that is, to align himself with a historical moment in which the fissures in the ideological structures of Western humanism became grotesquely apparent.

One must remember that 1898, the actual year in which Lorca was born, was considered by many Spaniards, particularly those of the generation that preceded Lorca's, as a disastrous and shameful moment in Spanish history. Their easy defeat at the hands of the Americans in the Spanish-American War of 1898 and the subsequent loss of Cuba, Puerto Rico, and the Philippines were matters that many of Lorca's fellow Spaniards took as an augur of not only the complete cessation of any notion of a Spanish "Golden Age," but also the onset of decades and perhaps even centuries of decline. As the Socialist politician and poet Fernando de los Ríos stated in 1926,

> It will be difficult for those listening to me to appreciate the terrible distress of mind felt by Spaniards in 1898; difficult . . . to appreciate the impact made on us mere children, who had just gone up to university, by that tremendous defeat, a defeat for which today we are immensely grateful, because in 1898 was found the psychological key to the intellectual, and even economic, renewal of Spain. (Quoted in Gibson, *Lorca: A Life*, 45)

For progressive Spaniards like de los Ríos and Lorca, the death of the Spanish empire at the hands of the upstart Americans signaled a release from the hidebound and claustrophobic traditions that many felt were the real causes of Spain's presumed lack of engagement with the rest of the world, particularly Europe and America. De los Ríos would travel to Germany to study during the first decade of the twentieth century, while Lorca's father, Federico García Rodríguez, became wealthy by investing heavily in land and agriculture, particularly the sugar beets that became essential crops in Spain as the country struggled to overcome its loss of access to the cheap sugar markets of Cuba. At the same time, however, while some Spaniards were able to forget their past humiliations and to prosper in the country's quickly developing social and economic realities, many others remained mired in a deadly combination of suffocating traditionalism, poverty, and regret, a regret born, I argue, out of the notion that Spain had lost not only its colonies during the war, but also its particularity, its distinctiveness.[11]

It is his ability to understand and articulate this process that has attracted generations of black intellectuals to Lorca. In the case of Bob Kaufman, we see an African American intellectual who both eagerly participates in the aesthetic rituals of surrealism and relishes the possibilities of aesthetic leveling. Kaufman's fascination with García Lorca turns, in fact, on the manner in which Lorca seems to come prepackaged as a sort of poetic trope, one that announces aesthetic possibilities built not only on a vibrant and enlivened individuality, but also a "stretched out" and inert symbolism. Lorca writes,

> Everywhere else, death is an end. Death comes, and they draw the curtains. Not in Spain. In Spain they open them. Many Spaniards live indoors until the day they die and are taken out into the sunlight. A dead man in Spain is more alive as a dead man than anyplace else in the world. His profile wounds like a barber's razor.[12]

For Kaufman, part of the beauty of Lorca is that he is always already dead, surviving "only in his poems, woven into the deeps of life." As a consequence, Lorca becomes infinitely available to Kaufman, who utilized the name of the poet in order to reference not so much the man or his work as a disembodied, ahistorical, asocial mood that allows Kaufman to convey strikingly beautiful, if somehow always vague, meaning and affect.

> Come, Love,
> Love, Come,
> Sing a river, Federico . . . García . . . Lorca . . .
> In Sarah's tents a Gypsy moon . . . Godless Spain's burning
>   noon . . .[13]

Here we see Kaufman at his surrealist best. He disrupts the theatrical diction of the romantics by refusing the conventional loveliness of a phrase like, "Come, Love," instead separating it into its constituent elements and reversing it. His poem "Like Father, Like Sun" flaunts a certain staccato rhythmic effect. The reader becomes prisoner to an enforced hesitancy. Even the matter of artistic influence is called into question through Kaufman's reconfiguration of the phrase "Like father, like son." From the title forward, the reader is put on notice that commonsense elegance has been jettisoned. Lorca is never treated as an individual. Instead the names Federico . . . García . . . Lorca are read as ill-defined imaginative elements. Thus the "Gypsy" exists only in the imaginary; Spain's burning noon becomes no more than the clever effect of pen drawn across paper.

The mechanical and ideological systems developed by European slavers and colonists, their repression and compression, their genius at placing the many at the service of the few, structured not simply the economic and martial lives of slaves and slavers, but also their artistic and cultural lives as well. For these reasons I have argued that in considering the work of García Lorca, it is particularly important that we remain attuned to ways that violence and war, especially the First World War, worked both to bridge and renew the cyclical processes of dehumanization that underwrite slave culture. As a young man, García Lorca, and indeed all conscious individuals in Spain, Europe, America, and much of the world for that matter, were preoccupied with the horrors that were unleashed by both the Germans and the Allies during the conflict. Five million soldiers died, while another eighteen million were wounded, with the Germans sustaining nearly one million casualties between March and November of 1918 alone (Stainton, *Lorca: A Dream of*

Life, 2). One wonders whether Western and Central Europeans came to know themselves by enacting on "their own" continent the very ghastly aesthetic practices they had honed in Africa and the Americas. "One eats, one drinks, beside the dead," remarked the French surgeon Georges Duhamel, speaking of the carnage he encountered. "One steps in the midst of the dying, one laughs and one sings in the company of corpses" (quoted in Stainton, *Lorca: A Dream of Life*, 2).

The similarity between what I have just described and the many hair-raising narratives of slavery and the Middle Passage that we have available to us are so obvious that one cannot but be surprised that more individuals have not discussed them. I must admit, in fact, that I find it altogether strange that so much in twentieth-century European and American literature—take, for example, Albert Camus's 1947 novel *The Plague*—treats not only violence, boredom, pestilence, and death but also suffocating enclosure as well, yet so few commentators have bothered to point out the obvious aesthetic and ideological connections between these works and the many structurally similar texts and images created by African captives.[14] Though it may be impossible to prove such a claim, I feel compelled to ask whether one of the most significant ideological dividing lines for modern Europeans and Americans is that point at which we turn to confront the various ghosts of our collective histories, only to find that a few of us see no clear distinction between the suffering of the enslaved and the madness of the many "good wars" that are continuously enacted in our names, while many others believe that there is some inherent distinction between the bullets, chains, whips, and cannons used to drive Africans into slavery and similar devices used in the presumably civilized missions to police, protect, expand, and augment the republican principles and capitalist practices of an enlightened West.

Nowhere, I would argue, was this division more palpable than in early twentieth-century Spain. While Lorca, his family, friends, and colleagues were all generally either opposed to war altogether or in favor of the French and more generally the Allies during World War I, many other Spaniards, as was clearly proven with the successful fascist revolt and the advent of the Franco dictatorship, were not. The point is that there were, so to speak, two Spains, an idea that had been a part of Spain's self-conception since at least the eighteenth century, but that was brought into greater focus by twentieth-century intellectuals such as the philosopher Miguel de Unamuno and especially the poet Antonio Machado, who had famously used the phrase *las dos Españas* in "Españolito," number fifty-three of his much-loved series, *Proverbios y cantares*, first published in his 1912 collection, *Campos de Castilla*:

> Ya hay un español que quiere
> vivir y vivir empieza,
> entre una España que muere
> y otra España que bosteza.
> Españolito que vienes
> al mundo, te guarde Dios.
> Una de las dos Españas
> Ha de helarte el corazón.

> (There is already a Spaniard who wants
> to live and starts to live
> between a Spain that dies
> and another Spain that yawns.
> Poor little Spaniard who comes
> to the world, God save you.
> One of the two Spains
> Will freeze your heart.)[15]

My desire to recognize in García Lorca the very *españolito* whose soon-to-be frozen heart Machado references stems, in part, from the fact that the literary legacy that binds Machado to Lorca is both very strong and very obvious. Machado was perhaps Spain's most commercially successful and critically acclaimed poet prior to Lorca himself. Lorca met the older Machado in 1916, when he traveled with Domínguez Berrueta, his professor at the University of Granada, and a group of other students on a tour of Spanish historical and monumental sites that went through the town of Baeza in northern Andalusia, where Machado lived. More compelling still is the fact that Machado's brief poem speaks so tellingly of Lorca's literally and figuratively traveling "to the world" in the name of Spanish culture, a culture that was, on the one hand, infinitely proud of his achievements while, on the other, scandalized by both his (homo) sexuality and his politics.[16] One might rightly argue, then, that to go forth as the voice of his country, to speak Spain, as it were, Lorca had to be at least somewhat conflicted, if not always particularly circumspect, about the matter of his various desires. Or in the more figurative vein that Machado's poem suggests, Lorca's talent and ability were themselves dependent upon a certain deadening of the poet, the icing of the heart that would allow him to become a suitable product for domestic and international consumption.

"To Fly Off without Direction"

García Lorca was an uneasy traveler. He was by all accounts profoundly afraid of boats and ships. Moreover, as Leslie Stainton has reported, he seemed surprisingly, even hysterically, afraid of everyday occurrences, particularly as these related to movement through space. Water, automobiles, traffic, and street crossings all loomed large and ominous in his imagination. "He often pleaded with taxi drivers to slow down," Stainton writes. "Morbidly afraid of crossing city streets he would latch onto a friend's arm and sometimes leap back to the curb in a panic after setting out into traffic" (Stainton, *Lorca: A Dream of Life*, 457). Lorca himself seemed at least partially aware of the phobias that travel could engender in him. Upon arriving in Buenos Aires in October 1933 and beginning a months-long stay in the city that would cement his international reputation and provide the financial independence from his parents for which he had long hoped, Lorca found himself somewhat dumbfounded, commenting to one of the many reporters who came to meet him at the dock,

> Please forgive me. It's just that when I travel, I don't know who I am. It's what I call the "discomfort of traveling," the discomfort of arrival and departure, when people drag you from one side to the other, and in a daze you respond mechanically and let yourself be pushed and pulled, oblivious to everything around you. (Quoted in Stainton, *Lorca: A Dream of Life*, 343)

And yet travel, the travel of the poet and playwright himself and even more importantly the travel of his considerable reputation, was a singular element in Lorca's life and work. This was while he was—and is—

known as an author who revealed a specifically Andalusian experience, who expressed in his best-known collection of poetry, *Romancero gitano* (*Gypsy Ballads*), a sense of the "hidden," intimate world of "Gypsies," and who, especially in the most famous of his plays (*Blood Wedding, The House of Bernarda Alba, Doña Rosita the Spinster, or The Language of Flowers*, and *Yerma*), was consistently concerned with the matter of the stifling/deadening effects of cloistering women within the closed and inward-focused homes, the *cármenes*, of southern Spain. Thus as Jonathan Mayhew has suggested, one of the great paradoxes attending the reception of Lorca and his work may be that he was seen as so infinitely translatable and transportable precisely because he was also seen as being so peculiarly Andalusian. Discussing Lorca's iconic status in the United States, Mayhew writes,

> My intuition is that Lorca's embodiment of Spanish cultural exceptionalism, far from being an obstacle, made him all the more useful to American poets. In the first place, he could satisfy the American hunger for cultural *difference* in a way that a poet from a less exotic locale—Belgium, say—could not. At the same time, Spanish cultural nationalism could provide an implicit model for an alternative construction of American culture.[17]

Mayhew's arguments for the importance of Spain in the production of the United States' self-conception are well taken. Even the most casual observer will note that American culture(s) share an unexpected structural similarity to the culture(s) of Spain in that they continually court a certain ideological distance from Europe while remaining eager to be recognized as vibrant, advanced, and singularly important to the modernity and continual modernization with which Europe is associated. In both Spain (with its presumably ancient rituals and long-established rhythms) and the United States (with its supposedly fresh thinking and capacity for change), one finds clearly articulated the notion that it is this very cultural difference that the rest of the world needs, this not quite fitting in that makes "us" so very valuable to "them."

Still, my focus remains on the correspondences between the representation of enslaved Africans (and their descendants) in so-called Western culture and similar forms of expression in Spain and the Iberian

Peninsula. As I argue in much of my writing, including elsewhere in this book, part of the struggle for African American intellectuals of the twentieth century involved the need to confront the fact that in order to gain access to communications media, particularly those of the highly capitalized markets of the United States, they often had to trade on the tendency to see Black Americans as evocations of a primitive and unchanging African folk culture.[18] The problem, however, is that while such a strategy might get one's books read, one's paintings exhibited, and perhaps one's bills paid to boot, it nonetheless ultimately works to limit what the black artist can say, to whom he can say it, and how. Moreover, for those many native Africans, (African) Americans, and other persons of African descent whose work has been imagined first and foremost as a struggle against the processes by which a plethora of individuals, institutions, and social structures (European, American, and otherwise) have attempted to circumscribe and domesticate (our) humanity, there is always an acrid, somewhat metallic taste left in the mouth when we are asked to reveal again the secrets crouched behind our (tribal) scars, no matter how high the retaining fees might be.

My intention is to demonstrate that Lorca was caught up in this very paradox, the paradox I attempted to name when I noted the fact that enslaved Africans had by necessity to privilege abstraction in their efforts to make sense of the viciousness of the basic structures of modernity. Part of what I find so exciting and enticing about Lorca is that he has left on the page, as it were, such a clear record of the everyday rites and rituals that one might utilize to circumvent these practices. As any number of commentators (most notably Lorca himself) have stated before me, he was not exactly the provincial genius of the land whom many have taken him to be.[19] Instead, he was an intellectual whose efforts remarked, often with surprising clarity, the complicated (aesthetic) legacies of slavery and colonization in Europe and the Americas, legacies that one might discern in the very primitivist impulses that I have just attempted to describe.

LT. COLONEL: And who are you?
GYPSY: A gypsy.
LT. COLONEL: And what is a gypsy?
GYPSY: Just about anything.

LT. COLONEL: What's your name?
GYPSY: Just that.
LT. COLONEL: What did you say?
GYPSY: Gypsy.

. . .

LT. COLONEL: Where were you?
GYPSY: On the bridge of all rivers.
LT. COLONEL: What rivers?
GYPSY: All of them.
LT. COLONEL: And what were you doing there?
GYPSY: Making a tower of cinnamon.

. . .

GYPSY: I've invented wings to fly, and I fly. Sulfur and rose on
    my lips!
LT. COLONEL: Ay!
GYPSY: Even though I don't need wings, for I fly without them.
    Clouds and rings on my tongue.
LT. COLONEL: Ayyy!
GYPSY: In January I have orange blossoms.
LT. COLONEL (SQUIRMING IN IRRITATION): Ayyy!
GYPSY: And oranges in the snow.
LT. COLONEL: Ayyyy! Blam! Blam! (He falls over dead.)
    *(The tobacco and coffee soul of the Lieutenant Colonel of the Civil
    Guard flies though the window.)*

    . . .

    *(In the courtyard of the barracks, four Civil Guards beat the gypsy
    boy.)*[20]

The complexity that one confronts when attempting to decipher the
codes of this poem is much simplified when one reads the work as emanating not only from a specifically Iberian milieu but also from the
more general context of the many colonialist and imperialist encounters
that have helped to establish humanist epistemological and aesthetic
practices. The poem works not simply because it represents the ugly encounter between presumed Spaniards and supposed Gypsies. Nor is the
work a wholly generic explication of the aesthetic/ideological structure
underlying the struggle between strong and weak. Instead, as with the

encounters between slaves and buyers, it speaks to the manner in which articulations—and counterarticulations—of power have been established by the difficulties inherent in the specifically Euro-American innovation of not only working to dominate the other, not simply robbing him of his name, but also and importantly of attempting to systematize this process such that one Gypsy, one slave, becomes indistinguishable from the next.

The text is brimming, indeed overflowing, with both measured confrontations and equally precise resistances that seem nonetheless to exist just outside the consciousness of the work's protagonists. The boy's mule-faced look (*mirada de mulo*) suggests that he is an impossible being created through the domesticating processes presumably undertaken most successfully by the Civil Guard itself. Yet he is a Gypsy, a traveler, the longevity of whose (Iberian) history challenges that of the "white" Europeans themselves, but who nonetheless makes no claims to sovereignty. This clumsy inexplicability is announced, however, within an impeccably paced, highly rhythmic poem in which this same Gypsy acts to establish a pronounced metrical certainty. Strangely, then, the pointed questioning by the Lieutenant Colonel, questioning that is meant to affix meaning to both boy and environment, only functions to unravel the received logic of the work. The more the Gypsy is allowed to speak, the more complex his sentences become, the more irritated and uncertain are the reactions of the Civil Guard. In the logic of colonial contact, the expansion of the iterative strategies of "the colonized" are inversely proportionate to the ability of "the colonizer" to speak at all; as the Gypsy gains his voice, as the rhythm of his song turns toward melody, the Lieutenant Colonel inevitably loses hold of well-established logics of articulation (Ay! Ayyy! Ayyy! Ayyy!) and dies.

> A gypsy
> Just about anything
> Just that
> Gypsy
> On the bridge of all rivers
> All of them
> Making a tower of cinnamon
> I've invented wings to fly, and I fly. Sulfur and rose on my lips!

Even though I don't need wings, for I fly without them.
Clouds and rings on my tongue
In January I have orange blossoms
And oranges in the snow.

I beg you to forgive this vulgar manipulation, this ugly amputation of Lorca's fine lyrics. Moreover, I must rush to say that I do not believe that it is possible for the so-called subaltern to speak in languages that are not already freighted with the detritus of colonialist and white supremacist domination.[21] I do, however, want to argue that part of what Lorca was attempting in this work, included in his 1931 collection *Poema del cante jondo* (*Poem of the Deep Song*), was to articulate the mechanics of antiphony, "call and response," that will be immediately recognizable to anyone with even the slightest knowledge of the traditions of flamenco to which Lorca is obviously gesturing, not to mention the blues, gospel, and jazz, with which we know he was fascinated at least since his trip to New York City in 1929. The stress here, however, is decidedly *not* on the sort of reciprocity for which these musical forms are so well known. This is not the *cantaor* trilling his lament to the answering chorus of guitars and castanets, nor is it the minister lining out the rhythms of his belief to an infinitely receptive congregation. Instead it is "deep song," that previously unimaginable elemental substance expressed from the throat of the Gypsy by the hostile entreaties of the Lieutenant Colonel. The beating that he receives in the barracks yard of the Civil Guard is intended not so much to punish him for what he has done as to shut him up, to repress again that unspoken, unspeakable knowledge that so threatens the logics underwriting the mechanics of an insistent and indeed violent systematization.

This hopefully helps you to understand why I have repeatedly—and insistently—argued that the problems that confronted the artists whom I discuss here were not so much aesthetic and psychological as historical and ideological. We still have not yet fully undertaken the work of dismantling the conceptual structures that allow us to maintain such an easy distinction between those "whites" slaughtered on European battlefields and those many "blacks" slaughtered on the equally bloodsoaked fields of European and American "development." What I credit Lorca with, then, is not some particularly self-conscious understanding of these matters, but instead the simple reality that he allowed himself to remain at least somewhat sensitive to the global nature of the structural complexities undergirding the debates around artistic form and practice that took place in Spain during the early part of the twentieth century. One begins to have more patience with Lorca's coyness and hesitancy in regard to the liberal Spanish assumption that everything that came from the metropolis (most notably surrealism) was not only good, but also somehow cleansed of the stench of human misery that suffused so much in the lives of Spain's largely provincial and agricultural population. The risk that he took in much of his poetry was to attempt to hold both of these beliefs in the same hand.

> The river Guadalquivir
> flows between orange and olive trees.
> The two rivers of Granada
> descend from snow to wheat.
>
> Oh love
> that left and did not return!
>
> The river Guadalquivir
> has garnet whiskers.
> The two rivers of Granada:
> one of tears, the other of blood.
>
> Oh love
> that left through the air!
>
> Seville has a road
> for sailboats;
> only sighs row
> on the waters of Granada.
>
> Oh love
> that left and did not return!
>
> Guadalquivir, high tower

and wind in the orange groves.
Dauro and Genil, little towers
dead in the reflecting pools.

Oh love
that left through the air!

Who would guess that the water carries
a will-o'-the-wisp of shouts!

Oh love
that left and did not return.

It carries olives and orange blossoms,
Andalusia, to your seas.

Oh, love
that left through the air![22]

There is something odd, not exactly right, about this seemingly quite simple and straightforward poem, "Ballad of the Three Rivers" ("Baladilla de los tres ríos"). On the one hand, the piece clearly celebrates both the stunning landscape of Andalusia (rivers and olive trees, towers and reflecting pools) and the popular artistic forms (ballads) for which the region is so famous. On the other, the work is insistently plaintive and vexed, lamenting in every other stanza a love that "did not return," that "left through the air." Tears and shouts vie with sailboats and orange groves for rhetorical prominence, suggesting a balladeer uncertain of himself, caught between a will to name the specificity of the place that he sings while also knowing that this location, perhaps all locations, gain substance—or perhaps better put, exchange value—only at the moment at which one leaves them. It follows that if we are to read this poem as a paean to Andalusia, we will have to admit that the poet, the singer, truly appreciates the beauty of Al Andalus only when he departs from it. More distressing still, this leave-taking cannot be figured as the romanticized ritual of sighs, good wishes, and handkerchief waving that all too often captivates the imaginations of Europeans and Americans. Instead, one notes here that there is blood in the water, an ugly forcefulness, "a will-o'-the-wisp of shouts," that tends to leave one a bit stunned, if not exactly trembling.

"Another Thousand"

I would like to pause for a moment in order to address one of the more tense silences that the careful reader of this chapter may have noted already. Specifically, though I have only tentatively touched upon the subject myself, it is clear that much contemporary Lorca criticism, particularly Ian Gibson's excellent biography, *Federico García Lorca: A Life*, and Ángel Sahuquillo's groundbreaking study, *Federico García Lorca and the Culture of Male Homosexuality*, has addressed with equal measures of sobriety and vigor the ways that Lorca's sexuality and sexual practice impacted both his art and that art's reception.[23] It seems, in fact, that one of the key fault lines in the revaluation of Lorca and his work in contemporary Spanish culture is precisely the question of whether it is best to foreground Lorca's homosexuality, thereby further challenging the disabling homophobia that was actively encouraged during the Franco dictatorship, or simply to acknowledge that García Lorca was one of the greatest poets and playwrights of the twentieth century, regardless of the nature of his desires.

For his part, Sahuquillo stands decidedly on the side of those who wish to name and celebrate Lorca's status as a sexual minority, making an important, if never quite fully developed, connection between Lorca's interest in traveling and travelers and the ways that this interest suggests what one might call a gay sensibility. Speaking of images of ships and sailors in Lorca's oeuvre, Sahuquillo writes,

> Lost in the censored pages of history, there is a long tradition of homosexual practices at sea. In the Spanish galleons, for example, there was a detailed code which specified the sexual freedom or loyalty of the men who "belonged" to each other during a trip. Its objective was to control jealousy in order to avoid fights and maintain order on board. (Sahuquillo, *Federico Garcia Lorca*, 77)

Sahuquillo's point is easily taken here. Given that depictions of sailors appear in much gay art (Rainer Fassbinder's 1982 film adaptation of Jean

Genet's 1947 novel *Querelle de Brest* comes most readily to mind) as well as the fact that both Ian Gibson and Leslie Stainton report that Lorca became somewhat more comfortable and open about his homosexuality after his (sea) voyage to the United States, Cuba, and Argentina, one might rightly conclude that Lorca's movement out of Spain allowed him to come to terms with his sexuality, and, moreover, that he utilized the rather common motif of the ship as a means to express this newfound liberation. Still, though I celebrate Sahuquillo's efforts to uncover hidden homosexual codes in Lorca's writing, I am also eager to make the simple observation that the ship was a central technology in the production of not only the modern conception of the homosexual but also the slave and his American descendent, the black, as well. Further, I must insist again that these processes of naming were not simply liberatory, but also reiterative and repressive—leveling, in de Certeau's language. The homosexual becomes a sort of generic, stretched out figure in much the manner of the black or the Gypsy, a modern (non)subject whose presence is as much a factor of his fungibility as any innate difference or peculiarity.

I will claim for homosexuals, therefore, membership in the always difficult to discern communities of traveling kin that have both supported and challenged the relentless violence that I have argued is *the* most obvious aspect of the various ideological structures supporting Western humanism. The homosexual, like the black, is a subject whose presence is constant and inevitable, but never fully appreciated or noted. His primary role is to support. In making these arguments I turn toward another of Lorca's famed dialogues, the obviously homoerotic "Diálogo del Amargo" ("Dialogue of Amargo"), in which an adolescent boy, Amargo, separated from his traveling companions, is repeatedly solicited by an unnamed rider during his journey to Granada. The work is at once somber and provocative, demonstrating Lorca's pronounced ability to demonstrate the tension and danger of overwritten desire. What troubles the reader, however, is the persistence and the veiled aggression of the rider, who counters Amargo's resistance by informing him that he has three brothers in the coastal city of Málaga who are vendors of knives: "Knives that find the heart all by themselves. Silver ones that cut the throat like a blade of grass."

RIDER: Do you want a knife?

AMARGO: No.

RIDER: But look, I'm giving it to you.

AMARGO: But I won't accept it.

RIDER: You won't have another chance.

AMARGO: Who knows?

RIDER: Other knives are useless. Other knives are soft and scared of blood. The ones we sell are cold. Understand? They go in looking for the hottest spot, and there they stop.

(*Amargo says nothing. His right hand grows cold as if it is holding a piece of gold.*)

RIDER: What a beautiful knife!

AMARGO: Is it worth very much?

RIDER: But perhaps you'd rather have this one.

(*He takes out a gold knife whose point shines like the flame of a candle.*).

AMARGO: I said no.

RIDER: Boy, climb up here with me!

AMARGO: I'm not tired yet.

. . .

RIDER: As I was telling you, my three brothers are in Málaga. How they sell knives! At the cathedral they bought two thousand of them to adorn all the altars and put a crown on the tower. Many a ship wrote its name on them. Down by the sea, the poorest fishermen get light from the luster of their sharp blades.

AMARGO: How beautiful it is!

RIDER: Who could deny it?

In the darkness the two lose their way, so that when they reach Granada, if in fact it is Granada to which they have come, Amargo finds himself confused by the lights of the large and lonely city, leaving the reader with the distinct impression that Amargo has been tricked. Is it Granada that awaits him or dangerous, captivating Málaga, where the rider's knife-wielding brothers attend the risk and promise of the sea?

RIDER: Up with you! Quick! Come on up! We have to get there before the break of day. And take this knife. I'm giving it to you!

AMARGO: Ay yayayay!

(The Rider helps Amargo up, and the two of them take the road into Granada. In the background the mountains bristle with hemlocks and nettles.)[24]

While it is clear that even as homosexual desire binds together Amargo, a youth separated from his companions, his corduroy jacket wrapped about his waist, a big silver watch ticking "dark" in his pocket, with the rider, purveyor of obviously phallic knives, one of whose points "shines like the flame of a candle," it is also clear that there is a heavy sense of menace that pervades the poem. Shining and phallic or not, these are knives that we are talking about, knives always looking for the hottest spot. As with the "Scene of the Lieutenant Colonel of the Civil Guard," one notes that for Lorca the Socratic dialogue is not only an erotic affair, but also a potentially violent one as well. Thus at the risk of restating the obvious, I will reiterate my claim that the aesthetic structures that Lorca displays here are wholly similar to those utilized by generations of masters and slaves in the market cultures of Europe, Africa, and America. The youth's name, Amargo (bitter), suggests a character aware of the danger inherent in practices of travel and trade, the often dangerous choices that one must make in the process of living one's life and confronting the loneliness of the world. Nonetheless it is this despair (this bitterness) that leads one "to the world." The poem speaks to the danger of overreaching oneself, becoming so lost in the beguiling dark of the *madrugada* that one might find one's brief trip to Granada with its protective, embracing mountains interrupted by a rider, with brothers at the coast in Málaga where traders might measure the weight of a boy's life with pieces of gold capable of turning the hands suddenly cold.

At his best, Lorca seemed to understand the ways both masters *and* servants involve themselves in a delicate dance of appraisal and subterfuge, domination and resistance. If you accept that Amargo had no choice, but to "go with the rider," with all the implications that this phrase holds, then it seems that the youth's artistry was established by his hesitancy. As is true with many others before and after him, his obstinate behavior was wholly dangerous in a world in which all odds were stacked against him. At the same time, however, it seems that the boy does gain at least a knife and a ride for his labor; small recompense, yes, but still emblems of a certain irritation that he has effected within the system, a refusal of the leveling and deadening that I have been at pains to represent.

I submit that what irritates Lorca here is not the fact that the boy is in danger, nor the reality that his dialogue with the rider suggests the turbulent, brooding tension that may be the very hallmark of adolescent sexuality. Instead, what concerns Lorca is again the *de*humanization that is so much a part of modern life. Amargo is no one special. He is any boy, lost, alone, a bit frightened and yet strangely invigorated on one of the many roads and pathways that lead to the shining balconies of unfamiliar cities. There is nothing spectacular about the decisions he makes; nothing remotely peculiar about his taking that knife, mounting that horse, entrusting his life to the uneasy exigencies of capital and trade. These are the same blandly dangerous decisions made by countless unnamed, barely remembered youths every day on every continent, as they accede to the rider's whispers and commands, perhaps loved, perhaps abused, perhaps both, with the deathly pall of hemlock and nettles in the bristling twilight erasing the evidence of ancient, established identity, locally valued presence. Thus Amargo's mother wisely and soberly reminds us in the poem that accompanies and completes this text, "Song of Amargo's Mother" ("Canción de la madre del Amargo") not to exhibit foolish, untoward histrionics, not to imagine that her son's absence, his inevitable departure, his "death," is anything out of the normal: "No llorad ninguna. El Amargo está en la luna." (Don't cry anyone. Amargo [bitterness] is on the moon.)[25]

Here is where one gets close to understanding what motivated Lorca's vexed depictions of homosexuals in a work like "Ode to Walt Whitman" ("Oda a Walt Whitman"). What Lorca always wants to privilege in his writing is what one might think of as an irreducible peculiarity, a (homosexual) identity that cannot be properly transported/translated from one port to the next. He wants to maintain some place, however limited, in which flesh might escape violation. In the particular case of Walt Whitman, Lorca notes the fact of the strange and rare poet's having helped to deliver his countrymen and countrywomen from the confines of rhymed and metered verse while also making the case that Whitman's legacy should not be delimited by the vigor of the Euro-American obsession with types and typology, the denial of the poet's specificity and peculiarity.

Not for a moment, Walt Whitman, lovely old man,
Have I failed to see your beard full of butterflies,
nor your corduroy shoulders frayed by the moon,
nor your thighs as pure as Apollo's,
nor your voice like a column of ash;
old man, beautiful as the mist,
you moaned like a bird
with its sex pierced by a needle.
Enemy of the satyr,
enemy of the vine,
and lover of bodies beneath rough cloth.

. . .

Nor for a moment, virile beauty,
who among mountains of coal, billboards, and railroads,
dreamed of becoming a river and sleeping like a river
with that comrade who would place in your breast
the small ache of an ignorant leopard.

Not for a moment, Adam of blood, Macho,
man alone at sea, Walt Whitman, lovely old man,
because on penthouse roofs,
gathered at bars,
emerging in bunches from the sewers,
trembling between the legs of chauffeurs,
or spinning on dance floors wet with absinthe,
the faggots, Walt Whitman, point you out.

He's one too! That's right! And they land
on your luminous chaste beard,
blonds from the north, blacks from the sands,
crowds of howls and gestures,
like cats or like snakes,
the faggots, Walt Whitman, the faggots,
clouded with tears, flesh for the whip,
the boot, or the teeth of the lion tamers.[26]

It is clear that through Whitman, Lorca is eager to relate what amounts to an almost pastoral conception of sexuality. In the process he is able to remain rigidly certain that "the old man's" desires and practices, "beautiful as the mist," were altogether distinct from what one finds articulated by "the faggots," blond, black, cats and snakes, gathering at bars, emerging from sewers, trembling between the legs of chauffeurs, flesh for the whips. For Lorca, writing out of his shock and fascination upon encountering New York for the first time in the collection *Poet in New York*, Whitman represents a compromise of sorts. This old, macho "Adam of blood," dressed like Amargo in proletarian corduroy, denotes the promise of America with its freshness and peculiarity while nevertheless remaining somehow aloof from the modern—and modernist—dehumanization that so bothered and frightened Lorca. Though Whitman might have sung his poems among "mountains of coal, billboards, and railroads," he continued in his originality. He was no slave, indistinguishable from the enervating systematization that Lorca encountered (or thought he encountered) on the infinitely rational, quadrangular blocks of New York. Instead he was a virile beauty, whose desire for his beloved was as feral as ignorant leopards, as ancient as sleeping rivers.

I must frankly admit at this juncture that I see Lorca's rhetoric in this ode as structurally indistinct from that of generations of American and European liberals who have run their own defenses of enslaved and colonized persons through a sort of active (and activist) nostalgia in which the name of the game is to resist at all costs the unveiling of the unknown and the unnameable. Thus Whitman must not be pointed out. He must not be called "that"! For to do so would be to concede that there is no language, no deep song that has not been soiled already by the vulgarities of modernization, systematization, repression, reiteration, and leveling. Or to mount a more generous reading of his aesthetics, one might argue that part of what Lorca achieves is a defense of the formal structures of the rituals of resistance with which he was so fascinated— indeed, that his fascination with so-called subaltern subjects was a factor of both the complexity of their speech *and* their silence. Unfortunately, however, this leads Lorca not only to stray far too close to those many individuals who would protest that a faggot is a faggot whether he has published some clever poems or not, but also to revert (even as he tries on the awkwardly fitting mantle of surrealism) to the very romantic tropes of a hyper-individualized (fixed) identity that he and so many others of his generation struggled against.

> That's why I don't raise my voice, old Walt Whitman,
> against the little boy who writes
> the name of a girl on his pillow,
> nor against the boy who dresses as a bride
> in the darkness of the wardrobe,
> nor against the solitary men in casinos
> who drink prostitution's water with revulsion,
> nor against the men with that green look in their eyes
> who love other men and burn their lips in silence.
>
> But yes against you, urban faggots,
> tumescent flesh and unclean thoughts.
> Mothers of mud. Harpies. Sleepless enemies
> of the love that bestows crowns of joy.
> Always against you, who give boys
> drops of foul death with bitter poison.
> Always against you,
> Fairies of North America,
> Pájaros of Havana,
> Jotos of Mexico,
> Sarasas of Cadiz,
> Apios of Seville,
> Cancos of Madrid,
> Floras of Alicante,
> Adelaidas of Portugal.
>
> Faggots of the world, murderers of doves!
> Slaves of women. Their bedroom bitches.
> Opening in public squares like fans
> or ambushed in rigid hemlock landscapes.
>
> No quarter given! Attention!
> Let the confused, the pure,

> the classical, the celebrated, the supplicants
> close the doors of the bacchanal to you. (Lorca, "Ode to Walt
> Whitman," 731, 733)

The strange thing, of course, is that Lorca's own movement between New York, Havana, Cádiz, Seville, Madrid, and Alicante was made possible by any number of "urban faggots" who prepared, opened (leveled, if you will) the way for the young poet's arrival. Moreover, Lorca himself, Lorca the traveler, was one of the means, one of many, by which these individuals came to understand themselves as part of an infinitely fungible "global" community. We should be careful, however, not simply to name Lorca as reactionary or old-fashioned and wash our hands of the matter. Instead, I suspect that what we are witnessing is real confusion on Lorca's part about just how profound and complicated the protocols of leveling actually are in modern society. The highly idiosyncratic, confused, pure, and classical subject is, in fact, an impossibility. It represents a refracted image of the socially dead slave. It is the infinitely pure figure of philosophy and sociology whose presence disrupts all critical and progressive political practices. The faggot, on the other hand, is like the black in that he both concedes and resists. He is a public character opening like fans in the squares of Santiago, Barcelona, Valencia, Granada, and Porto. Yet there is something untoward and undisciplined in his actions. All that trembling, spinning, and murdering of doves suggests an unchecked animality, a disloyalty to the most sacred of humanism's many conceits.

"Iré a Santiago"

Federico García Lorca never arrived in New York. There is some doubt, in fact, as to whether he left Europe at all. This is of course not to say that he did not stalk Manhattan streets, cross Brooklyn bridges, catch Harlem trains, or stumble toward the wet sobriety of ever-peaceful Vermont. On the contrary, it seems certain that a personage born on June 5, 1898, with the impossibly old-fashioned name Federico del Sagrado Corazón de Jesús García Lorca stamped inside his passport did, in fact, disembark from the S.S. *Olympic*, sister ship of the *Titanic*, on June 25, 1929, to be warmly greeted and soundly cheered by an eager crowd of friends and well-wishers. There is, moreover, record of someone bearing an uncanny resemblance to the famed poet and playwright enrolling as an unimpressive student of English at Columbia University, frequenting the city's many clubs and theaters (particularly enjoying the so-called black revues), presenting himself in literary Gotham (meeting both Hart Crane and Nella Larsen), and witnessing the grim shock of the October stock market crash. Nevertheless I must continue to insist that García Lorca never ventured as far as "our America." Though Lorca undoubtedly came to New York, he never truly arrived. Instead, as he crossed the deep, disinterested Atlantic, he prepared himself to meet not New York per se (one wonders whether this is ever really possible) but instead one of the city's countless simulacra that undoubtedly loomed breathtaking and *sur*real as his ship lumbered past the fine beaches of Sandy Hook and into the fretfulness of New York harbor.

Of course, like many well-educated Europeans of his day, Lorca already associated the city with countless comings and goings, crossings and misdirections. It must have seemed a place that existed outside human reality—"on the moon," if you will—while remaining the very emblem of where the world was headed. Lorca believed that in such a place you should not (at least not immediately) present your naked self. One might assume, therefore, that García Lorca was defeated by the complexity of New York City. Contravening his steadfast resistance to deadening, reiteration, and leveling, the very resistance on display in his evocation of what I have called "the known homosexual," the evidence suggests that before Lorca walked down the gangplank of the *Olympic* he carefully cloaked himself in a mantle of anxious resignation. "I look at myself in the mirror of the narrow cabin and I don't recognize myself," he wrote to friends in Spain. "I seem another Federico" (quoted in Stainton, *Lorca: A Dream of Life*, 221). Lorca, confronted by the unrepentant capitalist hunger of New York, seemed perfectly aware of the need to prepare some form of self-representation, some avatar that could be sold at market, even while attempting as best he could to protect the sanctity of his presumably inviolable essence. Moreover, the very fact that he never attained more than a rudimentary understanding of the English language implies that he not only accepted but also perhaps courted a certain distance from his "interlocutors." He kept mum behind the mask (the *lorquismo*) that he carried with him from Spain.

What may relieve the pessimism of this line of thought is the reiteration of my intent to read Lorca in intimate relation to an Atlantic cultural tradition bounded by slavery. I run my consideration of the artist and his art through an awareness of the forms of cultural agency and resistance available to the slave, particularly the slave at market. I will allow, then, that Lorca utilized the very traditions of dissimulation and masking that we note and often celebrate among enslaved persons and their descendants. This seems a simple enough claim to make. What is considerably more difficult to know is whether Lorca would have thought the same. I have discussed already "El niño Stanton" ("Little Stanton") and "Oda a Walt Whitman" ("Ode to Walt Whitman"), two of the poems included in Lorca's extremely influential 1941 collection, *Poet in New York*. In those treatments, I demonstrated the pseudo-surrealism that Lorca displays as well as the discomfort he exhibits with (gay) urban life. I will add that part of what distinguishes *Poet in New York* from earlier collections of Lorca's poetry is the fact that both his form and style seem to loosen significantly. He notably abandons his reliance on meter. The imagery that he creates tends more toward evocation (a beard full of butterflies; an apple's chaste longing to be pecked by nightingales) than specificity. One might argue, therefore, that regardless of the height of the buildings or the regularity of the streets, Lorca found little that was fixed in New York. He believed that the city was absolutely unlike the ancient fields of Granada, where a farmer's plow might unearth a Roman mosaic, or a short walk up a steep hill might land one in the breathtaking splendor of a centuries-old "Moorish" castle. Instead, the excitement of America was built upon the fact that there was "no there there," to borrow Gertrude Stein's apt phrase.

Lorca assumed that he was encountering a culture in the process of forming itself, a place full of wildness and possibility that was at once barbaric, uncouth, and modern. Overemphasizing both originality and primogeniture, Lorca's most potent desire during his brief stay in the United States seems to have been to unveil what lay behind the outrageous efforts of the American people to express the nature of their relationships to each other, their country, and the rest of the world. In a sense, he reiterated the presumed thinking of the so-called natives by which he found himself surrounded. He had come to a place overdetermined by memory of a migratory past. All action seemed to evoke displacement and our clumsy efforts to recall something recently forgotten. Writing to his family about a party at the home of Dorothy Peterson, the African American socialite and close friend to the novelist Nella Larsen, he commented,

> At the party there was a black woman who, without exaggeration, is the most beautiful woman I have ever seen. There just couldn't be greater perfection of features or a more perfect body. She danced by herself a sort of rumba accompanied by the tom-tom (an African drum), and seeing her dance was such a pure, such a tender sight, that it could only be compared to the moon coming over the sea or something simple and eternal in Nature. As you can imagine I was thrilled with the party. With the same writer I went to a Black night-club, and I remembered Mother, because it was a place like the ones you see in the cinema and which frighten her so much. (Quoted in Gibson, *Federico García Lorca*, 255)

I am not certain that one could produce a more straightforward evocation of the ideological and discursive structures of primitivism than this. The woman is perfect and beautiful precisely to the extent that she conforms to long-established ("ancient") conceptions of an unchanging African essence. She dances alone, thereby disallowing even the hint of sociality. It is almost as if she has magically appeared before the poet, along with the tom-tom, somehow transporting herself without aid of taxi or subway to the protected confines of the party. She is moon, sea, and eternal nature. Yet just when the poet's self-deception seems complete, he gives evidence that the images he invokes are hardly ancient, but just as vulgarly contemporary as the cinema that so frightens his mother.[27] It is clear that as gifted and advanced as Lorca was, he had not yet developed anything approaching a sophisticated conception of the mechanics of hybridity or transnationalism. Syncretism and cross-fertilization were underdeveloped ideas for him. The female dancer whom he encounters cannot be both African *and* American. Instead, as beautiful as she may be, she becomes in Lorca's fine prose a somewhat pathetic figure struggling to free herself from beneath the detritus of a leveling modernity.

I feel compelled to draw attention to the uncanny nature of Lorca's having encountered these images of a kinetic black beauty at least partially through the interposition of the Harlem Renaissance writer Nella Larsen. Though Lorca never seems to have noticed, Larsen was a profoundly talented practitioner of the delicate art of masking while also being one of her generation's most gifted, most piercing commentators on the ways that much within modern African American culture depends on the production of increasingly complex narratives of identity in which gestures of self-display are most often recitations of the necessity of maintaining the purity and inviolability of some private, elemental self. Born in Chicago in April 1891, Larsen (née Nellie Walker) was the child of a white Danish mother and a black West Indian father who Larsen claimed died when she was approximately two years old, leaving her mother free to marry her second husband, Peter Larsen. This relatively simple narrative is put into doubt, however, by Thadious Davis's biography of Larsen, in which she suggests that Nella's "birth father," Peter Walker, may have been one and the same as her "adoptive father," Peter Larsen. Thus Nella was either a "mixed-race" child whose familial status was thrown into disarray by her mother's marriage to Larsen's putatively "white" stepfather or the inconveniently dark daughter of a "mixed" family intent upon passing.

This line of thought was itself pointedly challenged by George Hutchinson in his 2006 biography of Larsen, in which he demonstrates the veracity of Larsen's claims regarding her birth, arguing that Davis's mistakes—and more generally the machinery of distrust that has grown up around Larsen's work and her biography—are reflections of our contemporary discomfort with Larsen's obvious "ambivalence toward the black bourgeoisie and the rhetoric of race pride."[28] What is certain, however, is that by the time Larsen reached young adulthood and matriculated in the Normal Department of Fisk University in Nashville, Tennessee, she was estranged from her family and well along the path of continual self-renewal, dissimulation, and masking that would result in her continual renaming (Nellie Walker, Nellie Marie Larson, Nella Marion Larson, Nella Larsen Imes, Nella Larsen) as well as the publication of two remarkably sensitive novelistic treatments of African American identity: *Quicksand* (1928) and *Passing* (1929).[29]

I would like to stretch both Davis's and Hutchinson's claims in order to suggest that underlying the awkwardness of Larsen's biography, an awkwardness exacerbated by her desire to maintain "a certain invisibility and mysteriousness as a form of self protection," is a profound sensitivity to the complexities of the ideological split between flesh and dream that I argue stands at the heart of the humanist enterprise (Hutchinson, *In Search of Nella Larsen*, 11). What Lorca encountered when he met Larsen in 1929 was hardly a woman who might act as an uncomplicated conduit to the reality of African American life. Mixed-race and "orphaned," Nella Larsen was attempting to articulate herself within normative structures of race, nation, gender, and sexuality in which her own jumbled identity was rendered largely unintelligible. As with the protagonists of both her novels, Larsen was a figure who was forced to play with surfaces and preconceptions because these represented, in a sense, the only games in town. At the party at which Lorca encountered Larsen, he witnessed a rather rigorously scripted racial theater in which the wholly ambiguous figure of Nellie Walker/Nella Larsen (Imes) modeled a newly established racial/ethnic stability. What Lorca could not—or would not—recognize was that, notwithstanding all his fantasies of having encountered real, unwashed Africanity, Larsen herself was effectively passing for black. She was modeling the upper-class, genealogy-obsessed racial identity that acted as the social glue for the community of well-heeled Harlemites in which she found herself ensconced. With the pleasant (*divertido*) and conveniently non-English-speaking Lorca as an exotically vibrant party favor, Larsen was able to demonstrate a (black) cosmopolitanism and worldliness that carried with it the taint of neither abandonment nor bastardy.

Tellingly, though Larsen, born five years ahead of the Supreme Court's infamous *Plessy* decision, is primarily known as one of the key lights of the Harlem Renaissance, she was (like the younger Salaria Kea) a professional nurse, having graduated in 1915 from the R.N. training program of Lincoln Hospital in the Bronx. Lincoln's curriculum was both rigorous and academic, offering students instruction in practical nursing as well as the philosophy and history of the increasingly prestigious profession. Upon graduation, Larsen left to become the head nurse of the John A. Andrews Memorial Hospital of the Tuskegee Institute in Tuskegee, Alabama. As with Kea, Larsen's status as a nurse—and a novelist—placed her at precisely that location where the clumsiness of the mind/body divide is most apparent. Indeed, I would expand George Hutchinson's idea of Larsen's "mysteriousness," to suggest that her biography models the treacherous path undertaken by generations of African American intellectuals as they have attempted to develop ideas of (black) subjectivity and consciousness from within the warped crucible of racialist ideology that underwrote the *Plessy* decision. As Larsen attended to her patients (and her characters), as she negotiated with administrators (and editors), as she instructed her staff (and her readers), she was forced to grapple with the very ontological, epistemological, and ethical complexities addressed by the Supreme Court justices as they assured the country that "the white" and "the Negro" were not simply myths, trumped-up lies designed to cover the rank exploitation standing at the heart of slavery and colonization, but instead solidly established "facts" of humanity, biological realities with a phenomenological weight so crushing that single drops of blood coursing dangerously through human veins were more than enough to seal the fates of both individuals and nations.

That on November 14, 1929, shortly after meeting Lorca, Larsen would submit a successful application to the Guggenheim Foundation in order to travel to France and especially Spain, suggests that the former nurse and newly successful novelist was aware of the ways that clever play within the interstices of received thinking about race, nation, and culture could provide modern intellectuals with badly needed, if peculiarly established, breathing room in which to negotiate the more vulgar aspects of the modern. The presence of a jovial, piano-playing, and sociable Spaniard, his skin only a shade or two brighter than that of the ostensible Negroes by whom he found himself surrounded, must have suggested to Larsen that, notwithstanding Lorca's fantasies of African primitivism dancing gleefully in the midst of Harlem apartments, the racialism that stands so menacingly at the center of humanist discourse is not so firmly established or insurmountable as one might imagine.

My criticism of Lorca is that he could not recognize among blacks the same coyness that he associated with at least some homosexuals. Instead, the only approach he seemed capable or willing to make toward the Black American was that of the anthropologist. He had, that is, to struggle within the vicious apparatuses of humanism in order to clear space for the precious, if wholly anachronistic, beings and objects that he felt himself called to protect.

> The mask. Look how the mask
> comes from Africa to New York.

They are gone, the pepper trees,
the tiny buds of phosphorus.
They are gone, the camels with torn flesh,
and the valleys of light the swan lifted in its beak.

It was the time of parched things,
the wheat spear in the eye, the laminated cat,
the time of tremendous, rusting bridges
and the deathly silence of cork.

It was the great gathering of dead animals
pierced by the swords of light.
The endless joy of the hippopotamus with cloven feet of ash
and of the gazelle with an immortelle in its throat.

In the withered, waveless solitude,
The dented mask was dancing.
Half of the world was sand,
the other half mercury and dormant sunlight.

The mask. Look at the mask!
Sand, crocodile, and fear above New York.[30]

One of the things that I value about Lorca is that he at least notes the masking that has been so valued and celebrated among slaves and their descendants. That said, I must wonder whether Lorca ever truly understood that masks are markers of hyper-sophisticated discursive processes. To mask oneself is self-consciously to utilize tropes of both fixity and improvisation, historical depth and modern leveling. My concern, therefore, is that without this sophisticated understanding, Lorca risked betraying even his own well-established aesthetic/ideological values.

A repeated though somewhat undeveloped claim of this chapter has been that Lorca's poetry was never fully surrealistic. He never gave himself over like Salvador Dalí to the unscripted imagery of the unconscious. I wonder, therefore, about the highly impressionistic imagery included in the poems of *Poet in New York*. One might argue that the theme (the structure) of the poem that I have quoted above, "Streets and Dreams" ("Calles y sueños"), is nothing if not "impossibility." "The valleys of light the swan lifted in its beak," "the hippopotamus with cloven feet of ash," "the laminated cat"—all of these seem the gestures of a poet concerned with the articulation of a grammar of the unreal, an only vaguely understood aesthetics of awkward gestures and improbable pairings. Still, I continue to doubt that Lorca was describing what he believed to be a fantasy world. Instead, he was attempting to name what he took to be the awkward and grating manner in which ancient, elemental culture was overwritten by the structures of modernity. The first stanza, "The mask. Look how the mask / comes from Africa to New York," does not suggest that the process of masking is ancient or eternal, but, on the contrary, infinitely modern, decidedly American. If "the ancients," the singers and dancers whom Lorca continually hails, were to survive in a time of "parched things" and "rusting bridges," in a time when anything of value might quickly and unceremoniously be turned to coin, then they would necessarily have to utilize the forms of dissimulation and trickery (the masking) that I have argued Lorca only half understood as he stuttered through the unforgiving streets of New York.

I will submit to you, therefore, that Lorca never seemed to recognize what a novice he was when it came to understanding the complexity underwriting the mixture of African and American cultures. The conception of subjectivity that he utilized in his depictions of (some) homosexuals seemed to evaporate when the poet was confronted with naming the antiquity of the black in relation to the modernity of New York. Lorca could not bring himself to understand that the syncopated dialogic models that one might encounter in Spain were quite similar to what one might find in the United States. He did not recognize that the masking practices, the dark rites and rituals of the New World blacks whom he celebrates, are much more committed, much more improbably profound than anything he ever allowed himself to imagine.

When the American black dons the mask, he does not so much hide his old self as become something altogether distinct and peculiar, something capable of bridging old and new worlds. When the practitioners of voodoo, Santería, or Obeah (persons whom Lorca undoubtedly regularly came across in the streets of New York and Havana) dress themselves in the raiment of their ancestors, they are not at play, they are not pretending. Instead they are, at least for a moment, the embodiment of a truth that is at once ancient *and* modern. They are, in fact, living gods coaxed into the dormant sunlight, beings walking through death toward the promise of rebirth.[31] If, moreover, as Lorca insists, Harlem has *un gran rey prisionero, con un traje de conserje* (a grand king prisoner in the suit of a doorman), then this king must have both his prerogatives and his "mysteries."[32] He knows that though he may be trapped, he is not alone in his dungeon. On the contrary, the slavers themselves, no matter how privileged or fat, remain profoundly ensnared within the structures of leveling and domination that they themselves have helped establish. Thus what may ultimately separate the dour king of the doorways whom Lorca stumbled upon in New York from his somewhat naïve interlocutor is that he has the simple good sense neither to flaunt his knowledge nor celebrate his ignorance.

> Cuando llegue la luna llena
> iré a Santiago de Cuba,
> iré a Santiago
> en un coche de agua negra.
> Iré a Santiago.
> Cantarán los techos de palmera.
> Iré a Santiago.
> Cuando la palma quiere ser cigüeña,
> iré a Santiago.
> Y cuando quiere ser medusa el plátano
> iré a Santiago.
> Iré a Santiago
> con la rubia cabeza de Fonseca.
> Iré a Santiago.
> Y con la rosa de Romeo y Julieta
> iré a Santiago.
> Mar de papel y plata de monedas.
> Iré a Santiago.
> ¡Oh Cuba! Oh ritmo de semillas secas!
> Iré a Santiago.
> ¡Oh cintura caliente y gota de madera!
> Iré a Santiago.

Arpa de troncos vivos. Caimán. Flor de tabaco.
Iré a Santiago.
Siempre he dicho que yo iría a Santiago
en un coche de agua negra.
Iré a Santiago.
Brisa y alcohol en las ruedas,
iré a Santiago.
Mi coral en la tiniebla,
iré a Santiago.
El mar ahogado en la arena,
iré a Santiago.
Calor blanco, fruta muerta.
Iré a Santiago.
¡Oh bovino frescor de cañavera!
¡Oh Cuba! Oh curva de suspiro y barro!
Iré a Santiago.[33]

Much of what attracts me to this poem, "Son de Negros en Cuba" (which Greg Simon and Steven White translate as "Blacks Dancing to Cuban Rhythms," but which I prefer to name simply "*Son* of Blacks in Cuba"), is, in fact, its rhythm, its sound. I too would like to go to Santiago (*iré a Santiago!*), land of palms, bananas, storks, silver coins, flowers of tobacco, coral, rotting fruit, and sugarcane. One must wonder, however, why García Lorca remains so insistent that he will arrive there in *un coche de agua negra*, a car of black water. In Cuba, where the word *negro* (black) might be uttered one moment as the most profound slur and the next as the gentlest of gestures between lovers, you would be well advised to always pay strict attention to diction and shadings of meaning. Even more to the point, the fact that Lorca ends his brooding collection *Poet in New York* with this burst of rhythm and conviviality suggests, I believe, not so much that the author finally escaped the vulgarity and repression that he found in New York, but instead that he fooled himself into believing so. About Havana Lorca writes,

But what's this? Spain again? Universal Andalusia again?
It's the yellow of Cadiz, a bit stronger, the pink of Seville just turning carmine and the green of Granada with a slight, fish-like phosphorescence.

Havana emerges among bamboo groves and the sounds of maracas, Chinese horns and marimbas. And in the harbor, who comes to meet me? The dusky Trinidad of my childhood, the one who "went walking one morning along the quayside in Havana, down the quayside in Havana one morning went walking".

And here come the Blacks with their rhythms, which I suddenly realize derive from our great Andalusia—friendly Blacks, with no anguish, who show the whites of their eyes and say: "We are Latins." (Quoted in Gibson, *Lorca: A Life*, 282–83)

That is to say, Lorca has once again arrived nowhere. He seems, in fact, never to have left "universal" Andalusia. Instead, trapped behind a mask that he clearly forgot he was wearing, Lorca could see (and perhaps more importantly, hear) Cuba only as the evocation of the manufactured images of liberated exoticism ("Trinidad went walking one morning along the quayside") so popular in the *habaneras* of his youth. Thus the many blacks in the harbor seem to exist only for him. They are never working or fighting, thinking or plotting. They have no secret desires, no private anguish. Instead they become indistinguishable from the familiar and comforting sounds that they make, sounds that never suggest labor or loss, but instead only a friendly, wide-eyed, grinning acceptance of the poet and the culture that he believes he represents. "We are Latins!" they sing, perhaps coaxing a coin or two from the relieved traveler as they disencumber him of his bags.

Still, even as I chastise Lorca for turning toward primitivism upon encountering New World black subjects, I nonetheless imagine a writer struggling to discern the underlying complexity of Western humanism's many processes and conventions. In fact the question for generations of scholars has been how to read—and write—Africa, America, Europe, Black, White, English, and Spanish into the same sentences. Moreover, I must admit that my own tendency to turn toward the formal while maintaining that what is most important for me are matters of history and society, speaks itself to the complexity of plainly naming the truth of our collective culture, the simple fact that slavery, colonization, and the racialist structures that attend them underwrite—and articulate—*all* modern aesthetic practices, no matter how complex or aloof they may appear.

I will remind you then of another story, another set of rhythms to which one might attend as we attempt to broaden the historical and ideological contexts that Lorca evokes in "*Son* of Blacks in Cuba." In 1898 Black American soldiers arrived in Cuba, indeed in Santiago itself, to take up the unlikely task of fighting the good fight of American imperialism while also liberating not simply themselves but also the whole of the benighted, dispersed African people from the yoke of racist, imperialist oppression. They found that though they came well equipped with guns and mortar, cannon and shot, what they really needed but often lacked were the proper words. Though Cuba might have been "liberated" from the yoke of Spanish oppression, it was not exactly freed. Instead, the imperialist structures of the United States were substituted for those of Spain. The underlying social and ideological tensions, the jarring breaks in the basic rhythms of the island, remained firmly in place. No matter how wildly they danced nor how loudly they sang, the blacks in Cuba were never as naïve as Lorca seemed to believe. In 1953 Fidel Castro, friendly blacks to his left and right, also arrived in Santiago, leading an ill-fated attack against the Moncada Barracks. A handful of men died, dozens were injured or imprisoned, while many more would meet similar fates before the final overthrow of the dictatorship of Fulgencio Batista in 1959. Still, the ever-singing blacks seem always to suffer. One must wonder, therefore, what they might have said to the poet if he had really been of a mind to listen; what warnings they may have offered, what occult rites they might have shared before he left behind the pinks and greens of smiling Havana, boarded a haunted ship (*un coche de agua negra*), arranged himself in a narrow cabin, his heart still at least half frozen, and suffered the long journey back to the increasingly dangerous cacophony and volatility of a divided Spain.

Postscript

In a mid-August trip to Granada, in no mood to leave the delicious comfort of hotel air-conditioning, I found myself walking during the ugliest part of the day the mile or so down a small roasted slope, fumes and exhaust wild against my face. My destination was the Huerta de San Vicente, the former summer home of García Lorca's family, to which he

retreated at the beginning of the Spanish Civil War as the rebels continued their relentless march north.

Trotting through the small house of pleasant furnishings, ugly paintings, and impressive kitchen plumbing, our group (two young Greek
couples towing a bored three-year-old, a pair of French retirees, and me)
arrived with something like breathless expectation at Lorca's small sleep
chamber, a room dominated by a single bed covered by his mother's
handmade lace and the maestro's stately writing desk, where, we were
assured, he penned some of his most brilliant works. The guide admon-
ished us once, twice, thrice not to touch the desk, as it was a precious
object that must be kept whole and unchanged for generations to come.
Hanging above it was a large replica of a poster advertising La Barraca
Teatro Universitario of the Unión Federal de Estudiantes Hispanos, the
traveling theater troupe that Lorca once directed and whose activities
were thought contemptible by many conservative Spaniards. Blame it on
the heat or perhaps my growing impatience with the preciousness with
which the memory of García Lorca is treated in Spain, but I touched the
desk. I touched it three times in order to pair the guide's scolding "nos"
with my own clumsily mischievous "yeses." On the third pass she caught
me and launched into an obviously rehearsed, if still quite irritated, dis-
sertation on the preciousness of Lorca in the Spanish national patrimony. I stood glum and sophomoric, certain in my desire to maintain a
vibrant "living" vision of Lorca and comforted by the fact that the guide
and I were the only Spanish speakers in the room. Recognizing that she
was failing either to educate or shame me, our chaperone, giving in to
antique frustration, quickly turned on her heels and led us to the gift
shop. On the way out, both the three-year-old and I took the opportunity to finger the lace bed cover.

I am not certain that I have ever had quite as explicit an interchange
about the competing meanings and values attached to the idea of the
archive than this one. On this my second trip to Granada, I once again
found the city irritating. Red-faced tourists herded through the gardens
of the Alhambra, bloodless flamenco, poorly prepared "typical" Spanish food, no place to get one's underpants washed, and that stunning
heat that everyone insisted had originated in Africa all made me wonder
why all the bother, what could possibly be achieved by this hectic pres-

ervation, this continual recitation of fun house images of Andalusian tradition. Arrive at the bus station, take a taxi to the center, pull out one's maps, and begin the search for García Lorca and you're much more likely to find "Federico," the wondrous master of Spanish *duende* who was not so much shot by partisans of a government that then remained in power for the next forty years as sainted through a sort of agent-less process of martyrdom.

A scant two years before García Lorca's murder, as the political situation in Spain was dangerously close to reaching the bloody point of no return that would initiate the civil war and lead to the death of half a million persons, Lorca was sitting in a Madrid restaurant when he suddenly noticed none other than José Antonio Primo de Rivera, founder of the Spanish fascist party, Falange Española (Spanish Phalanx), whose members were distinguished by their blue shirts. Primo de Rivera also saw Lorca, artistic director of La Barraca, whose members always dressed in blue themselves. The fascist leader, clearly aware of Lorca's importance to the country's quickly changing self-conception, hastily wrote a note on a napkin and handed it to a waiter, who delivered it to the startled writer. It read, "Federico. Don't you think that with your blue coveralls and our blue shirts we could between us forge a better Spain?" Intensely disturbed, Lorca placed the napkin in a pocket and decided to ignore the matter. When asked by a companion what the fascist leader had written, Lorca's irritated response was, "Don't say anything to me. Don't say anything" (quoted in Stainton, *Lorca: A Dream of Life*, 390).

Travel to contemporary Granada and you will find the Huerta de San Vicente as well as a good number of cafés and bars that bear the Lorca name or that traffic in the images with which he is most associated. You will also find the name of José Antonio Primo de Rivera inscribed in granite at the grand Santa María Cathedral at the center of the city. The fascist hero, killed by the Republican government during the civil war, was rewarded for his efforts by having his name carved into dozens of Spanish structures by the government of Francisco Franco. Thus one might rightfully say that the process of memorialization that I am attempting to demonstrate is built upon a profoundly thin conception of history. One martyr is as good as another.

García Lorca was a writer looking for means by which to resist the leveling and deadening of human subjectivity that I have argued is one of the most pernicious legacies of both Atlantic slavery and Western humanism. He was concerned to push his aesthetic projects toward radical internationalism and ever more rich understandings of the historical complexities that produced Europe, Africa, and America. Nonetheless, he continues to be consumed as a figure whose usefulness stands largely on the ability of current generations to ignore the deep interconnection between his philosophy, his politics, and his aesthetics. We treat him with the same formal structures utilized by slavers to evaluate captives at market. The poet, like the slave, is a being entirely composed of reflective surfaces, a cipher ever ready to be filled with meaning. The blinkered and parochial nature of much within the so-called humanities and human sciences, the frankly segregated manner in which we perform our work, continues not only to marginalize the contributions of Africans and persons of African descent to world history, but also to encourage shockingly frail and two-dimensional treatments of so-called elite European culture. We can no longer afford to support the lie of (white) European exceptionalism that stands at the heart of humanism. To do so forces us to produce narratives of modern history and culture that are as sadly repetitive as they are mediocre, narratives that are rightly critiqued as having little value in a world in desperate need of structures of thought and feeling that might enable complex understandings of the basic arrangements of modern society. I fret, however, that we have little stomach for such procedures. We have been lulled by an artificial prettiness in our appreciation of aesthetics; so much so, in fact, that we seem all too often to be more than willing to turn away from the great complexity of a figure like García Lorca, only to offer a sort of dry-mouthed worship, a shrill and stuffy fetishization of a desk that can never be touched.

3

Langston's Adventures in the Dark

I am here to remind you that the Negro's position as outcast is his most powerful human driving force, a force which
hurls him forward towards a wider horizon that is more universal, more just, towards a horizon for which all honorable
men are struggling today.
—Nicolás Guillén

Regardless of their affiliation to the right, left, or center,
groups have fallen back on the idea of cultural nationalism,
on the over integrated conceptions of culture which present immutable, ethnic differences as an absolute break in
the histories and experiences of "black" and "white" people.
Against this choice stands another, more difficult option: the
theorization of creolisation, metisssage, mestizaje, and hybridity. From the viewpoint of ethnic absolutism, this would
be a litany of pollution and impurity.
—Paul Gilroy

In naming the ethics and aesthetics of Langston Hughes's attempt to
paint the complexity of the interracial and intercultural engagements
that establish both so-called Western humanism and the many embodied resistances to its most vulgar ideological structures, I would state
again that the promise of modern subjectivity was established not only
by capitalists in New York, London, or Madrid, nor by their cultured
compatriots and apologists in the sheltered enclaves of Cambridge, New
Haven, or Salamanca, but also by the multiethnic, multilingual crews—
and cargoes—of the ships that attempted the Middle Passage. There
can never be an unsoiled articulation of human subjectivity. There
can never be an announcement of who we are that does not stumble
upon the staccato rhythms of (mis)understanding and (mis)calculation

that are perhaps the most consistent legacies of humanist articulations of modernity. It is in this sense that Paul Gilroy's lovely and strangely compelling phrase, "litany of pollution and impurity," catches in my imagination as I find myself confronted with the question of whether it is possible to produce innovative work around race, slavery, colonization, and cosmopolitanism while also continuing to privilege "clean" modes of intellectual inquiry. The theorization of creolization and *mestizaje*, the imagination of the profundity of the Atlantic, is by necessity a dirty affair, one that forces intellectuals to recalibrate their methods and methodologies in order to gain access to those locations that have been excluded (one is wont to say excreted) by the over-integrated conceptions of culture that both Gilroy and Guillén bemoan.

Here I will repeat Giorgio Agamben's idea of the anthropophorous animal, that being not yet become a subject that supports Man's various world-making projects; that (non)individual whose negation acts as the central and most cherished, if often least acknowledged, procedure within the systems of mastery that form humanism. It is this only partially articulated subject whose presence I am attempting to acknowledge and illuminate in these pages. In doing so, I have become increasingly frustrated with not so much the limitations as the hostilities that structure the so-called humanities and human sciences. Given the brutality and clumsiness that typify many institutionalized modes of intellectual inquiry, modes encapsulated within ethically frail disciplines, we may have gone as far as we can with traditional considerations of the lives and creations of conventionally established intellectuals, black or otherwise. The project of Black Studies is disabled from the outset precisely to the extent that it is built upon the celebration of a well-groomed transatlantic black cosmopolitanism capable of keeping company with calcified traditions of elite American and European culture. Slaves, soldiers, emigrants, refugees, and migrant laborers, all figures whom I read as Man bearers, are woefully underrepresented in our most cherished intellectual endeavors, largely due to the fact that our disciplines have only a limited ability to recognize the modes of their articulation. As a consequence, the unchecked desire to establish what we might think of as biographical certainty around the most celebrated of modern intellectuals, the will in the cases of Federico García Lorca and Langston Hughes to master and destroy the undisciplined matter of their never quite fully articulated sexualities, their ill-fitting flesh, is itself built upon a determination to establish and celebrate an intellectual/ideological inevitability, the very thing one confronts at the locked gates of some grand institution of higher learning while waiting impatiently for an undergraduate with enough hospitality and temerity to turn the lock.

The personnel with whom we must concern ourselves were often defeated. They existed—and exist—at those locations thought to be outside society. They were benighted. They were dirty and impure. They were never more eloquent than when they were bartering their own flesh, their own human potential. Part of what we have to ask ourselves as progressive critics, then, is whether we are as committed to giving up on heroic intellectual and cultural narratives as we claim to be. To do so involves not simply throwing out old-fashioned concepts of distinction and peculiarity but also jettisoning the very celebratory notions that have fueled so much within our work. These gummy, clumsy sentences are at best improvisational. We do not know where we are going. We have no clear idea of what lies ahead. The focal point of all black intellectuals, all modern intellectuals, *all* intellectuals, dispersed as we are in the void of diaspora, must ever remain on the possibilities inherent in divination, interpretation, translation, misunderstanding, and misprision. Albert Memmi asks, "Is it certain that this language which stammers today is unable to develop and become rich?"[1] More important still, does an eloquence established by capriciousness and bloodlust not grate on the ear?

Mon-nee

In the summer of 1923, a twenty-one-year-old Langston Hughes arrived off the west coast of Africa as part of the multinational crew of the S.S. *Malone.* He soon found himself at Sekondi, the Gold Coast port town established by the Dutch in 1640 in order to service the ships that carried cloth, jewelry, cooking pots, and guns to the Asante. They then reversed direction, bearing precious minerals, timber, and slaves to Europe and the Americas. Bored and rambunctious, Hughes and his shipmates found that Sekondi continued its traffic in gold, rubber, and timber, even as it had stopped the exportation of slaves. This did not mean, however, that the town had fully given up its traffic in human flesh. Hughes describes a brisk business in prostitution, the majority of whose practitioners were quite young, quite small, sometimes prepubescent girls with "bushy hair" and "henna'd nails," to whom hungry sailors were directed by African boys claiming that the girls were their sisters, boys who patiently waited for their clients outside the girls' huts, or slept on floor mats beside the coupling pair if the seaman had the inclination and the money to spend the night.

Though at least two generations of critics, including both Jay Saunders Redding and Arnold Rampersad, claim that Hughes is surprisingly guarded in his two autobiographies, I would counter that his description of the young prostitutes of Sekondi is relentless.[2] "In front of one hut three white sailors from a British ship were bargaining with an old woman," he writes. "Behind her, frightened and ashamed, stood a small girl, said to be a virgin. The price was four pounds. The sailors argued for a cheaper rate. They hadn't that much money" (Hughes, *The Big Sea*, 119). You will forgive me for pointing out that the logic of the sailors was impeccable. The value of small African girls in what we cynically call the open market has never been high. And perhaps more to the point, there continues to be some confusion about what is actually being bought and sold. Even Hughes seems to wonder about the claim of the girl's virginity. In the racialist logics that underwrite so much within modern culture and thought, to place the words "black" and "virgin" against one another would seem at best oxymoronic, at worst ridiculous. What most titillates, however, what piques the interest of Hughes's readers, is the suggestion that something much more valuable, more discrete, than sex was being sold at Sekondi, something that ultimately could not be either properly measured—or named.

Hughes tells us that during the night, as the ship remained anchored off the coast, two girls, petite ladies of the evening, rowed a small boat out to the *Malone*. One of them was taken by the "bo'sun" to his private cabin. The other was left in the quarters of the crew to quench the desire, the modern wanting that continues to be so very difficult either to acknowledge or articulate.

She lay there naked and held up her hands. The girl said: "Mon-nee!" but nobody had any money.

Thirty men crowded around, mostly in their underwear, sat up on bunks, watched, smoked, yelled, and joked, and waited for their turn. Each time a man would rise, the little African girl on the floor would say: "Mon-nee! Mon-nee!" But nobody had a cent, yet they wouldn't let her get up. Finally, I couldn't bear to hear her crying: "Mon-nee!" anymore, so I went to bed. But the festival went on all night. (Hughes, *The Big Sea*, 108)

What I want to resist in my reading of this passage is reiteration of wholly stale critical procedures. Yes, Hughes describes the sexual abuse, the rape, of a child. Yes, that abuse is facilitated by both misogyny and white supremacy. Yes, the scene is not only homosocial, but decidedly homoerotic, the tension and thrill of the moment maintained not only by the splayed nakedness of the girl, but also by the sailors themselves, their underwear, anticipation, and sweat working together to achieve the tumescence of transnational passion. Still, as I have stated repeatedly, I am unconcerned in these pages with established fact, the so-called known world. Instead, I would suggest that we read the sailors' actions— and the girl's for that matter—as a sort of vulgar, if profoundly effective, critical practice.

It would be easy to turn away from the girl's nakedness, to retreat from the obscenity attaching itself to the child's flesh in order to find some means by which to seal the ideological tear this image produces. Indeed, there are many humanist practices that allow for the nonconsideration of the black, the female, the colonized, and the enslaved. Within the range of images Hughes gives us—the sexual predation of men, the systematic exploitation of Africans, the easy consumption of children— one finds no method by which to imagine a life for a female child outside the bowels of a ship traveling the Atlantic. She remains on that floor, in that boat, her presence distorted and pathetic, yet the actual ideological structures that support all this remain clean.

Though Hughes never bothers to say so, it is obvious that what haunts this scene is the specter of the Middle Passage. The multiracial crew, the naked African girl were lost together atop the aloofness and depth of the Atlantic, their revelry a type of theater, a ritualized evocation of a never quite palpable certainty. Like the believer who calms his fretfulness through the wearing of crosses or the fingering of beads, what the crew attacks is both much more and much less than a dark-skinned African girl hungry for money. Instead, what they attempt to defeat is the sense of possibility that she represents, that spectacular and elusive virgin animality that might leave both men and cultures forever adrift. They press her down, moor and anchor her just as their predecessors carved their bows into images of half-naked women, wooden breasts providing proof of a life, a culture, a past greater than the ocean's unnamed mystery.

Humanism's greatest achievement has been the vicious tethering of flesh to a dream of transcendent Manhood. Our judgment of Hughes ought to turn, therefore, on an assessment of how clearly he notes this fact. I want not simply to deploy well-established liberal critical modes in which the point is to name the unceasing oppression of females and people of color, wring one's hands a bit, then retreat once more to the real work. Instead, I will make the simple point that the monuments to culture and civilization that dully hang in overpriced museums or sit dusty and unread in underutilized libraries are not, in fact, primary locations for the articulation of human being. On the contrary, we must focus first on those nodal points, those archives, that exist *outside*—and in contestation of—already calcified precincts of high or traditional culture, thereby allowing for the flexibility and mobility necessary for the constant innovation that is presumably the hallmark of modernity.

I will acknowledge, then, that the image of Langston Hughes as *pícaro*, as a peripatetic, disinterested traveler willing to leave a young girl alone to confront—and accommodate—her many tortures, marks him not only as an unethical, even vulgar, figure, but perhaps as a sad intellectual as well. Like Lot's wife, the artist who turns his head away from the rough, the loutish, and the rude risks becoming inert, dull, useless in the face of the many pressing tasks confronting contemporary thinkers. Much of the spirit of *Archives of Flesh* is drawn from the belief that one must do one's analyses on the run, make room for unexpected encounters with the marginalized, the restricted, and the repressed in order to recognize that Western humanism is built upon complex and contradictory assemblies in which capitalism and white supremacy are subverted, however haphazardly, by the grubbiest, most benighted examples of animal ingenuity and will.

By way of forgiving Hughes, I celebrate not only his willingness to treat images of tortured and abused "low" women so capably, but also his deft use of farce and slapstick in his explorations of humanism's grimy underbelly. Returning from his voyage on the *Malone*, Hughes carried with him a large red monkey named Jocko. Deciding to make the best of the situation, Hughes's stepfather presented the animal at a local pool hall. Arriving with hair combed and sporting a fetching sweater, Jocko was placed in the middle of one of the tables so that the crowd could examine the beast with pleasure.

> Dad put him down on the green pool table, holding him by a long leash. But the noise and the people and the smoke and the shouting were too much for Jocko, surrounded on the table by the crowd. He uttered a yell of fright and began to run frantically back and forth on the pool table as far as his leash would permit. The crowd roared with laughter, and the ring of dark faces closed in on poor Jocko, closer and closer, frightening him so badly that suddenly he could no longer control himself, and without warning his bowels began to move all over the table. (Hughes, *The Big Sea*, 136–37)

The ape, finding himself molested by an eager crowd of assailants/onlookers/interlocutors, quite logically shits. He expresses, extracts, moves, and articulates. Indeed Jocko's communications are only a whisper less articulate than those of the young prostitute pressed to the floor in the bowels of the S.S. *Malone*. Trapped in a situation that cannily replicated the theatrical procedures of the slave auction, the minstrel show, and the human zoos that had gone out of vogue in Europe and the United States scarcely a generation before his American unveiling, Jocko names the substance and quality of the U.S. encounter with Africa and Europe without so much as managing a single articulate twitch from his inelegant tongue.

I have made this detour through the absurd and the rude in order to remind my readers that images of prostitutes and other presumably defiled and defeated women do not simply demonstrate how poorly understood these benighted figures are in narratives of modernity and Western humanism. Nor is the point to remark the fact that the clear distinction between Man and beast is quite seriously troubled when one takes account of the intricacies of race, class, gender, and ethnicity. Instead I argue that it is the vulgarity, the ape-like "ugliness" of the prostitute, that allows her to demonstrate with often stunning clarity the many unspoken *lived* realities of the most absurd aspects of humanist ideology. Or to retreat to the vernacular, Hughes's female characters literally "talk shit."

Prostitutes stand not at the periphery of modern society, but at its dead center. They personify the complex interplay between bright fantasies of solidly established tradition and the dark, sullen acceptance of human ignorance. I mean to offer the figure of the prostitute as the marker of a complex process by which dominant conceptions of human value are continually established through spectacular displays of violence and repression. The policing of so-called profligate, abnormal sexual exchange has as much to do with the denial of the most vulgar aspects of the ritualized defeat of human animality as with any real concern to name and relieve misery. The buying and selling of women and girls is not a demonstration of that which exceeds humanist discourse, but instead one of the clearest articulations of the methods by which the unscripted potential of the flesh can be noted, confronted, corralled, and exploited.

As a correspondent during the Spanish Civil War, Hughes tells of the mandatory blackouts in Madrid as fascist rebels, greatly aided by the Germans and Italians, bombed the city, using any visible light to direct their shells. Undeterred, the *madrileña* prostitutes, their houses deprived of electricity, would take to the streets around the Puerta del Sol, particularly the block behind Madrid's only skyscraper, the Telefónica. There, in the dark, they plied their trade to hundreds of waiting soldiers, many of them members of the international brigades that had come to defend the liberty, if not always the chastity, of Republican Spain.

> The darkness up and down the street would be pinpointed by the tiny flames of dozens and dozens of matches being lighted by soldiers to peer into the faces of the prostitutes walking in the dark. The black-out canyon of the street danced with little flames of hope, burning briefly, then flung to the ground as some young soldier, lighting a match at the sound of a seductive voice, found himself peering into a broken-down witch's face.[3]

What I would point to here is not the rather open and untidy secret of the centuries-long and quite often officially sanctioned relationship between soldiers and prostitutes. Moreover, I hope that it is obvious that I am unlikely to blush when faced with the fact that sex is frequently the currency of international travel and tourism. I am struck, however, by how careful Hughes is in his framing of this scene. The continual reference to light and dark, the tiny flames that inhabit but never fill the "black-out" canyon, even the occasional explosion of an artillery shell, giving "a sudden burst of light, enough for a soldier to see a woman clearly, and perhaps pick out a partner for his needs," repeats the desperate yet barely acknowledged struggle of modern subjects with the most basic, most obvious truths of history and humanity. I am stunned that Hughes is able to move so effortlessly in his two autobiographies from images of African girls being raped aboard ships to prostitutes plying their trade in unlit gloom. Both images detail the invisibility of the social and cultural interaction that mark so much within humanism. Taking full advantage of the dark and dirty images displayed in his texts, Hughes points simultaneously toward the violent articulation of Manhood and the repression of anthropophorous animality while suggesting a process existing in the dark at/in which the conventions of domination and aggression might be held in abeyance.

If I might be allowed to venture so far as to announce the tragedy of this scene, I would suggest that what defeats the promise of shared humanity is, in fact, the light. The bombs and matches hide much more than they reveal. They turn the simplest of our sins and pleasures, the animal coupling of women with men, toward an ideological complexity that has proven repeatedly to be deadly, more than capable of extinguishing both light *and* dark. Marx warns us that "the social revolution cannot draw its poetry from the past, but only from the future. It cannot begin with itself before it has stripped itself of all its superstitions concerning the past."[4] I would add here that one of the more profoundly enervating of these superstitions is our irrational fear of the dark, a fear established, I would argue, on the assumption of both unknown dangers *and* pleasures. As with these scenes of prostitutes at Sekondi and Madrid, the continual struggle to transcend and transform the Man bearer seems compelled by a will to destroy awareness of human animality while never fully losing contact with it. We search in the dark for those not yet tamed aspects of our humanity, those rare moments in which the rigors of Manhood, the harshness of the blazing light, might be ever so slightly relaxed.

Hughes punctuates the previous passage by telling us that the young women of Madrid breathlessly gave themselves to their lovers in anticipation of the city's imminent defeat by Franco's forces, only to be counted as whores when the promised fall did not come. He also relates the rumor that the rebels' shock troops, "dark" North African Muslims, "Moors," who stand so solidly in the Spanish "national" imagination, had been promised their pick of the Castilian women should the city be defeated. "IMAGINE," said the *madrileños*, "that rebel Franco bringing Mohammedans to Spain to fight Christians! The Crusaders would turn over in their graves" (Hughes, *I Wonder as I Wander*, 349). What seems obvious here is that it is quite difficult, perhaps impossible, to separate disgust from desire. Should an off-white hand reach toward the raven-haired beauty of his beloved, he would find himself touching the very embodiment of delinquency and defeat. And even more importantly, had the benighted Spaniards—radicals, liberals, and conservatives alike—allowed themselves to relinquish hold on their desperate fantasies of European belonging, that ever-elusive promise of whiteness, in order to reconcile with the African, the Mohammedan, the dark, Spain might have been spared the killing, the poverty, the shame, and retribution that continue to grip both it and the continent to which it so tenuously clings. What it seems that Republican Spaniards did, however, was hedge their bets. They decided to mask their own cynicism, their own implication in the relentless violence of an always unstable Manhood against an ill-defined human animality. Women are raped and sold *as* cattle there by the Mohammedans. Here we do nothing more than create remarkably beautiful lamentations of the fact.

> Come now, all you who are singers,
> And sing me the song of Spain.
> Sing it simply that I might understand.

> WHAT IS THE SONG OF SPAIN?

> *Flamenco* is the song of Spain:
> Gypsies, guitars, dancing

Death and love and heartbreak
To a heel tap and a swirl of fingers
On three strings.
Flamenco is the song of Spain.

I DO NOT UNDERSTAND.

Toros are the song of Spain:
The bellowing bull, the red cape,
A sword thrust, a horn tip,
The torn suit of satin and gold,
Blood on the sand
Is the song of Spain.

I DO NOT UNDERSTAND.

Pintura is the song of Spain:
Goya, Velasquez, Murillo,
Splash of color on canvass,
Whirl of cherub-faces.
La Maja Desnuda's
The song of Spain.

What's that?

Don Quixote! España!
Aquel rincón de la Mancha de
Cuyo nombre no quiero acordarme . . . .
That's the song of Spain.
You wouldn't kid me, would you?
A bombing plane's
The song of Spain.
Bullets like rain's
The song of Spain
Poison gas is Spain
A knife in the back
And its terror and pain is Spain.

Toros, flamenco, paintings, books—
    Not Spain.
The people are Spain:
The people beneath that bombing plane
With its wings of gold for which I pay—
I, a worker, letting my labor pile
Up millions for bombs to kill a child—
I bought those bombs for Spain!
Workers made those bombs for a Fascist Spain!
Will I make them again, and yet again?[5]

Hughes runs through many of the most precious images of Spain and the Spanish people: flamenco, Gypsies, guitars, the bellowing bull, the red cape, Goya, Velázquez, Murillo, Don Quixote are all represented. Yet the very breathlessness of his verse belies the idea of a clearly discernible "song of Spain." The contrapuntal pacing, the give and take between the ever-persistent questioner and his increasingly hesitant interlocutor, leads one to imagine a certain skepticism regarding Spain's reality. ("What's that?" "I do not understand.") There is what one might call a conceptual flat-footedness on display in the poem, an inability to register the piece's romantic imagery. Finally we are left with the certainty that the officially sanctioned markers of Spanish culture, "*Toros, flamenco*, paintings, books," are, in fact, "not Spain." Instead, Hughes turns toward the people, resolving the ideological conflict that I take the poem to represent in favor of the lived reality of *modern* individuals.

If you have followed my arguments thus far, you will understand that those bombs bursting above Spanish heads are themselves not only part of a desperate attempt to disrupt and delay the inevitable dispersal and rejection of even the most cherished aspects of so-called traditional cultures, but also precise examples of the central modes of modern cultural articulation. The effect for Hughes's readers is that they have their attention abruptly turned from monumental examples of Spanish culture and toward the vigorous attack and violation of "animalized" humanity that forms such an essential, if so rigorously ignored, part of Western humanism. Fascism has never been solely a collection of ideologies or stunningly efficient procedures of violence, but instead the unacknowledged inter-articulation of profound brutishness with the most carefully and delicately packaged objects of national culture and patrimony.

It is telling that Hughes returns repeatedly to the image of bombs bursting overhead in his attempt to examine the discursive and ideological structures that gird both modern forms of exploitation and the never fully articulate *resistance* to that exploitation. Bombing imagery appears in "Air Raid: Barcelona," "Moonlight in Valencia: Civil War," "Madrid," "Shall the Good Go Down?," and "Stalingrad: 1942." More interesting still, Hughes's use of this trope is not restricted to those several poems that treat conflicts in Spain and Europe more generally. In "August 19th . . . A Poem for Clarence Norris," an elegy for one of the black teenagers convicted of rape and sentenced to be electrocuted in the infamous Scottsboro case, Hughes describes the dreadfulness of the exploding bomb in order to relate the horrific miscarriages of justice that Norris and many other African Americans suffered to the global oppression of working and poor people.[6] "Stop all the leeches / That use their power to strangle / Hope, / That make of the law a lyncher's / Rope, / That drop their bombs on China / And Spain, / That have no pity for hunger or / Pain."[7]

Following Hughes, one imagines that the first and still most potent word established in the "Atlantic vocabulary" was "mon-nee," that our cultural practices have been produced between the very teeth of capitalist exploitation. It seems to me, then, that the time has come for us to stretch the central conceits of Black Studies to their very limits. It is true that our enslaved ancestors formed new modes of relation and belief from out of the detritus of their lost traditions. What remains largely unspoken, however, is the simple fact that modern forms of European culture were also established by the history of contact, conquest, colonization, and travel to which we attach many names, most notoriously "the Middle Passage." Or, to push my readers beyond the boundaries of polite irritation, the celebrated objects of Goya, Velázquez, Murillo, Cervantes, Picasso, and Lorca are themselves examples of slave culture, cleverly wrought articulations of complex procedures by which the repression and exploitation of humanity are at once ritualized and ignored. Turning again to this work's main conceptual conceits, we would be well advised to locate our criticism not within disciplinary structures that work to name and celebrate Man's many splendors, nor at sites of official—and expected—dissent, but instead at those locations, those archives, where the obvious repression of the anthropophorous animal, the flesh, is most apparent. Thus the slave, the sailor, the black, and the prostitute are key figures in the disloyal and discontented critical project that I have launched, because their modes of unheralded articulation get as close as anything to unveiling the complexity of Western humanism's many obscurantist discursive structures.

Before leaving this matter, I would like to return to the point that I made in both the introduction and the first chapter about the fact that the African American interest in the plight of Republican Spain pivoted on the assumption that the fight against fascist aggression there was but a continuation of the fight against fascist aggression on the African continent, particularly the invasion of Ethiopia by Mussolini's forces in 1935. I would state again that part of why I find the connection between Africans, Americans, and Spaniards so compelling has to do with the reality that the transatlantic discursive and intellectual interchange between modern Spaniards and African Americans represents at its core an attempt to restructure received notions of geographic and cultural distinction. As I demonstrate throughout this book, progressive Spaniards and African Americans have been central to the efforts to disrupt the sophistry underwriting the idea of a white Europe and a black Africa. I would add that intellectuals like Hughes and Lorca struggled to resist the lie that there is some clear distinction between the most vicious aspects of slavery, colonialism, and white supremacy and a sort of preciously maintained official culture. A strike for or against the Spanish people was for Hughes and the community of intellectuals whom I take him to represent never simply a local event. As we have seen, their attempts to assist Spain were indistinct from their efforts to redeem Ethiopia.

In "Too Much of Race," Hughes tells us, "Those who have already practiced bombing the little villages of Ethiopia now bomb Guernica and Madrid. The same Fascists who forced Italian peasants to fight in Africa now force African Moors to fight in Europe. They do not care about color when they can use you for profits or for war."[8] The point, of course, is to name the fact that the structures of global capitalism—of which slavery and colonialism are but the most obvious—are maintained, at least in part, by a sort of discursive sleight of hand by which the practitioners of economic and military aggression easily recognize their similarity, while those whom they exploit often come to fetishize what they take to be inherent and insurmountable differences of race, religion, and ethnicity. Thus, though I have some sympathy for Arnold Rampersad's suggestion that Hughes's several treatments of the Italian invasion of Ethiopia could be seen to vacillate equally between racial-ist or "Africanist" modes and more genuinely internationalist forms, I nonetheless continue to believe that Hughes never accepted the notion of (black) African primitivism or provincialism. Instead, I read Hughes generically, arguing that his fretful stance in relation to Ethiopia is itself evidence of his struggle to advance a universalist (post)humanist cri-tique in which Africans and Africanity are central.

> The little fox is still.
> The dogs of war have made their kill.
>
> Addis Ababa
> Across the headlines all year long.
> Ethiopia—
> Tragi-song for the news reels.
> Haile
> With his slaves, his dusky wiles,
> His second-hand planes like a child's.
> But he has not gas—so he cannot last.
> Poor little joker with no poison gas!
> Thus his people may learn
> How Il Duce makes butter from an empty churn
> To butter the bread
> (If bread there be)
> Of civilization's misery.[9]

The strange, uncivilized thing about this poem, "Broadcast on Ethio-pia," is that Hughes seems altogether unwilling to allow a heroic concep-tion of Ethiopia. It is precisely not a tragic, benighted location, perfect in its simplicity and refinement, with an emperor of whom all children of the African diaspora might rightly be proud. Instead, nearly forty years before Selassie's overthrow in 1974, Hughes created a decidedly unflat-tering picture of the presumably beloved leader. He is drawn as an ineffective personage, one with slaves and "dusky wiles," whose war and statecraft seem at once vain and childish. Instead, as I maintain throughout this chapter, Hughes places his hope on the innately adaptive qualities of "the anthropophorous," Ethiopian and Italian alike. They stretch beyond both the limitations of their natal communities and the rigid discursive structures separating Man from human. In the process they do not necessarily conquer misery, but at the very least they come to understand the tricks, discursive and otherwise, that maintain men like Il Duce and Ras Tafari in their undeserved positions of power.

Hughes made these same ethical and aesthetic protocols brilliantly clear when he related the details of his rupture with his erstwhile patron, Charlotte Osgood Mason. Mason, like many of her generation, was self-conscious about what she took to be the excesses of modern society, excesses that presumably worked to produce a certain spiritual and cultural rootlessness among contemporary Americans and Europeans. She decided, therefore, to commit her considerable wealth to supporting and developing primitive and aboriginal art forms, chiefly those produced by Plains Indians and African Americans, including a number of the most famous personnel of the so-called Harlem Renaissance, especially Hughes, Zora Neale Hurston, and Alain Locke. "She wanted me to be primitive and know and feel the intuitions of the primitive," Hughes writes.

> But, unfortunately, I did not feel the rhythms of the primitive surging through me, and so I could not live and write as though I did. I was only an American Negro—who had loved the surface of Africa and the rhythms of Africa—but I was not Africa. I was Chicago and Kansas City and Broadway and Harlem. And I was not what she wanted me to be. So, in the end it all came back very near to the old impasse of white and Negro again, white and Negro—as do most relationships in America. (Hughes, *The Big Sea*, 325)

At the risk of overreaching myself, I will argue that the structure of the relationship that Mason wanted from Hughes was exactly the structure of the relationships that British and American sailors wanted with adolescent prostitutes on the coast of West Africa. What Mason desired, like many before and after her, was that the African American creative intellectual deny that his creations were, in fact, produced through work—not inspiration, not soul, not some bestial essence, but work. She insists upon a particularly American class of aesthetic solipsism. The (black) laborer's struggle, perseverance, and exhaustion can never be seen for what they are, but instead only as inspiration, spirit, and soul. Viewed in this light, even a black individual with Hughes's remarkable talents can be seen as a resource, one whose suffering exists primarily as the evocation of universal forms of knowing that might be discerned and fretted over but never properly challenged.

Recognizing this fact might hopefully help you to understand why I have been so concerned in this chapter to make plain the laboring of prostitutes. Much of the drudgery of the trade is that, as with captive Africans forced to dance and sing onboard ships, one must toil without ever seeming to do so. The same can be said of all manner of African and American laborers. As Frantz Fanon reminds us, the colonizer desires that the slave be "full of enthusiasm," never remarking in his or her comportment awareness of any exploitation.[10] One of Hughes's great mistakes, then, was that he forgot to take heed of the truism among colonized and exploited persons that revealing one's awareness of the basic structures of domination, bringing into the light evidence of abuse and resistance to abuse, evidence of things unseen, can be a dangerous and even deadly gambit.

> I cannot write here about that last half-hour in the big bright drawing-room high above Park Avenue. That beautiful room, that had been so full of light and help and understanding for me, suddenly became like a trap closing in, faster and faster, the room darker and darker, until the light went out with a sudden crash in the dark. (Hughes, *The Big Sea*, 325)

Hughes's mistake in his relationship with Mason was not so much that he inadvertently forced her to return him to the hold with the rest of the captives, but instead that he forgot that the light and beauty of that room above Park Avenue were designed specifically to divert attention from the reality that he was, in fact, in custody. He had come to inhabit just a bit too fully the naïve primitivism that Mason required of him, never daring to see that once he began to question the exploitation that underwrote Mason's patronage, she would be forced to return him to the pens.

There is ample evidence to support the assumption that Mason began to tire of Hughes when she started to suspect that he was capable of producing not only evocations of folk consciousness but also rather caustic and piercing critiques of the very modern class pyramid on top of which she so ostentatiously perched. In December 1931, at the height of the Depression, Hughes published his bitterly sarcastic "Advertisement for the Waldorf-Astoria."

BLACK MOB FROM HARLEM. DROP IN AT THE WALDORF THIS
   afternoon for tea. Stay to dinner. Give Park Avenue a
   lot of darkie color—free for nothing! Ask the Junior
   Leaguers to sing a spiritual for you. They probably
   know 'em better than you do—and their lips won't be
   so chapped with cold after they step out of their closed
   cars in the undercover driveways.
     Hallelujah! Undercover driveways!
     Ma soul's a witness for de Waldorf-Astoria!
(A thousand nigger section-hands keep the roadbeds smooth,
   so investments in railroads pay ladies with diamond
   necklaces staring at Sert murals.)
     Thank God A-mighty!
(And a million niggers bend their backs on rubber plantations, for rich behinds to ride on thick tires to the
   Theatre Guild tonight.)
     Ma soul's a witness!
(And here we stand, shivering in the cold, in Harlem.)
     Glory be to God—
     De Waldorf-Astoria's open![11]

Naïvely, and perhaps lulled into recklessness by the midwinter light cascading over the Manhattan skyline, Hughes presented this angry, relentlessly dark poem to his patron in order to solicit her opinion. Her response, as she sat framed by windows overlooking Park Avenue amidst a richly tasteful riot of furniture and art, was to tell her protégé that the work was more propaganda than poetry. Soon thereafter, reiterating her disappointment at the gloomy turn in her talented young charge's practice, she excused Hughes, a last check in hand, from her stable of favorites.

The rejection by Mason was to prove a decisive moment in Hughes's development as an intellectual. It was only then that he was forced to acknowledge fully the true relationship of art and culture to society. He was compelled to act upon the belief that art ought not to represent an escape from the realities of class and race exploitation, but, on the contrary, should attempt to make plain the discursive and ideological contradictions that this exploitation produces. Hughes articulates new modes of cultural analysis, new archives, for his various audiences. He tells us that after he was driven from Mason's presence, "poetry became bread; prose, shelter and raiment." Literature became not that which was goodness and light but instead "a big sea full of many fish" (Hughes, *The Big Sea*, 335). As a still developing and increasingly radical intellectual, Hughes began to understand that his experiments with literature rightly and necessarily continued the very muddling and risk taking that had been enacted by both enslaved Africans and their captors as they made the journey between the presumably old world and the supposedly new.

If my own reading of Langston Hughes has been celebratory or hagiographic, it is because I am intrigued by the many ways he risked, and perhaps courted, the mistrust of readers and patrons alike. Of necessity we have had to learn the syntax of glossolalia, the art of speaking in tongues. At the same time, however, I do not want my comments to be understood as simply a celebration of the ambiguous or the uncertain. Though I claim no particular allegiance to Africa, Europe, or America, I nonetheless boldly announce the ascendancy of those of us who have been outcast, displaced, shunned, and exiled. I claim, in fact, that Hughes's much-heralded embrace of Hispanic culture was motivated not only by a sort of black *wanderlust*, but also a deeper acknowledgment of the necessity of breaking and syncopating the rhythms of humanist discourse.

> In the days of the broken cubes of Picasso
> And in the days of the broken songs of young men
> A little too drunk to sing
> And the young women

A little too unsure of love to love—
I met on the boulevards of Paris
An African from Senegal.

God
Knows why the French
Amuse themselves bringing to Paris
Negroes from Senegal.

It's the old game of the boss and the bossed,
Boss and the bossed,
amused
and
amusing,
worked and working,
Behind the cubes of black and white,
black and white,
black and white
But since it is the old game
For fun
They give him the three old prostitutes of
France—
Liberty, Equality, Fraternity—
And all three of 'em sick
In spite of the tax to the government
And the doctors
And the Marseillaise

Of course, the young African from Senegal
Carries back from Paris
A little more disease
To spread among the black girls in the palm huts.
        disease—
From light to darkness
disease—
From the boss to the bossed
disease—

From the game of black and white
  disease
From the city of the broken cubes of Picasso
  d

    i

  s

e

  a

    s

  e.[12]

It is difficult for me to understand why this sophisticated and self-consciously modernistic poem of Hughes's, "Cubes," has received so little attention by his many critics, biographers, and translators. Apart from Seth Moglen's excellent 2002 treatment of the work, there has been scant critical attention paid to it.[13] This is though the text possesses many of the elements for which Hughes is rightly famous: travel, concern for the poor and working classes, sensitivity to both Latin and African cultures, and most importantly for our efforts here, fascination with the play of light and dark. Hughes deploys not only his signature free verse style, but also an extremely evocative graphic representation of movement between and across cultures. The separation of the word "disease" into its composite parts, those seven (lucky?) letters, demonstrates an author not simply attempting to relate the dispersal of pestilence, but also and importantly to reach, however awkwardly, toward a new language that might help him to name what must have been infinitely apparent as he encountered his black African doppelgänger on one of the lovely boulevards in the City of Light.[14] What the two undoubtedly knew but could not easily speak was the old game of "boss and the bossed, amused and amusing, worked and working." They looked into the manufactured faces of slavers and colonizers alike and found them lacking. For this crime, legions of women and men have fallen under gun and whip, knife and prod. Many others have found their most cherished labors reviled, or worse yet, ignored.

It seems, then, that there were but few avenues open for this radical man of letters. He had to turn toward the vulgarities that one might utter in the dark, toward the whispered, muted forms of discourse that might allow a brown-skinned poet to recognize and plainly name even the much-celebrated Western maidens Liberty, Equality, Fraternity as little more than diseased prostitutes. This, however, was no easy gambit, for as is evident in "Cubes" itself, one of the most durable tenets of white supremacy is that the black, the aboriginal, the Arab, the Asian, is already the very marker of vulgarity, the sign of cultural and ideological infection. Worse yet, all too often these agents of illness and disorder seem to lack even the good sense to keep quiet about these well-known, if not easily or properly spoken, facts. As with Hughes, the most inelegant among them seem ever ready to proclaim in their clumsy, thick-lipped manner the most inconvenient of truths. They continue to resist magnanimously proffered integration into the precincts of respectability, to lurk about the dusky edges even as their erstwhile masters invite them to play in the light.

Struck Deep in Spanish Earth

I assume that my readers are fully aware of the controversy that attended Arnold Rampersad's publication in 1986 and 1988 of his two-volume biography of Langston Hughes, in which he claimed that there was no evidence in the archive to support the widely shared belief that Hughes was homosexual. I hope, moreover, that the resonance of this controversy with the equally fraught matter of how to address Federico García Lorca's sexuality is apparent. The debates surrounding Rampersad's claims were still circulating as late as 2002, when the second editions of his two biographies were released.[15] I might add that on the several occasions in which I have presented excerpts from this chapter, I have been asked, no matter the purported content of my presentation, whether I possess some knowledge that might satisfy a choking desire to know "was he" or "wasn't he." In the face of all this, I have begun to suspect that we remain far too comforted by the assumption that no matter the complexity of the questions that we confront in our cultural studies, these might ultimately be resolved through reference to biography. We have been sold the idea that one might truly know a man through the detritus that he leaves in his wake. Here I will remind you of the arguments I made in the first chapter regarding the highly politicized nature of our archival practices. The point of all that collecting and cataloging is never just the revelation of some undisputed truth, but also the need to support commonsensical conceptions of culture, politics, and identity. In the case of Hughes, we might assume that we have gotten hold of him, taken his measure, once we have properly consumed the whispers and rumors that always precede his many arrivals. I hope that it is obvious, moreover, that this tendency to assume intimate knowledge of Hughes translates the regimentation, or leveling, of the modern homosexual against which García Lorca so vigorously struggled in his short, brilliant career. What most irritates me, however, about the procedures that I am attempting to describe is that they so precisely replicate the structures of repression, denial, and counter-articulation that I have argued stand at the center of humanist aesthetic processes and that are in such desperate need of reformation.

"If I see Mr. Hughes I'll recognize him right away, because I have his characteristics. He is a forty or forty-five year old, fairly thick, almost white skinned man, with a little English moustache decorating fine, 'bitter' lips."[16] With these words, Nicolás Guillén, the famed Afro-Cuban poet and one of Hughes's closest allies in the Hispanic world, initiated not only his introduction of Hughes to the Cuban public but also a rather wry critique of the forms of studied expectation and gossip that accompany the transnational intellectual on his journeys.

> In fact: when Mr. Hughes appeared we were met by a small, thin twenty-seven year old youth of light brown *trigueño* color who did not have an English moustache, nor one in the style of any other nation. He just seemed a Cuban *mulatito*, one of those inconsequential mulattoes pursuing some course of study at the National University who spend their lives organizing small, intimate parties at two pesos per ticket. However, behind this lives one of the spirits most sincerely interested in the things of the black race and a very personable poet without any other concern than to observe his people, to translate it, to come to know and to love it. (Guillén, "Conversación con Langston Hughes," 172–75, translation mine)

The stress here is on translation, or more precisely on the assumptions that one must conquer—or at the very least massage—in the *course* of translation. The "black" poet whom Guillén eagerly awaited in Havana had to be reconciled with the racial codes of his host nation. Hughes was one of the most celebrated, most regularly translated American poets in the Spanish- and Portuguese-speaking world. But as Vera Kutzinski has quite convincingly argued, the very fact that Hughes is often taken to have a simple or innocent conception of the intricacies of African, American, and Atlantic aesthetic and iterative practices has allowed him to be translated in ways that might properly be described as flattened in an effort to create him as a useable and consumable product. In his most translated poem, "I, Too," first published in *Survey Graphic* in 1925, Hughes boldly articulates the realities of racism and white supremacy as they existed—and exist—in the United States:

> I, too, sing America.
>
> I am the darker brother.
> They send me to eat in the kitchen
> When company comes,
> But I laugh,
> And I eat well,
> And grow strong.
>
> Tomorrow,
> I'll be at the table
> When company comes.
> Nobody'll dare
> Say to me,
> "Eat in the kitchen,"
> Then.
>
> Besides,
> They'll see how beautiful I am
> And be ashamed—
>
> I, too, am America.

When one reads the 1926 translation by José Antonio Fernández de Castro, a prominent and politically progressive editor of Cuba's *El Diario*, one finds that the work has undergone rather profound changes in order to address a different set of social and racial mores in early twentieth-century Cuba. The first stanza reads:

> Yo también, honro a América
> Soy el hermano negro
> Me mandan a comer a la cocina
> Cuando vienen visitas
> Pero me río,
> Como bien
> Y así me fortalezco.

Without belaboring the point, one is struck by Kutzinski's rather insightful observation that part of what takes place in de Castro's translation is that he makes the work *more* instead of less "racial."[17] That is to say, de Castro renders the speaker of the poem "black" (*negro*) instead of "dark," gesturing toward the fact that in Cuba, also a white supremacist and color-conscious country, but one with nothing like the strict division of "black" and "white" persons that existed in the United States, the notion of sending someone from a formal meal simply because he had, as Americans might say, suffered a touch of the tar brush would have seemed a bit preposterous.

More generically, I would stress the fact that what both Guillén and de Castro negotiate as they present Hughes in the pages of *El Diario* are the very racialist ideological structures that undergird the articulation of Western humanism. In order to enter into public discourse, in order to be recognized, one must negotiate the knotty questions surrounding one's flesh and how it might be properly narrated, packaged, and readied for use in the maintenance of humanism's operative assumptions. In the Atlantic world in which Hughes traveled, this meant that the body's specificities were "neutralized" through reference to shockingly clumsy racial protocols. Writing to his friend and patron Noel Sullivan during a 1934 trip to Mexico to attend to his recently deceased father's estate, Hughes reported that he had been detained at the Mexican border because his entrance permit did not state that he was colored. After a weekend of waiting and the payment of a seventy-five-dollar bond, the papers were finally marked "mestizo," and Hughes was allowed to continue his journey.[18] The indecisiveness of the flesh had been conquered.

Approach the fortified frontiers of Europe or America wearing a dark-skinned, kinky-haired body, and one provokes an uncanny stress. The question of whether or not the thing toeing its way toward the gate is wild or tame must always be broached, if never exactly settled.

I would point out yet again that one of the things that Hughes was continually forced to confront in his career was the assumption on the part of "foreign" and domestic audiences alike that they knew—or at least should know—his characteristics. Like the prostitute whose face must first be examined in the weak light of a recently struck match, Hughes's suspect flesh had always to be checked for defect. Note the foreign journalist's card issued to Hughes by the Spanish Ministry of State on July 30, 1937, upon his arrival in the country to report on the civil war (see figure 3.1). Featuring a handsome photo of a thirty-five-year-old Hughes, it reads:

Ministerio de Estado

Jefe de la Oficina de Prensa

Certifica que Langston Hughes figura inscrito en el Registro de Periodistas
    Extranjeros de esta Oficina como corresponsal de "Globe Magazine", "Afro-
    American" de Baltimore, y "Call Post" de Cleveland.

Valencia, 30 de Julio de 1937.

What is so thrilling about this particular piece of ephemera in the Hughes archive is how powerfully the images and the language resonate with the efforts of African Americans, particularly African American men, to be recognized as modern subjects (New Negroes) following the close of slavery. As with black soldiers eagerly participating in the Spanish-American War, the document reminds us that the only proper relation of the (primitive) subject to the state is one of regimentation. To be a man, one must be *known* as a man. The official language utilized in Hughes's press card does nothing to obscure the ideological/ontological transformation that awaits Hughes on the borders of Republican Spain. He approaches the country as a figure (*figura*) in need of inscription onto one of the official registries of state power, the Registro de Periodistas Extranjeros (Registry of Foreign Journalists). Moreover, the card suggests no particular interest in Hughes's personal data, ignoring his age, weight, date of birth, and country of origin, but putting great emphasis

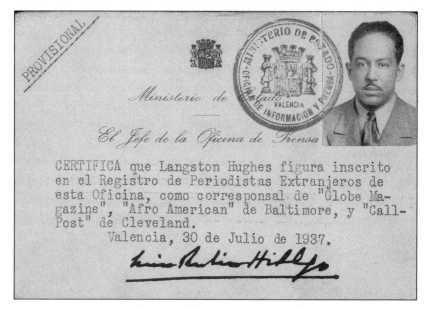

CERTIFICA que Langston Hughes figura inscrito
en el Registro de Periodistas Extranjeros de
esta Oficina, como corresponsal de "Globe Magazine", "Afro American" de Baltimore, y "Call-
Post" de Cleveland.
Valencia, 30 de Julio de 1937.

Figure 3.1. Langston Hughes's Spanish press card, dated July 30, 1937. Langston Hughes
Papers, Beineke Rare Book and Manuscript Library, Yale University.

on the several journals that supported his transfer to—and transformation within—Spain. Like the African American soldiers fighting as part
of the international brigades, Hughes's status in the country is indistinguishable from the documentation that surrounds him. That the card is
marked "provisional" needs no comment.

I make these points because they help us focus on the will to represent human subjectivity that has roots deep in practices of enslavement whereby African subjectivity was reduced to marks in ledgers,
practices that have been continued in state-sponsored identification/
articulation protocols whose disciplinary features become extremely—
and violently—apparent when "wild" anthropophorous subjects find
themselves incapable of fitting within rigid norms. Those of us who are
interested in the work of Langston Hughes are much less bothered by
the fact that he might have been homosexual than by the equally vexing
reality that his considerable archive remains so sloppily ineloquent on
the topic. Hughes's actual biography, a biography that demonstrates remarkable flexibility and willingness to recalibrate his personality, indeed

literally to translate himself, tends not to support the calcified protocols and long-established conventions available to us for the assessment of modern individuals.

Tellingly, the basic strategies with which we narrate the life of Langston Hughes are taken largely from Carl Van Vechten's introduction to Hughes's first collection of poetry, *The Weary Blues* (1926). Even as Hughes's work was translated into the Spanish language and his personage was introduced into Spanish contexts, there remained a certain "Van Vechtian" formality in the ways that the young poet might be approached. One of the first extensive treatments of Hughes in the Spanish language came in the March 1930 issue of *Revista de la Habana*. It reads in part:

> L.H. had lived in more than twelve locales in both his mother country and abroad, including Mexico City, Kansas, Buffalo, Colorado, Topeka, Cleveland, Chicago, etc. After graduating from high school he worked as a messenger and a farm laborer. He returned to Mexico. He was then a student at Columbia University. He fled from the university. Enlisting as a sailor, living like the men of the rivers and the seas, on the Hudson, the Atlantic, in the Canary Islands, on the western coast of Africa. Suggestive names captivated his ear and were always engraved on his spirit: Dakar, Burutu, Azores, the Afortunadas, the Bay of Luanda, Calabar, Lagos, the Belgian Congo. . . . He returns to New York and to the sea again: Holland, Paris, arriving with seven dollars in his pocket where his first desire was to leisurely visit the Louvre and the theater of the Opera. . . . Door man in a night club of Montmartre. Second cook in a restaurant frequented by tourists. . . . In Venice his money and passport were stolen from him. He became absolutely destitute. In Genoa: obligatory fights with the "black shirts." Wine, figs, and pasta. He enlists again as a sailor. Naples from a distance. Sicily, the islands of Lipari. And Spain. "Divine Spain." Valencia and again New York. The year 1924. In a public dance he meets the same night that he arrives his great introducer to the world: Van Vechten.[19]

Of course, anyone who had read Van Vechten's earlier introduction would have recognized that this essay, penned again by José Fernández de Castro, owed much to the earlier efforts of Hughes's friend and patron. Moreover, Hughes himself would later rehearse many of these details in his two autobiographies. Even more importantly, however, one begins to see that Hughes, even and especially as he detoured toward Havana and the Spanish language, had to negotiate the fact that his celebrity was supported by a well-established, even traditional edifice of words and images. In his efforts to (re)produce himself, to come to voice, he seemingly had become the very embodiment of the picaresque character who has fascinated generations of readers ever since the intro-duction of Cervantes's Quixote. At the same time, however, if Hughes wanted to do something more with his art than simply reiterate com-monsense notions of the artist as adventurer or outsider, he had to create counterstrategies, a corrosive vocabulary that might allow him to find a voice strong enough to rise above the cacophony of fantasies and projec-tions in which he found himself immersed.

I sense now that the moment has arrived for me to beg your forbear-ance. In order to continue the somewhat experimental and hopefully dialogical conceits of this book, I must admit that I am in trouble here, confused, stuck, and just a bit frightened. Thus far I have written a largely celebratory assessment of Hughes, gladly discovering along the way that treating him as an internationalist and a Hispanophile helps to deliver him from the trash heap of surprisingly dull, infinitely respectable writ-ers to whom brown-skinned children of my generation were directed as they prepared their much-anticipated Easter Sunday orations. But there is another Hughes who lurks about these pages, one whom I find myself avoiding like some friend or lover with whom things have gone inexpli-cably sour. There is the Hughes of the Jesse B. Semple stories, which I still find decidedly simple. There is Hughes the hack, writing librettos and poetry at a breakneck pace in order to pay the mortgage on his Harlem brownstone. And more difficult still, there is the Hughes who seemed to cower and capitulate as he was summoned before the U.S. Senate during the height of the anticommunist hysteria for which the United States has yet to atone; the Hughes who thereafter studiously avoided being linked to radical individuals and organizations, including the great W. E. B. Du Bois, lest he find himself incapable of making a living. Finally, there is my self-conjured image of Hughes as a man who freed himself from the primitivism of Charlotte Osgood Mason only to "submit" to the equally stifling, if perhaps somewhat more discreet, primitivism established and policed by editors and "publics" on both sides of the Atlantic.

I was led to this bit of dismal self-awareness by the pointed questioning directed at me when I presented an earlier version of the previous chapter in an infinitely comfortable room on a sprawling campus in the state where I was born. The most rigorous of my questioners, a woman of sharp intellect and ready laughter, noted that at the end of that chapter I seemed to retreat from my generally positive assessment of Federico García Lorca. She heard a certain irritation in my tone as I remarked Lorca's "inability" to understand fully the masking practices of the African Americans whom he encountered during his trip to the United States in 1929. I wonder now what she would make of my tortured admission that, quiet as it's kept, I sometimes also find Hughes irritating.

In my own defense—and Hughes's, for that matter—I would counter that though I clearly understand Hughes as a progressive writer, one whose experiments with politics and aesthetics I readily celebrate, I nonetheless remain cognizant of the fact that both art *and* politics are created in relation to real and imagined publics. Thus, my efforts in this chapter and throughout *Archives of Flesh* are designed to complicate our understanding of the discursive universes to which we belong. Most specifically, I have attempted to remain ever cognizant that captive Africans, starved and sweating in the dark of the Middle Passage, self-consciously, forcefully, and irremediably shaped the discursive landscapes that modern-day intellectuals inhabit. I have claimed repeatedly that the denial of this fact has been maintained not only through laughably simple procedures of logic, but also through the most sophisticated forms of violence evident in the formal practices of Western humanism. That we do not have the benefit of a full knowledge of the languages that our enslaved forebears created in order to imagine a world that might include you and me does not in any way suggest that these languages do not, in fact, have a profound impact on our everyday discursive practices.

If the critical and cultural work of progressive intellectuals is to have any real weight, it will necessarily have to court processes of defamiliarization that might allow us to imagine and mimic the much more difficult and serious work of chained Africans, establishing and asserting new forms of identity, society, and culture in the heat and stink of slavery's pit. It is key that we begin to treat the sense of being out of place that many of us confront as not simply some horror to be bemoaned, but instead as one of the structuring—and generative—realities underwriting the most potentially productive of our efforts. "I am here to remind you that the Negro's position as outcast is his most powerful human driving force, a force which hurls him forward towards a wider horizon that is more universal, more just, towards a horizon for which all honorable men are struggling today." We must not only accept but also provoke the irritation that I have just admitted having. We must remain ever wary of triumphant, celebratory, and therapeutic modes of criticism if we are to remain truly committed to moving beyond the horizon, past the littoral.

Predictably enough, we remain befuddled and uncertain. What we have gained from Hughes, however, is a renewed sense of the stakes involved in our attempts to direct the course of our travels. He has taught us the trick of how one might admit to one's genius and yet survive long enough to teach others something of the strangely (un)certain rhythms of an artistic and intellectual practice still in the process of naming itself. Moreover, he has boldly entreated us to allow our clumsy tongues to taste the sweetness and uncertainty of "strange" languages and "foreign" cultures. He dared to weep for whites trapped beneath the beautifully iridescent bombs of a trembling Spain. He touched Africa with his right hand and Europe with his left and declared himself at home in the world. He reminded us that our sufferings—and our joys—are not ours alone, but the planet's. More bravely still, he whispered to us an impossible promise: within the veil of our dark ignorance, our black history, we will find the unnamed land, the unknown victory for which we have produced so many misunderstood songs.

> Proud banner of death,
> I see them waving
> There against the sky
> Struck deep in Spanish earth
> Where your dark bodies lie
> Inert and helpless—
> So they think
> Who do not know
> That from your death
> New life will grow.

For there are those who cannot see
The mighty roots of liberty
Push upward in the dark
To burst in flame—
A million stars—
And one your name:
    Man
Who fell in Spanish earth:
Human seed
For freedom's birth.[20]

4

Primitive at the Plantation's Edge

The *Studia* must be reinvented as a higher order of human knowledge, able to provide an "outer view" which takes the human rather than any one of its variations as Subject . . . to attain to the position of an external observer, at once inside/ outside the figural domain of our order.
—Sylvia Wynter, "The Ceremony Must Be Found: After Humanism"

As a result of rallies we got courses in "black literature" and "black history" and a special black adviser for black students and a black cultural center, a rotting white washed house on the nether edge of campus.
—David Bradley, "Black and American, 1982"

There comes a time when the only thing that one can do is admit defeat. Standing at the tail end of a Black Studies movement established as part of the articulation of anti-segregationist, anticolonialist African and African American political and cultural insurgencies, one is made painfully aware of a sort of necessary and inevitable social and professional marginalization structuring the everyday existence of the so-called black scholar. The broadly imagined ethical outlines of even the most valued projects of black intellectualism continue as ornamental, overly moralistic, never quite fully valid aspects of the industry/government/ education complex that we decorously name the American academy. Accommodated in ever more brightly colored, if distantly placed and institutionally vulnerable, houses, the black, African, Africana scholastic project has only the most limited means by which it might affect a sort of inchoate articulation. When times are good and the funding secure, the history, thought, and culture of the peoples of the African diaspora might be taken as a sort of reiteration of the central conceits of American and European cultural and intellectual orthodoxy. A single red/brown/yellow/blue face appearing intermittently in recruitment brochures or faculty lounges boastfully reminds us of the meritocratic liberalism that presumably underwrites the basic structures of our most cherished educational and intellectual institutions. More impressive still, the scholar of Black Studies might make great use of an apparently never too tired for service "plus one" account of black subjectivity in which the most traditional ideas of universalism, cosmopolitanism, and Western humanism are presumably broadened and deepened through the indication that some representative black individual "was there." And when times are lean and narratives of scarcity rub harshly against notions of open-minded largesse, one might enact again and yet again a sort of hysterically ineffectual theatrical rebellion, identifying the many always easy to uncover moments of racialist hostility and insensitivity that are among the most profoundly resilient aspects of American and European society.

Still, regardless of the modes of attack and address, only the most limited consideration of Africa and the African diaspora can be discerned in the best-supported and most cherished precincts of the humanities and human sciences. There is so little awareness of the broad ideological structures on which the various practices of professional humanists are established that it becomes difficult to imagine that we might either critique or redirect basic modes of research and study. Broach the topic of lists, fields, and curricula with the most generous of colleagues, and you will very likely be met with a hand-wringing and apologetic, if firmly conventional, story of limited resources, fixed traditions, bureaucratic obstacles, and the rigid expectations of a harshly disciplining market. At the moment of challenge, humanistic studies are imagined to exist not so much as a complex of ideologies, discourses, and institutions with an identifiable and relatively short history, but instead as an impossibly distant force, almost metaphysical in nature, that we are able to approach with only the most unstable of intellectual prosthetics.

The crisis of humanism is first and foremost a failure of the political and ethical imaginaries that stabilize the labor that one presumably does as a practitioner of the humanities and human sciences. It is the ever more vertiginous social reality confronting intellectuals who approach their work through a sort of willed ignorance of the ideological organization of the *Studia*. As I have suggested, the philosophical and ethical arrangements of humanism become much clearer once one appropriates the historical understandings given us by Michel Foucault and amplified by Sylvia Wynter, once we recognize that not only are the conceptual and instrumental arrangements that we use to teach, research, write, and publish decidedly new phenomena, but are also inextricably tied up with the violent extraction of value and labor. In a sense, then, we in the United States are lucky to have so little opportunity to cover over the absolutely intimate relationship between universities, colonization, and enslavement. Step onto the campus of one of the country's great sites of learning, and you are quite likely stepping onto a plantation, an institution in which the expression of so-called high culture was—and is—fueled by the literal entrapment and internment of Africans and their descendants.[1] Those gates and guards through and by which we pass are not simple adornments, but instead absolutely necessary safeguards within a set of protocols designed to distinguish (African) chaos from (European) order. The disciplinary structures most commonly associated with the humanities operate first and foremost to yoke the "free-floating" energy of the untidy (Negro) to a process by which a disembodied universalist (white) order might be named. The trick, of course, is to accomplish this particular procedure without seeming to do so. There is good reason that there has been so little discussion of the relationship between the history of Atlantic slavery and the development of the disciplines. That procedure would invite consideration of the rather uncanny overlap of these institutions' developmental timelines, coming to maturity as they did in the nineteenth century and fracturing in the twentieth. Even more to the point, a truly historicist and anti–white supremacist examination of the history of the humanities and human sciences would necessarily have to take into account not only the fact that the descendants of the enslaved and the colonized continue to do the unseen, unwanted, irrational work of the university, dumping trash cans, cleaning toilets, and preparing meals, but also that the scholars whom they service incessantly, even manically, reiterate a set of intellectual protocols built precisely on never noting that their cleverness and disinterestedness are often themselves examples of brittle misunderstanding(s) of the conditions of their own labor.

It comes as no surprise, then, that Black Studies should be so studiously ignored as it stands mocking and mocked at the plantation's edge.

Fascinating in its vulgarity and decrepitude, the rotting whitewashed house seems to point in two directions at once, naming a desiccated past while demanding a certain horrified attention in the present. Wynter writes,

> It is within the same governing laws of figuration and its internal logic that the Black Culture Center was proscribed to exist on the nether edge of the campus. It functioned as the target stimuli of aversion, with respect to the Euroamerican order of the center of the campus, which is then enabled to function as the object stimuli of desire. The relation, functioning dually at empirical and valorizing levels, if stably kept in phase, ensures the stable production of the same shared endogenous wave-shapes, in Black students as well as Whites—the same normative seeing/valuing, avoiding/devaluing behaviors. Hence the paradox that, after the turbulence of the 1960s and the 1970s the Black Culture Centers in their nether-edge-of-the campus place function to enable the recycling (in cultural rather than racial terms) of the Order/Chaos dynamics of the system-ensemble.[2]

Here I take some solace in the conditional nature of Wynter's most damning observation. *If* the fraught relations between Black Studies and the "Euroamerican order of the center" are stably kept in phase, *then* we condemn ourselves to the reiteration of those normative behaviors and modes of thought established in the crucibles of enslavement and colonization. The very presence of the shabby house at the edge of campus remarks the possibility of rupture within these systems. It suggests modes of knowledge and articulation that if not elegant are at least not so wholly and innocently disconnected from the means of their own replication as to exist in a sort of creative stasis, operating like the disciplined, defeated professor of literature whose tepid passions never quite reach the level of either offense—or brilliance.

While I knowingly, even lovingly, embrace the disorder that is Black Studies, I cannot bring myself to celebrate that embrace. Sitting here on the ugly side of campus, collecting my thoughts in rooms that though not obviously rotting are nonetheless likely to be swept away come the next great wind, I know that my efforts must be read as at once marginal and suspect. I "have every interest in challenging an order of figuration" that programs my own negation (Wynter, "The Ceremony," 49). Yet mine is not a blameless opposition. I do not naïvely celebrate the obvious fraying of the humanist project. Nor do I yearn for an easy re-organization of priorities, the moving of the white house to the center. Instead I am seeking, however haltingly, the reinvention of the *Studia* in a manner that would allow for the articulation of a fully universal humanism and the dismantling of the deeply embedded white supremacy that so firmly establishes American and European intellectualism. In doing so, however, I must by necessity recognize the Black Studies apparatus itself as having been established within the order/chaos ideological nexus that lies at the heart of the humanities and human sciences. Thus in the necessarily radical practices of disarticulation that one hopes will soon and very soon take up our attention and our energies, it is quite unclear whether the rotting house will survive.

What this means practically is that, like many others before me, I have attempted to utilize methods developed in the particular context of African American Studies to address texts and contexts outside traditions that hold fast in North Carolina and New York. I am interested less in identity than process. As a consequence, I have found it relatively easy to shift my focus from "black" America to "white" Spain. What I am most earnestly attempting to achieve, however, is not simply an easy acknowledgment of the historical and cultural overlaps between Spain and African America, but instead something akin to a new hermeneutics, a new mode of reading that is at once diagnostic, corrosive, and reparative. I shift my gaze back and forth between my two interlocutors, the black and the Latin, the American and the European, because I am thrilled by the possibilities inherent in their *in*articulate-ness, the ways neither can be fully or comfortably housed within the Man/human, Man/anthropophorous animal nexus. It is the clumsiness of the African American/Spanish pairing that most intrigues me. I suspect that the necessary tentativeness of the theoretical and critical apparatus that one must create in order to maintain the combinations that are at the center of this book is itself a necessary procedure for the intellectual interested in finding a new ceremony that might allow us to gain "the outer view," to rid ourselves of the mediocrity of thought and action that stands so ostentatiously and ignobly at the very heart of the humanist enterprise.

The Unthinkable

All that matters now is to keep thinking the unthinkable and
writing the unprintable and maybe I can break through this
motherfucking race barrier that keeps us niggers suffocated.
—Chester Himes, *My Life of Absurdity*

Late in 1964 the African American novelist Chester Himes traveled
through Spain and north Africa with his life partner, Lesley Packard,
stopping long enough in Alicante to buy a piece of land at Moraira-
Teulada, where the couple would eventually build a house, Casa Griot,
named for their much-loved Siamese cat. By September 1968, they had
begun in earnest the process of moving permanently to Spain. Chester
and Lesley married there in 1978 and lived on the peninsula until they
both died, Chester in 1984 and Lesley in 2010. Though Himes's name
is almost synonymous with the history of those African American
artists and intellectuals who settled in France, particularly Paris, presumably to escape the more severe forms of racist violence that they
might encounter in the United States, Himes spent more than sixteen
years in Spain after having passed a decade further north. Five of his late
works were published while he resided in Moraira-Teulada: the novels
Blind Man with a Pistol (1969), *Black on Black* (1973), and *A Case of Rape*
(1980), and two fascinating volumes of autobiography: *The Quality of
Hurt* (1973) and *My Life of Absurdity* (1976).[3] Another novel, *Pinktoes*,
was published in 1967, a year before the couple's permanent move to
Moraira-Teulada. Perhaps even more importantly, early in 1954, fourteen years before finally settling permanently in Spain, Himes arrived on
the island of Mallorca, escaping with his lover, a woman he refers to in
the memoir as Alva Trent, from the relentless cold and the astoundingly
bold racism of 1950s London. The two carried with them the defeat of
not having been able to publish the work that they had written together,
The Golden Chalice, a fact that Himes attributed to the American publishing industry's hostility to the couple's interracial status. In revolt,
Himes decided to publish a novel that played right along the cutting
edge of white fantasies about black sexuality and black/white sexual congress. "I'll give them something to hate me for," he wrote. "I'll give them
a book, because this is the kind of thing they can really hate me for."[4]

The result was Himes's extremely provocative, woefully underexamined fifth novel, *The End of a Primitive*.[5]

Building upon the arguments of the cultural critic Jodi Melamed, I would suggest that *The End of a Primitive* was not so much a bridge between the naturalist aesthetic that dominated Himes's early works and the farcical, hard-bitten nature of the crime novels for which he is justly famous, but instead a culmination of the author's ongoing attempts to engage his audience through deployment of a set of *dis*articulations, modes of address and representation designed to occupy so fully the racialist/white supremacist common sense as to make plain the many structural cleavages, the absurdities, that hold it together.[6] Himes understood and reiterated the very spatial metaphors, the images of enclosure, darkness, physical deprivation, and shrinking that have been so successfully—and successively—utilized in African American literary and cultural practice. He allowed himself to dwell in the half light, the stench, the damp, the cold, and the heat of the hold long enough to push beyond aesthetic and ideological constraints established by what he understood to be a wholly hypocritical literary/critical apparatus. He pressed forcefully in the novel against the Man/human binary not by reiterating the typical Afro-American call for inclusion in the so-called human family, but instead by embracing the charge of bestiality, allowing the name calling embedded in the phrase "black beast" to overwhelm his narrative, to make evident the profoundly anti-human vulgarity that lies at the heart of the common sense of white liberal respectability.

I will state again that I am not interested in the production of a more equitable, racially liberal, and diverse humanities project. I agree with Cary Wolfe that the purported pluralism that is so loudly trumpeted by humanism's many disciples ultimately works to strengthen the basic ideological structures supporting white supremacy and capitalist exploitation.[7] Instead, I call for a radical Black Studies and an invigorated Critical Archive Studies as parts of broad-based efforts to disrupt the Man/anthropophorous animal binary. I am eager to move beyond the knee-jerk fear that the black might be called animal or beastly. Indeed, to subscribe to the idea that men, no matter the hue of their skin, stand above animals is simply to retreat to slightly less noxious articulations of humanism's structuring conceits.

Much of what fascinates me about Himes was that his escape to Spain represented not simply an attempt to avoid the harsher varieties of anti-black violence, but also an effort to seek new modes of subjectivity in which the black intellectual might finally give up on the untenable/unthinkable project of taming and mortifying his own flesh. He did so through self-conscious reference to Spain's marginal status in what one might call euphemistically the "European imagination." The peninsula represented for Himes the very cursed promise of eccentricity implied in David Bradley and Sylvia Wynter's images of the rotting white house. His open disdain for the country in which he was able to establish the only stable home he had ever had was itself an emblem of the focus and resiliency necessary for an intellectual who understood that, though he might achieve fame and even some measure of prosperity, the means of his survival were not simply inadequate but toxic. Himes's biographer James Sallis reports that the author hated Spain. He found it to be equally as racist as the American South but not nearly as efficient. In letters written late in life, Himes offered a steady stream of anti-Spanish invective, describing the country as a tomb and a trap. In a note dated July 29, 1975, to his agent, Roslyn Targ, wife of his editor at Putnam, William Targ, he lamented that, as he would be dead within a month, his first priority must necessarily be the completion of his second autobiography, *My Life of Absurdity*. Writing feverishly from his home in Moraira-Teulada, he carped that he was "almost totally helpless" and that Lesley had "lost interest in keeping me alive." Spain, notwithstanding the cheerful sunshine and great beauty of Alicante, had become a snare. "I cannot get out of Spain," he droned. "I would not trouble you with this if it were not deadly serious. I cannot get any help from any one. Please think of me with charity."[8] Himes repeated his apparent desperation the following year on July 17, 1976, writing that Lesley had "taken total care of me for the past ten or more years and . . . and it is hard on her because I HATE SPAIN."[9]

What strikes one when reading Himes's complaints about his life on the Costa del Sol, complaints that he stridently restated from at least 1968 onward, is not simply the fact that he wrote from locations that many would consider paradisiacal, but also that he remained thoroughly productive during this period. Though he claimed to Roslyn Targ in the summers of 1975 and 1976 that he was on the verge of death, he did not, in fact, die until some eight years later, after having published two splendid autobiographies. Whatever other deficits Spain may have had, it had become for Himes a sort of metaphor for the strange, indeed vertiginous, reality he faced as an artist whose physical and mental abilities were declining while he nonetheless began to achieve both financial comfort and something akin to canonical stature. In his 1976 letter to Targ, he listed the assets that he was eager to leave to Lesley: $44,000 deposited in Credit Suisse, $1,700 deposited in Barclays, $10,000 on deposit in Morgan's Paris, a furnished house with swimming pool on two plots of land in Moraira, another empty plot nearby, and two little cars. He then closed by again reiterating his loathing for the country. In a postscript, Lesley entreats the Targs to visit them in Alicante, noting that filled with trees and sea breezes, the garden was particularly pretty:

> There are days when we have lots of fun playing our cassettes and sitting around the pool. Also Mike and Sarah are over here very often. They have both had a very successful show together in Altea and sell reasonably well. An American collector bought 12 of his drawings. Not so bad!! (Chester Himes letter to Mrs. Roslyn Targ, July 17, 1976)

It is clear that Himes found it exceedingly difficult to reconcile long-established sensibilities and sensitivities with the process by which his talent—and his life—had been monetized, the ways his rather famously desperate efforts at both security and self-expression had been actualized not in New York nor even Paris, but on the very edge of the Iberian Peninsula. Though he did not often reflect upon the matter, Himes had settled rather surprisingly close to the African continent. He rested more or less comfortably at a location not at all distant from the slaving stations of centuries past. He had taken up residence at the plantation's edge. Sitting with an adoring wife by the refreshing pool of a lovely home, the pages of an unfinished autobiography ready at hand, he had come to know the uncanny comfort that one might achieve while attempting to resist the forgetting and self-deception that are the blood price of an ill-fitting respectability.

The desperate vertigo evinced in Himes's letters to Targ echoes the very strange state of affairs that led him to Mallorca in the winter of

1954. He had met his lover Alva Trent Van Olden Barneveldt a little less than a year earlier as the two traveled onboard the *Ile de France* toward Europe and the renewed lives that they hoped to find there. When Trent met Himes in one of the corridors of the ship, her first words were, "Don't leave me! Please don't leave me!" She then apologized for her strange behavior, stating that the ship provoked severe attacks of claustrophobia (Himes, *The Quality of Hurt*, 153).[10] Feeling sorry for her and acting on his awkward sense of chivalry, Himes helped her to her cabin, then rushed above deck to vomit over the railing. Just out of a disastrous—and spectacularly abusive—relationship with Vandi Haygood, the woman on whom the character Kriss in *The End of a Primitive* is based, Chester felt strangely attracted to Alva. Their quickly developing affair represented a sort of minimalist carnival of boundary crossings. Meeting inside a tightly sealed tube of metal vainly/valiantly pulling itself across the Atlantic, they retreated, however ineffectually, from the sterility and severity of the nation that had handled them both so roughly. They were intensely aware of the breeching game they performed. Alva was just as comfortable stealthily making her way to the third-class cabins as Chester was to the first. Her dazing story of betrayal and defeat demonstrated a woman as ready as any to renounce the privileges of race and class.

Born to a prominent Philadelphia family, Alva met her Dutch husband just before the Second World War while she was an exchange student in Bonn. Giving birth to four girls in quick succession, she attempted to escape with them to the United States when the Nazis invaded the Netherlands and her husband became a collaborator, working as the dental surgeon for the staff at the Maastricht headquarters. Successful in getting only three of the children out of the country, she returned to her husband, eventually suffering a string of nervous breakdowns before retreating again to the United States and divorcing him. But, as the divorce was not recognized by the Dutch government, she had no obvious legal right to the girls, whom she had left behind. In April 1953 she booked passage aboard the *Ile de France*, hoping to meet her husband and convince him to allow their children to come back with her. In a close, ill-lit hallway punctuated by rows of tightly sealed doors, she met a seasick novelist and ex-convict, Chester Himes.

There was something surprisingly elegant about Chester and Alva's retreat to Mallorca. The island, located off Spain's northeast coast, had been one of the last redoubts of Republican resistance. In the interim between the war and Himes's first visit it had become, along with the other islands of the Baleares, a retreat for artists, radicals, and homosexuals seeking a place in which they might live more or less unnoticed by the Falangist government in Madrid. By the time Himes made his own clumsy approach, Mallorca had long since ceased to be a site of open conflict. Its quaint villages were destined to become locations for the most sublime tourism, touching emblems of Spain's industrial retardation. Chester and Alva found themselves at the lip of a sort of gilded pit. Himes, defeated and in retreat from the realities of American racism and anti-intellectualism; Alva, abandoned and damaged, frantic to establish an alternative to the hubris and humiliation of white bourgeois domesticity—the two could hope for no more than the slow sink into regret and dissipation that was the island's ultimate gift.

And yet there can be rather strange surprises for those of us forced to the plantation's edge. One becomes increasingly aware that the horror and dis-ease that presumably define the half-life begrudgingly offered to the repudiated and disavowed are themselves reflections of the shocking instability of the logics underwriting the Man/human binarism. Soon after Alva married her husband, they went to a Paris hotel, where he desperately attempted to consummate their marriage. Later describing the scene to Chester, she explained that as her husband's penis was too large, she was unreceptive to his advances. Frustrated, he forced her to undergo an operation at the hands of his medical school friends in order to rectify the problem. He booked a separate room, keeping her alone, only coming for daily sex visits. The exercise was a success, but Alva would later complain, "You know, my husband made me pregnant five times but never made me an orgasm" (Himes, *The Quality of Hurt*, 161). The legitimacy of the children whom the couple produced was a thing established upon a level of force and coercion not distinct from that which passes between master and slave. There was a deficit of pleasure. In the place of intimacy, violence stood; instead of dripping lust, respectability persisted. The father smiling brightly at precious daughters sees in their cheerful faces evidence of his own throbbing rupture. His great success is that he has escaped the vulgar and illogical (re)productive possibilities of human flesh. He has retreated from the carnivalesque world of animals, slaves, and prostitutes and into a realm of ordered largesse in which, thanks to the ministrations of those skilled medical school friends, his daughters have been both born physically and reborn socially without suffering the taint of their mother's beastlike hysteria. If Man and human must come together, awkward and unacknowledged, in the production of progeny, they certainly cannot be expected always to get along. The joy of self-reiteration might be cunningly disrupted by the mechanics of the animal body, the relative size and shape of a never quite to be trusted penis.

Much of my attraction to Himes turns on the fact that he was so obviously self-aware and self-conscious about the hysterical forms of propriety that rigidly structure much within humanism, including much of the Black Studies enterprise itself. With each jerk of his pen, Himes meant to overturn useless models of respectability in favor of iconoclastic forms that continually remind one of soiled flesh, a none too distant prehistory in which our ancestors inhabited their hordes with their faces covered in shit. As much in *The End of a Primitive* as his autobiographies, Himes seemed most anxious to find a means by which not so much to mend the Man/human, Man/animal break as to demonstrate its artificiality. In both their composition and their coupling, Chester and Alva attempted to find a hermeneutics that might allow them to bring meaning to their suffering. Their creative practice was decidedly ceremonial. Out of the ashes of their abandoned project, *The Golden Chalice*, Chester sought to disavow the common sense of the *Studia*, producing in *The End of a Primitive* a work designed to soothe its author as well as to alert its readers to processional alternatives in the structures of their lives that might prove slightly less caustic to human animality than the brittle racialism and woman hating that so suffuse Western humanism.

Rising early, drugging himself with coffee and Dexamyl, then retreating to his writing desk in the garden of one of the small houses he shared with Alva, Chester found unexpected solace in his craft.

> I wrote slowly, savoring each word, sometimes taking an hour to fashion one sentence to my liking. Sometimes leaning back in my seat and laughing hysterically at the sentence I had fashioned, getting as much satisfaction from the creation of this book as from an exquisite act of love. That

was the first time in my life I enjoyed writing; before I had always written from compulsion. But I enjoyed writing *The End of a Primitive* . . . for once I was almost doing what I wanted to with a story, without being influenced by the imagined reactions of editors, publishers, critics, readers, or anyone. By then I had reduced myself to the fundamental writer, and nothing else mattered. I wonder if I could have written like that if I had been a successful writer, or even living in a more pleasant house. But one can write under such conditions for only a very limited time; in fact under such conditions one writes with the driving inspiration to get the hell out. (Himes, *The Quality of Hurt*, 302)

With every turn of phrase, Himes revels in the *non*productive nature of his writing. He reaches toward a classical conception of human subjectivity in which there is no easy distinction between hours of fashioning, hysterical laughter, acts of love, and the "driving inspiration to get the hell out." The effect is an almost religious revelry in which each word scratched onto the page carries exact meaning, a phenomenological weight unequal to the reactions of editors, publishers, critics, or readers. The ceremony of the writing desk is a thing that exists in itself for itself. It is a process not dissimilar from the discursive possibilities available to the unsold slave as he retreats to the relative comfort of his cell. What one sounds at such moments is an expression of a humanity temporarily relieved from rigorously scripted performance techniques designed to reiterate and obscure the viciously exploitative capitalist exchanges that establish anthropophorous animality and then yoke its possibilities to those of Man. The slave may express, but never transcribe, the unthinkable and the unprintable. Much of the value of the whitewashed house at the edge of campus, the value of Himes's retreat to Spain, is that the sublingual soundings of humans not yet become Men might be contained there and referred to later if profit can be made.

These same structures of thought and feeling are feverishly repeated in *The End of a Primitive*. The novel follows forty-eight hours in the lives of two characters: Jesse Robinson, an out-of-luck black novelist deeply embittered by the limitations imposed on his talent and craft; and Kristina (Kriss) Cummings, a forty-something white divorcée and employee of the India Institute, an organization modeled in part on the famed Rosenwald Fund, the liberal foundation that underwrote African American intellectual life through direct grants to individuals such as Gordon Parks, Elizabeth Catlett, Claude McKay, Charles Drew, Augusta Savage, Katherine Dunham, Ralph Ellison, W. E. B. Du Bois, James Weldon Johnson, Langston Hughes, and Chester Himes. The work is provocatively autobiographical, representing Himes's earlier affair with Vandi Haygood, former acting director of fellowships for the Rosenwald Fund, a position that she took over from her husband, William C. Haygood, while he served in the army during the Second World War.[11] All of these details are meticulously reproduced in *The End of a Primitive*, as is the fact that Himes and Haygood had had an earlier tryst in Chicago.

What truly startles, however, what unnerves the reader who has followed the long arc of Himes's career, is how ruthless and un-glossed Himes's prose is as he describes his interactions with Haygood in *The Quality of Hurt* and then repeats the structure of these actions in *The End of a Primitive*.

> When she went to Chicago to visit some old lover after telling me she was going to Washington, D.C., on business, I hurt her seriously. Physically, I mean. I began slapping her when she admitted the truth and all the hurts of my life seemed to come up into me and I went into a trance and kept on slapping her compulsively until suddenly the sight of her swollen face jarred me back to sanity. (Himes, *The Quality of Hurt*, 136)

> He sat on the side of the bed with his back to the dead body. . . . "You finally did it, son," he said. . . . End product of the impact of Americanization one Jesse Robinson—black man. Your answer, son. You've been searching for it. BLACK MAN KILLS WHITE WOMAN. All the proof you need now. Absolutely incontrovertible behaviorism of a male human being. Most human of all behavior. Human beings only species of animal life where males are known to kill their females. Proof beyond all doubt. Jesse Robinson joins the human race. Good article for the *Post*: he joined The Human Race. All good solid American *Post* readers will know exactly what you mean: were a nigger but killed a white woman and became a human being. (Himes, *The End of a Primitive*, 205)

There are three rudely suggestive claims that Himes makes in these passages that bear repeating. First, he equates status as a human (Man) as indistinguishable from the abuse, exploitation, and murder of one's human partners. Jesse was once a nigger, but he "killed a white woman and became a human being." Second, in Himes's own attack on Vandi Haygood, he claims to have gone into a trance, a state regularly described in both *The Quality of Hurt* and *The End of a Primitive*. Part of what makes systematic violence possible is the ability to deny the killing rage that motivates it. Though fierce aggression is a key element in the reproduction of the main structures of our social, cultural, and philosophical practices, it can never (should never) be acknowledged as such. Finally, and perhaps most disturbing of all, the hands doing all that slapping and extinguishing of life are not pink but brown. It seems that the modern black subject is not only just as capable of anti-human viciousness as his white counterpart, but also much like brown-skinned African American soldiers taking aim at brown-skinned Filipinos, there is a distinct need for such action. The African American is never more of a Man than when, walking away from dazed bellicosity, he finds his lover's face bloodied and bruised.

One might see very well then the necessity of Sylvia Wynter's call for a new ceremony, one in which there is no longer any need for such acts of hostility. In heeding this claim, however, we ought to be perfectly aware of the stakes. (Black) Manhood is given meaningful structure precisely through negative reference to black flesh. It is not the beast that attacks his beloved, but Man. Himes's literal defacing of Vandi Haygood, Alva's husband's efficiently medicalized attacks on his wife's virginity, Jesse's eventual murder of his lover, Kriss—all of these are acts of Man(ly) aggression, "the most human of all behavior." What must have been profoundly stressful for Himes writing in the middle of the twentieth century, just as the country was decidedly changing its constitutional narratives such that some blacks might achieve a bracketed Manhood status, was that the unthinkable and unprintable realities, the very realities that Himes so desperately attempted to name, were those which resisted the violence of Manhood by referring to a repressed (black) animality.

I Submitted Myself to That Yoke

Of course what I felt then as an ape I can represent now only
in human terms.
—Franz Kafka, "A Report to an Academy"

Animal imagery is so omnipresent in *The End of a Primitive* as to form
a sort of static background. Jesse lives in a rooming house dominated by
gay men. In his relentlessly homophobic descriptions he is ever careful
to remind his readers of their animal attributes. His flatmates are all
birdmen. The youngest of them has beautiful "doe eyes." In the main
hall of the apartment there is "a stuffed owl which appears so shockingly
lifelike in such natural surroundings that Jesse often wondered how the
birdmen would dare venture from their nests" (Himes, *The End of a
Primitive*, 39–40). For her part, Kriss is not above the most vulgar articulations of white fantasies of black bestiality. "If we still owned slaves I'd
pay a year's wages for you," she tells Jesse after many hours of drinking
and unrelieved sexual tension. "I'd keep you in my bedroom for a pet
and give you a gold collar and nameplate" (165). And as Jesse himself
becomes more and more desperately drunk, he continuously references
black humanity's kinship with apes. Irritated when Kriss tells him that
an old lover is coming over for drinks, he goads her by suggesting that
she search for more partners "in the jungle," adding that should the
stock of humans not prove adequate, "there are the apes" (181). Continuing the joke later in the evening, he announces that he is "going to
write the biography of the great white ape who rules all the black apes in
the jungle." He completes the ill-conceived joke with the claim that "Of
course the title will be, *Gone with the Apes*" (183). Finally deflecting the
criticism of the other guests, he answers that he'd "been an ape too long
to change now—feeling mighty uncomfortable as a human being" (188).

There is an obvious arrangement of irritated and outraged play on
display here. Instead of retreating behind more palatable narratives of
black cultural retardation, Himes restates the simplest of racial slurs.
The black's inferiority can never be overcome, as, unlike the white, he
cannot settle the knotty problem of his bestiality, the cunning of his animal flesh. Repeating the most solidly established forms of racialism, he
represents the black/animal as a being not yet become an actor. Instead,

it exists as an elemental actuality outside history and culture that can be discerned with only the most peculiar of discursive and technological strategies. The black/animal *must* remain "outside," "on the edge," as it is from this position that it becomes available as the most necessary, most potent prosthetic within the Manhood arsenal.

At once amused and enraged by the limitations put on his life and career by this particular structure of thought and feeling, Jesse pens a very brief, very clumsy, and very funny short story both to distract himself and to make visible the dominant ideological structures of Euro-American racialism.

> The nigger woke, sat up, scratched at the lice, stood up, farted, pissed, crapped, gargled, harked, spat, sat down, ate a dishpan of stewed chitterlings, drank a gallon of lightning, hated the white folks for an hour, went out and stole some chickens, raped a white woman, got lynched by a mob, scratched his kinky head and said, "Boss ah's tahd uh gittin' lynched. Ah's so weary kain keep mah eyes open," and the Boss said, "Go on home an' sleep, nigger, that's all you niggers is good for." So he went back to his shanty, stealing a watermelon on the way, ate the watermelon rind and all, lay down on his pallet, blinked, yawned and went to sleep hating the white folks. (63)

The humor that fuels this story is built around the bluntness of the racialist common sense, the steadiness and sobriety of the white supremacist archive. The nigger is a fundamental and rudimentary creature. It has no particular motivations and cannot be said to desire. Instead it exists as pure repetition. It wakes, eats, drinks, rapes, steals, gets lynched, and hates white people in a timeless process punctuated only by the occasional interventions of the Boss. Its dumbness is absolute. If it forms ideas larger than a confused hating of (white) Man, this remains impossible to discern, as the philosophical structures available within the *Studia* are blind to the possibilities of animal thought. That said, I want to make it plainly clear that what I am after here is not a retreat from notions of black bestiality. Instead what interests me are the possibilities inherent in fully inhabiting the ideological contradictions that support the "necessary" distinction between Man and animal.

Jacques Derrida makes a similar claim as he comments on the discomfort of being watched by his cat as he stands naked in the bath, a discomfort made stranger still by the fact that the cat is itself naked, though, in Derrida's figuration, not nude.

> There is no nudity "in nature." There is only the sentiment, the affect, the (conscious or unconscious) experience of existing in nakedness. Because it *is* naked, without *existing* in nakedness, the animal neither feels nor sees itself naked. And therefore it isn't naked. At least that is what is thought. For man it would be the opposite, and clothing derives from technics. We would therefore have to think shame and technicity together, as the same "subject." And evil and history, and work, and so many other things that go along with it. Man would be the only one to have invented a garment to cover his sex. He would be a man only to the extent that he was able to be naked, that is to say, to be ashamed, to know himself to be ashamed because he is no longer naked. And *knowing* himself would mean knowing himself to be ashamed. On the other hand, because the animal is naked without consciousness of being naked, it is thought that modesty remains as foreign to it as does immodesty. As does the knowledge of self that is involved in that.[12]

I would like to remain focused for a moment on the shame/technicity nexus that Derrida describes. Specifically, I suggest that the only way that such an idea can be said to have any logical stability is if we admit a rather surprisingly limited idea of human technique. Shame is understood as a form that is counterpoised to an ill-defined nature, that thing which is separate, that stands aloof from the discursive. The problem, however, is that ever so difficult to read cat. Being but not existing within its nakedness, it is established as a thing that stands wholly opposite to Man. Yet the descriptions that Derrida utilizes represent it as hopelessly implicated within human technicity. Its domestication is the ticket that allows its privileged admission into Derrida's bathroom. One imagines a collar, a bell, well-groomed fur, and manicured claws all testifying to centuries of Man's manipulation. Its function is precisely to reflect the very self-consciousness that is so much on display in Derrida's prose. It has been produced to provoke human self-reflection, to help operationalize the mechanics of shame. Moreover, one would be well advised to remember that we have no actual access to *Felis catus* here, but instead a representation of the same.

Only very recently can there be said to be any general disarticulation of the notion of the African and the black as warped or uncooked versions of the human animal. At the core of so-called Western humanism one finds an impressively resilient will to maintain racialist practices and procedures that reiterate the anthropophorous animal/Man binary. To cease to do so would so clarify the connections between slavery, colonization, and white supremacy in the articulation of the humanities and human sciences as to risk even further eroding their already decidedly weak claims to social relevancy. The expected response to this claim is to call foul, to point to the black's embrace of order, the snugly fit nature of his shamefully pulled on clothes. Such procedures have helped us gain hard-won positions in the still proliferating whitewashed houses dotting the nether edges of American campuses. What I believe to be a much more interesting—and perhaps more efficacious—move, however, what I hope might get us closer to the new ceremony for which Wynter calls, would be to refuse these old techniques, to give up on our constant efforts to have black Manhood and black respectability recognized. Instead, as a first move in the production of a post-humanist Black Studies project, we should recognize that the human/animal, order/chaos binary is such a desperate gambit that not only can it no longer be particularly useful in the articulation of anticolonialist, anti–white supremacist intellectual insurgency, but also it is clearly inadequate for the work of naming and projecting advanced notions of human subjectivity.

Man is not a singular reality, but instead a technique of the human. The preciousness with which so many approach the humanities and human sciences is itself an emblem of the fragility of the Manhood trope. Having lost hold of the fact that the hu(Man)ities are but extensions of a set of aesthetic/prosthetic procedures designed to compensate for an original wounding, that tearing and incapacitation that Octavio Paz claims attended the human species' development from the commonality of apes with their faces bent toward the ground to the isolation of an individuated and isolated bipedal collection of (non)animals, we confuse the all too shallow conceits of the *Studia* for original, incontrovertible truth. In this way our imaginative faculties become increasingly dull, our ethics remarkably cynical.[13]

I am supported in my claims by Franz Kafka's impressively underappreciated short story "A Report to an Academy." Published in 1917, the account presents the details of Red Peter, a speaking ape who appears before a scientific association to give the details of his capture and transformation from ape to "human." The work relentlessly undermines notions of Man's nobility and instead precisely graphs the humanization process on a grid marked by domination, submission, diminution, and leveling. "To give up on being stubborn was the supreme commandment I laid upon myself," Peter testifies to the Academy. "Free ape as I was, I submitted myself to that yoke."[14]

That Kafka so stubbornly plots Red Peter's story along the familiar narrative outlines of slavery and colonization has the effect of not only naming the vulgarity of the Euro-American history of conquest, but also of making plain the ways that the humanities and human sciences (the Academy) are themselves first and foremost systems of domination and suppression. Red Peter's status as a near human is built upon the relinquishment of his stubbornness. In order to appear as a valued guest before the Academy, one must be wholly willing to place one's neck inside the trap. In the process, however, Peter loses access to those modes of discernment and articulation that have not been vetted within the Academy's disciplinary procedures. That is the point. While practitioners of the humanities and human sciences are ever eager to demonstrate the often impressive advances in knowledge achieved within their various procedures, they remain largely unconcerned with the striking amount of knowledge that is not so much ignored by their disciplinary structures as repressed. Red Peter's narrative sounds thin, expected, almost banal to the contemporary reader. There is very little that is intimate about the history that he recounts. Instead, what he achieves is the expression of the wholly expected set of narrative protocols that attends any ape's movement from the bestial to the human. "I belong to the Gold Coast," he announces. "For the story of my capture I must depend on the evidence of others" (Kafka, "A Report to an Academy," 246).

What Peter names, of course, is nothing more fanciful than double consciousness. Articulation is an exercise in forgetting. Red Peter's access to the singularity of his existence has been canceled in favor of a complex discursive technique that allows him to project a finely wrought simulacrum of his former self. As a consequence, he harbors no resentment about what was done, noting good-naturedly that he has "drunk many a bottle of good red wine" with the leader of the expedition that shot and captured him (246). The only alternative records of the original assault are the very wounds to Peter's flesh. His name is *Red* Peter and not simply Peter, the name of another performing ape of his generation, because he carries a "large, naked, red scar" on his cheek, persistent emblem of the bullet to the face he received on the day of his capture (246). A second bullet hit him below the hip, giving him a permanent limp and the rather unsettling habit of taking down his trousers in polite company in order to show his guests the entry point. Any symbolization of the very real and quite recent violence underwriting the studied disinterestedness of the Academy is to be avoided. It is not so much that by demonstrating his scar Red Peter risks offering a glimpse of ape genitals, but instead that this action reveals a competing narrative, an alternative discursive mode, an archive of flesh that might prove the lie of the Academy's monopolization of (human) knowledge.

Peter was transferred from the Gold Coast to Europe by ship—in his case, the *Hagenbeck* steamer—where after the ordeal of his wounding and capture, he woke to find himself in a steel and wood contraption so low and narrow that he was forced to squat with "knees bent and trembling all the time," while the bars of the cage cut into the "flesh behind" (246). Trapped below deck, his body treated as a hindrance, a thing to be jettisoned in the acquisition of Manhood, he was forced to take up the most complex of modern tasks. He approached his own ape flesh as an object distinct from his personhood. The anthropophorous animal must be made and remade, born and reborn. Not only must we imagine this strange form, but we must also constantly gird ourselves against fully recognizing how splendidly ludicrous this imaginative structure actually is. Sneeringly distinguishing between the enlightened concept of liberty and the "way out" that he sought as he squatted trembling in his cell onboard the *Hagenbeck*, Peter speaks of the strange representations of freedom that so delight contemporary Europeans:

> In variety theaters I have often watched, before my turn came on, a couple of acrobats performing on trapezes high in the roof. They swung themselves, they rocked to and fro, they sprang into the air, they floated into each other's arms, one hung by the hair from the teeth of the other. "And that too is human freedom," I thought, "self-controlled movement." What

a mockery of holy Mother Nature! Were the apes to see such a spectacle, no theater walls could stand the shock of their laughter. (249)

The human freedom that presumably floats above one's head in an old-fashioned circus tent is itself a profoundly naïve aestheticization of the body's domination, a desperate reaction against the spontaneity, disloyalty, and uncertainty that accompany our aloof and treacherous flesh. More vulgar still, the spectacle that Peter describes does an obviously sloppy job of occluding the distinction between freedom and a sort of comfortable acquiescence. Like Himes, dissatisfied by the side of his pool in Moraira, Red Peter has given up all connection to the ideal in order to access the possible. "I deliberately do not use the word 'freedom,'" he informs the Academy (249). Instead he opts for a simple and infinitely practical "way out." He wishes to exit that cage, walk above deck, and avoid the worst aspects of his capture and debasement. Eventually coming to understand that there was no escape for him, but instead only progressively more comfortable forms of incarceration, he made a choice between two available options: the zoo or the stage. "I said to myself: do your utmost to get on the variety stage; the Zoological Garden means only a new cage; once there, you are done for" (253).

I wish to read Red Peter's entrance onto the stage, his willingness to present himself as a stylishly attired and comfortably housed freak, in direct relation to the activities of scholars of the African diaspora sitting (squatting?) more or less comfortably in offices at the plantation's edge. Moreover, the irritated tone that travels with this simple pairing ought to be taken as evidence of my fear that the price for achieving positions at either margin *or* center is often a passivity and dulling of our critical sensibilities that seriously limit our creativity and negatively add to the continued erosion of the coherence and utility of the humanities and human sciences. As with the constantly inebriated characters in *The End of a Primitive*, we are only able to enact and reenact base forms of viciousness in the absence of sober reflection. Worse still, we often seem to have forgotten that we are drunk. Tellingly, Kafka suggests that the attainment of that signal element of human exceptionality, speech, is itself an extension of the human animal's ability to quite effectively drug itself. Even after achieving the doubled self-consciousness that allowed

him to repress the will of a free ape living in the Gold Coast and substitute in its stead the complex wounding of its avatar, "Red Peter," the
creature left crouching in that cage, the being seeking desperately for
some way out, found it exceedingly difficult to master two of the most
common behaviors of the human animal: speech and the consumption
of alcohol.

Peter had been given diligent instruction in both speaking and drinking by a sailor who recognized in the captive the possibility of human
consciousness. Instead of readily responding, however, the ape perceived the man's vocalizations as nothing more than incessant grunting
and the bottles of alcohol that he offered as revolting poison to be hurled
immediately from the lips in shock and rage. The trick, however, was
again to give up on the precision that is implied by the term "freedom"
and instead to accept the dulling and reduction of animal possibility that
mark the "way out."

> I took hold of a schnapps bottle that had been carelessly left standing
> before my cage, uncorked it in the best style, while the company began to
> watch me with mounting attention, set it to my lips without hesitation,
> with no grimace, like a professional drinker, with rolling eyes and full
> throat, actually and truly drank it empty; then threw the bottle away, not
> this time in despair but as an artistic performer; forgot indeed, to rub my
> belly; but instead of that, because I could not help it, because my senses
> were reeling, called a brief and unmistakable "Hallo!" (252–53)

Where Kafka and Himes meet is in the unyielding manner in which
they point to the many intricate and intimate modes of violence that
help to establish the fiction of a humanity that exists outside nature,
and also in their insistence that our most basic discursive modes do not
represent advances over our "animal natures," but instead retreats from
the basic realities of our species being. Eloquence, at least the eloquence
celebrated by the academicians examining Red Peter, is a factor of intox-
ication, proof of the senses reeling. Speech is the device that helps to
stanch the wounds left when consciousness has been ripped from the
ape's body. "The Negro" in the cell, the shack, the white house is itself an
attempt at suturing. It is the always half-slurred aestheticization of the
viciousness that underwrites our most cherished projects of philosophy

and criticism. As a consequence, its elementary mumblings are always inchoate, if also somehow surprisingly attractive.

Kafka's genius in "A Report to an Academy" is made more apparent still when we consider that by transplanting Red Peter from Africa to Europe on the *Hagenbeck*, he focused his readers' attention squarely on the figure of his contemporary Carl Hagenbeck, a German impresario in the mold of P. T. Barnum, who from the 1870s forward produced ethnic shows featuring Nubians, Inuits, Patagonians, Sioux, Samoans, Somalis, Maasai, and many other exotic individuals to awestruck audiences in Germany, France, Austria, Switzerland, England, Belgium, Sweden, Norway, Italy, the Netherlands, and Argentina. The fact that Hagenbeck was also an importer of unusual animals, providing stock to Barnum himself, should be enough to alert you to Kafka's keen awareness of the lack of distinction between the anthropological and the zoological. Hagenbeck regularly donated objects that he collected for his shows to ethnological museums and eventually became a member of the Berlin Society for Anthropology, Ethnology, and Prehistory. More telling still, he was concerned both as entrepreneur *and* anthropologist with controlling the risk posed by the possibility that his exotics might directly communicate with the audiences that arrived to view them.[15] As Hilke Thode-Arora writes, "To guarantee the smooth running of the show, he preferred most of his performers (with the exception of a few translators) to be unable to speak a European language, fearing that contact with the spectators might stir them up, inciting revolt or conflict" (Thode-Arora, "Hagenbeck's European Tours," 169). The intemperate fear that Thode-Arora reports is one and the same with the shock that one might receive upon discovering not so much that the primitive might, if given enough opportunity and motivation, indeed speak, but also that the very fact of its iteration demonstrates the flimsiness of the fiction of "Man." A single "Hello" from a prepossessing Somali both proves the lie of European superiority and makes plain the paths of violence and bloodshed that allow the loquacious meeting of Man and anthropophorous animal to take place.

This allows us to understand even more clearly the joke of Himes's using images of apes attempting *not* to echo tinny rhetorics of (un) freedom in *The End of a Primitive*. In addition to Jesse's drunken comments about Kriss's sexual appetites and his own subhuman social status, Himes creates a splendidly clever narrative device that efficiently paces the novel while allowing for delicious critique of the ideology of Man. Kriss's favorite television program is one in which a newscaster interviews a talking chimpanzee who predicts current events. What is fascinating about this maneuver is that while it obviously recalls the history of African Americans in U.S. broadcasting, a history that reveals the freakish conceptions of human subjectivity that underwrite American-style white supremacy, it also actively resists both Derrida's clumsy articulation of animal presence as but a reflection of human subjectivity and Kafka's pessimistic representation of an animal subjectivity that remarks itself only through techniques designed to suppress all forms of knowledge that do not reiterate the dominance of Man.

The chimpanzee that appears and reappears in *The End of a Primitive* is at once critical and aloof. Its presence is a continual reminder of the fact that, notwithstanding the rhetoric of Man's absolute dominance, there are many locations in the physical and social worlds that can never be fully noted by and within the techniques available to us within the *Studia*.

> "On November 4, 1952, Republican nominee for President, five-star General of the Army, Dwight D. Eisenhower, will be elected President of the United States by an overwhelming landslide of 442 electoral votes and a popular vote of 33,938,285, the largest popular vote in the history of *your* Republic, thereby giving Senator McCarthy a mandate to rid the nation of its mentality," the chimpanzee stated with extreme boredom. After all, this would bear no effect on chimpanzees—chimpanzees didn't think. (Himes, *The End of a Primitive*, 24)

The work that Himes accomplishes here is something altogether distinct from the repetition of the usual complaint that whites conceive of blacks as some lesser species of animal, a conceit only barely relieved by the depressingly common liberal claim that black individuals and communities are not biologically deficient, but instead simply culturally and socially underdeveloped. Instead the giggling, jeering critique that Himes offers is one in which he suggests that especially at those moments of absolute certainty, the anthropophorous animal continues in its semi-wild state. It is impossible to integrate a nonthinking animal into Man's most precious discursive structures, nearly impossible to explain what establishes the boredom of a beast whose articulation is nothing more than autonomic recall of the most basic forms of human iteration.

Throughout this book I have argued that practitioners of Black Studies should not only actively pursue the discovery of new archives, but also approach the materials they encounter with radically imaginative forms of critique. While I sometimes covet the comforts that one might find at the plantation's center, I am also painfully aware that the work of decolonization, the difficult task of confronting and dismantling the structural and ideological legacies of white supremacy and capitalism, are retarded precisely to the extent that we embrace and repeat structures of thought that allow for unexamined articulations of a clear distinction between Man and animal. Part of what so attracts me to this image of a talking and bored chimpanzee is that Himes loads it with questions of limitation and compromise that are absolutely necessary to our understanding of how humanists might begin to articulate something more than the most cynical, stunned, and defensive arguments for their relevancy. Ever contained within the limitations of an only half-watched television set, the chimpanzee is articulate only to the extent that it warps the modes of presentation available to it. Moreover, the presence of this "character" demonstrates a hopefulness within Himes's aesthetic, a belief that one might gain something powerful and provocative by paying attention to the dumb beast's vocalizations. After all, unthinking, bored, and aloof or not, this chimpanzee does not simply report the news, he predicts it.

Belying the often casual modes in which they are presented, animal interlocutors can represent unforgiving articulations of the ways that practices of colonization, enslavement, incarceration, and internment rebound upon "innocent" Americans and Europeans, whose discursive and ideological structures consistently prove inadequate for the project of preparing them for the everyday repetition of violence and repression that is perhaps the most obvious legacy of both Atlantic slavery and Western humanism.

"On July 1 responsible officials of the United States will charge that slave labor exists in Russia on a scope unknown in the history of man." . . .

"On September 8 a woman named Bella V. Dodd will testify before a Senate Internal Security subcommittee in New York that there are fifteen hundred Communist party members teaching in schools throughout the nation." . . . "On May 21 fascist Spain will be admitted to UNESCO." . . . "On October 16 U.S. Secretary of State Dean Acheson will urge the U.N. to continue to fight in Korea as long as is necessary to stop aggression and restore peace and security." . . . "On November 8 police will fire on black rioters in Kimberly, South Africa killing fourteen and wounding thirty-nine. African blacks will be protesting against government segregation policies of African blacks in Africa. . . . Police will shoot into a mob of ungrateful African blacks, impressing them with white man's goodwill toward African blacks who respect white man's rule in Africa," the chimpanzee concluded, yawning with an air of extreme boredom. After all, no one was shooting down chimpanzees. (Himes, *The End of a Primitive*, 90–91)

Slave labor in Russia, denunciations of communists, the embrace of fascists, the continued violation of the Koreas, and the murdering of black Africans exist for Himes in a singular and indivisible ideological and discursive field that I suspect is still extremely difficult for many of us either to discern or comprehend. The disinterestedness of the chimpanzee, his yawning announcement of yet another tragic loss of black "human" life, models for Himes's readers the inability to move beyond consideration of strictly defined precincts of European and American culture, an inability that—no matter how clumsy or limited—often stands in for what is often referred to as cosmopolitanism. At the same time, the chimpanzee has the decency to at least depart from liberal obfuscation and deflection. As a consequence, his predictions are delivered with a clarity and precision that allow for something more than the repetition of the *Studia*'s dominant techniques.

Half high on coffee and sedatives in his Mallorca garden, Himes took delicious pleasure in the composition of these tongue-in-cheek representations of animal articulation. Living as an exile unable to conform to either the complexities of white supremacy or the banalities of anti-intellectualism, Himes—like Kafka before him—embraced the comforts offered by the expression of the absurd. Though he did not achieve "freedom" per se, he was able to erect a discursive apparatus supple enough to articulate in one breath the commonplaces of woman hating, anti-black racism, and the all too easy normalization of (Spanish) fascism. Like a chimp hurling its feces at pink, hairless faces bobbling behind heavy glass, Himes knows and announces the constant threat of violence that he is under, yet he does not make the mistake of assuming that the bloodthirstiness of his captors is a demonstration of either impressive intellect or advanced culture.

Placing into the ape's mouth a joke about the U.S. government's role in the stabilization of Franco's government, the castaway writer attempted a domestication of the rhetorics of statecraft and geopolitics that might allow his readers to understand that they need no special vocabulary to discern the order of things, but instead simple good sense—the humility and composure passed down from their enslaved ancestors—in order to see the masters resplendent in their nakedness and yet not laugh.

Chimpanzee: There was great poverty in Spain and the Franco government couldn't get a penny from the U.S. and they had a grave beggar-problem similar to your Negro-problem which had to be solved, besides which Franco's uniforms were getting somewhat frayed. So the Generalissimo met with his ministers to see what could be done about these problems, especially about the problem of his uniforms. After a week's deliberation, the ministers suddenly struck upon a foolproof solution. In a body, they rushed to the palace and demanded an immediate audience with the Generalissimo.

—"What's the answer, boys?" he asked.

—"Declare war on the U.S.!" they chorused exultantly.

Generalissimo Franco considered the suggestion. He thought of the prosperity in post-war Japan and Germany. It seemed to be a flawless solution. But he was assailed by one grave doubt.

"But what if I win?" he asked. (Himes, *The End of a Primitive*, 201)

One imagines Himes alone in his garden, head back, eyes closed, cackling laughter spewing from a wide open mouth as he relishes the profundity of the humor on display in this brief passage. The punch line turns on the fact that not only could Franco win, he did. The burning, anti-fascist sentiment that motivated two generations of (black) intellectuals and led many to initiate intimate, even lifelong, associations with

Spain and the Spanish people proved inadequate to the task of stopping the Falangists in their paths. Himes's very presence on lovely and demoralized Mallorca proved that fascist thought and politics could be quite easily normalized within the complex of liberal institutions that structure European and American society.

The real joke, however, was the fact that part of Franco's genius was his ability to recognize that ruthless exploitation and violence have *always* been stunningly successful social—and cultural—gambits. The success of the Falangist campaign could come as a surprise only to those individuals whose humanity had not recently been called into question. Having started his military career fighting against Moroccan insurgents, Franco was fully cognizant of how shock troops and heavy bombing might both scatter militants and demoralize the general population. Much of the horror of the great European wars was established by the shock suffered by persons previously treated as Men upon realizing that the violence methodically meted out to the enslaved and the colonized could be used just as effectively against them. Like Red Peter drunk on cheap schnapps, many Europeans and Americans were—and are—surprisingly slow to understand that the boundaries of violence are infinitely flexible. The mechanics of slave society are regularly applied against populations of pink-skinned individuals whether they can decipher the phenomenology of the whip's sting or not.

I call for a recalibration of Himes's status as a sort of half-canonized African American writer. We need desperately to consider the whole of Himes's oeuvre and not simply his rightly celebrated crime novels. Even more to the point, Himes's deployment of marginal characters— animals, homosexuals, prisoners, criminals, detectives, and a dizzying assortment of lost individuals such as Kriss Cummings and Alva Trent—should not be taken as simple evidence of the author's desire to demonstrate a colorfully evocative demimonde, but instead as an effort to resist normative ideologies of order. The blind spots and silences of dominant modes of thought and address are made spectacularly apparent through the deployment of absurdist elements that reveal the even more absurd structures of violence and naïveté that underwrite so much within the *Studia*. Though Himes rightfully lamented the difficulty he faced as an immensely talented black artist attempting to support himself and gain audience, it would be incorrect to assume that this state of affairs can wholly account for his career-long deployment of marginal characters and outrageous situations.

Early in *The End of a Primitive*, Jesse overhears one of his gay flat-mates (he of the great doe eyes) lamenting, "I feel so unnecessary!" (41). An easy reading of this statement would be that Himes is allowing his character to lament the profound redundancy faced by a creature as odd and useless as a black gay man living in 1950s Manhattan. What I suspect Himes was actually after, however, was a simple articulation of the fact that the lack of solidity and depth that the character bemoans is an essential element within the structures of Western humanism. To the extent that one is a well-articulated citizen of the United States, Spain, and that crop of countries that we deign to consider peers, we are all redundant. Himes laments not so much primitivity as the compromises required of those who achieve status as modern and human. Jesse is fully actualized as an American and a cosmopolitan at precisely the moment that he kills Kriss. Drugged, defeated, and naïve, the ape gains its Manhood through a loss of substance and good common sense. One begins to understand very clearly why it took nearly thirty-five years for the unexpurgated version of Himes's fine novel to be published. At a moment when liberal society in the United States wanted nothing more than to integrate Negroes into something approximating the American mainstream, Himes presented them with a work in which the conceits of the center (that fashionable apartment on Gramercy Park where Jesse gained his majority by plunging a kitchen knife deep into his lover's drunken body) were revealed to be remarkably unappealing. Failed novelist and defeated black that he was, Jesse was so much better as a primitive than he was as a Man. For Himes, the benefits of "entering the human race," the comforts of a fine villa in Moraira-Teulada, came at far too high a price. Instead, the castaway author relishing the brilliance of the light tripping across the Mediterranean and satisfied with the charms of a vanquished and discarded white woman decided to hedge his bets, to resist a least for a bit the beguiling pleasures of New York and Paris and to tarry a bit longer on the plantation's edge.

5

Richard Wright in the House of Girls

How poor indeed is man.
—Friedrich Nietzsche, *Thus Spoke Zarathustra*

There is a staggering, provocative, and ever so slightly macabre moment
of instruction guarding the gates of Richard Wright's enigmatic treatment of mid-twentieth-century Spanish society and culture, *Pagan
Spain*. Wright reports that in the final days of her life Gertrude Stein,
"racked with pain and with only a few days to live," solemnly counseled,

> "Dick, you ought to go to Spain. . . .
> "You'll see the past there. You'll see what the Western world is made of.
> Spain is primitive, but lovely. And the people! There are no people such
> as the Spanish anywhere. I've spent days in Spain that I'll never forget. See
> those bullfights, see that wonderful landscape."[1]

What startles and sends the alert reader scampering to consult his notes
and reevaluate his assumptions is just how easily the codes of influence
and mastery on display might be interpreted and broken. Stein, deathly
ill and tugging girlishly "with the fingers of her right hand a tuft of hair
on her forehead," seems most concerned to pass on to Wright the mantle
of genius and intellectual leadership that she so ably wore during the
previous four decades. Her dominance of the development of American
modernism was indisputable.[2] It was made more impressive still by the
fact that she lived most of her adult life in Paris as an unmarried woman,
a lesbian, and a Jew. The very pretension of the comments that Wright
ascribes to her, "You'll see what the Western world is made of," suggests a
woman who has long since delivered herself from marginality. Not only
does she know what the Western world is made of, but she also knows
where to find it. More startling still, Wright's narration of this scene
works to place Stein's genius against the background of her insistent and

vengeful flesh. The many images of a stout, short-haired woman, covered from head to foot in heavy, concealing clothing, are eclipsed by a picture of a weak, girlish body garishly forcing itself into Wright's narrative and thereby making itself no longer useful as an "invisible" vehicle of a presumably disembodied Manhood.

For his part, Wright stands beside Stein as an apt and deserving pupil, one with the combination of intelligence, endurance, and humility necessary to carry on even as his mentor falters. What we see is nothing less than a manhood ritual. With the last of her strength, Stein invites Wright to the center. The exiled African American writer whose two major works, *Native Son* and *Black Boy*, literally name the author's minority status, his childishness, has now been hailed as a quintessential modern, one whose only major fault is his lack of familiarity with the primitive. Stein's imperative syntax—"go to Spain," "See those bullfights, see that wonderful landscape"—reiterates not only her confidence in her interlocutor, not simply their equality, but also their singular presence among a transnational literary and cultural avant-garde.

Still, the forcefulness of the language that Wright deploys is seriously undermined when one takes into account the timing. Stein died in 1946, while Wright did not make his first trip to Spain until 1954, eventually publishing *Pagan Spain* in 1957. I wonder, therefore, if the vigor of Stein's advice rests less with Wright's desire to fulfill the dying wishes of a dear comrade than with the extremely productive rhetorical work that her words do. What I argue is that the best way to break the rather breathtaking critical silence that attends *Pagan Spain* is to pay careful attention to the ways that it is not simply an example of the grand novelist's indulging himself with a journalistic writing experiment in the style of Truman Capote's 1966 "nonfiction novel," *In Cold Blood*.[3] Nor does it represent Wright's aloofness in relation to the aesthetic experiments that helped to distinguish European and American fiction of the mid-twentieth century. Instead, in this meticulously planned—if only haphazardly researched—project, Wright was attempting to disestablish those conceptual structures that effectively worked to obscure the distinctions between the white, the European, the modern, and the universal. He did so, moreover, by relentlessly reversing the terms of Euro-American exceptionalism, not only ascribing backwardness, provincialism, and indeed paganism to the Spaniards, but also reserving for himself status as Western, modern, cosmopolitan, and—importantly for the arguments that I make in this chapter—male. He achieves this through reference to rather precise cartographies of difference in which the paganism and primitivism of Spain are always framed as closed, cloistered, inside, and inaccessible. Thus images of women, hungry in their desire to free themselves from the restrictive confines of traditional society, abound in this text. In the process Wright offers an impeccable rescripting of many of the dominant tropes of capture, exploitation, abuse, and complicity that have structured our understandings of Euro-American colonization and Atlantic slavery.

If the bifurcation of human being into its animal and intellectual aspects is itself a primary artifact of post-1492 procedures of colonization and enslavement, then it follows that in his most basic, most clumsy resistance to this reality, the enslaved/colonized subject might at the very least be expected to claim that the line dividing Man from human has been too haphazardly drawn. When the black cries, "I am a man!" he does not so much disrupt the hierarchies of human being with which we are concerned as assert his right to rise within them. What Wright is after in *Pagan Spain*, however, is somewhat more ambitious than this. As I have argued already, he attempts to turn the tables, refusing common-sense cartographies in which humanity is always associated with the colonized world, particularly Africa, while Manhood is strictly limited to Europe and its outposts. Taking advantage of a loophole of retreat, Wright, the (black) American living in France and writing about a "marginal" European country that he only briefly visited and whose dominant languages he never learned, is nonetheless able, at least temporarily, to place his blackness under erasure in order to announce the cosmopolitanism and theatrical aloofness that are the very markers of Manhood. In doing so, he actively works to rehearse many of the tropes associated with slavery and colonization: excessive religiosity, obsequious deference to power, infantilized sexuality, suspicion of strangers and nonconformists, and most especially the systematic exploitation of women. For Wright, it is the Spaniard and not the Negro who deserves the pity of the missionary and the anthropologist. The problem, of course, is that this line of thought leaves the clumsy distinction between Man and human very much intact. What one finds most chilling about Wright's efforts in these arenas is how easily—and ignorantly—he places himself in the position of the (white European) chronicler of the marginal and the primitive, a sort of mid-twentieth-century Marlow casting his bemused gaze from a safely distant perch atop the Pyrenees.

In preparation for the composition of *Pagan Spain*, Wright created a prospectus, "An Outline Tracing the Treatment of Material on a Proposed Book on Spanish Life, Tentative Title, *Lonesome Spain*."[4] Therein he describes his plans for a book of eight sections: "Life after Death," "Gods for Sale," "The Underground Christ," "The Love of Death," "The World of Catholic Power," "The Pagan Heritage," "Flamenco, Sex, and Prostitution," and "Spain in Exile." Upon publication, the book contained only five sections: "Life after Death," "The Underground Christ," "Sex, Flamenco, and Prostitution," "The World of Pagan Power," and "Death and Exaltation." One of the things we can easily discern from the selections that Wright was forced to make as he pruned nearly 50,000 words from the 150,000-word manuscript that he submitted to Paul Reynolds, his editor at Harper and Brothers, was his understanding that the intellectual environment that he described was one in which the conceptual and ethical problems confronting Western humanism were met by equally pressing issues of how one might exist beyond the restrictions of human flesh.[5] Death, religion, sex, and exaltation, including ecstatic art forms like flamenco, were central to Wright's understanding of Spanish society and culture. The Spain that Wright describes is a remarkably kinetic location. Everything and everyone is in motion. Thus Wright's treatment of Spain is altogether impressionistic. As with his commentary on pre-independence Ghana in the seminal 1954 work, *Black Power*, Wright finds himself much more capable of describing the disembodied forces that he finds in Spain versus the blunt, everyday realities of the many individuals whom he encounters.[6]

Understanding this reality gets one closer to understanding why Wright has so little to say about how Spaniards of the 1950s coped with the aftermath of the Spanish Civil War. He fails to offer any considered discussion of the geopolitics that sent the country lurching through a shockingly bloody civil war that ended only fifteen years before he edged the nose of his Citroën across the French-Spanish border. One of the most serious criticisms that one can make of Wright is that, like Hegel briefly considering what he took to be the native African's absence from the ever forward-moving march of world history, he could never fully recognize anything akin to either Spanish individuality or creativity. The paganism that Wright represents is essentially a marker demonstrating that "the fundamental customs, habits, and emotional attitudes of the people have not altered and are not likely to alter for centuries" (Wright, "An Outline"). In this sense, the Spanish Civil War could not be said to be the explosion of competing economic and cultural forces that pitted Marxists, anarchists, intellectuals, urban workers, and landless *campesinos* against royalists, large landowners, the military, and the Guardia Civil. Nor could it be said to have been the first important salvo of fascist Germany and Italy in their decades-long efforts to dominate the rest of Europe. Indeed, the involvement of foreigners in the war is never mentioned. Instead, the conflict was explained by Wright as entirely a matter of what one might think of as an elemental bloodlust. He quotes at length an interview he conducted with a prominent Spanish journalist, one Señor G., who begins their conversation by informing Wright, "The Spaniard is an animal that is spoiled from the cradle. We are made to feel that we are something precious, something that needs no improvement" (Wright, *Pagan Spain*, 239). One might easily see then how for Wright, the 1936–1939 civil war could easily be understood as the articulation of a certain *under*civilized humanity whose primary purpose was to reflect and define the frank and aloof Manhood that both Wright and his Spanish interlocutor demonstrate.

What I am attempting to show is the fundamental structure of *Pagan Spain*'s narrative strategy. I would hazard to guess, in fact, that Wright was able to produce such a long manuscript not in spite of the fact that the ex-Communist author eschewed materialist analysis, but *because* of it. What this awkward analysis of Spanish culture did for Wright was to free him to experiment with a much more obviously modernistic style. The language and imagery that he deploys are recognized as but reflections of timeless realities that can be said to exist only for themselves. Wright's descriptions were significant only to the extent that they demonstrated universal truths about the human condition that might be applied not only in Spain, but also in much of the so-called primitive world. The master is not writing in order to change Spain, but only to describe it. "I don't agree with the setup in Spain, but my job in this book is not so much to condemn as to understand and present my understanding to others" (Wright, "An Outline").

Writing Spain became for Wright an exercise in approaching thin, immutable surfaces and then recording his marvel at the infinitely multiplying reflections they provoked. One can begin, therefore, to understand the motivations underwriting Gunnar Myrdal's grumpy, only half-complimentary letter thanking Wright for having dedicated the book to him:

> If you will permit me to offer a criticism, my feeling is that this is really only a preface to the serious, penetrating and enlightening analysis of the Spanish situation which you should write. What you give are flashes of insight, incisive impressions by the stranger. . . . I want you to write a bigger and deeper book. Do not forget that this is meant as praise, both for your present installment and, still more, for your potentialities of human analysis! (Quoted in Rowley, *Richard Wright*, 485)[7]

Even as I readily agree with Myrdal's basic claims, I would push against his logic a bit by reminding you that *Pagan Spain* was hardly an anomalous part of Wright's oeuvre. On the contrary, it was the third installment in a three-part series of what we might think of as sociological travelogues: *Black Power* (1954), *The Color Curtain* (1956), and *Pagan Spain* (1957). Myrdal's sense that with *Pagan Spain* Wright had only just begun a project ostensibly devoted to the examination of the structural and cultural realities of Spanish society misses the point. As Wright traveled through Spain, he was attempting to continue the work on colonization and decolonization that he had initiated in *Black Power*, his 1954 study of the transition of the British Gold Coast colony into the independent nation of Ghana. This was almost immediately followed by *The Color Curtain*, Wright's examination of the institutionalization of the Non-Aligned Movement as represented by the Afro-Asian Conference held in Bandung, Indonesia, in April 1955. At the same time, Wright was obviously aware of the quickening pace of the civil rights movement in the United States and sensitive to the dynamic geopolitical confluences that drew together the 1954 *Brown v. Board of Education* decision, the 1955 Bandung Conference, and Ghana's independence in 1957. What he was after in *Black Power*, *The Color Curtain*, and *Pagan Spain* was less an examination of the specific political, economic, and cultural realities of the nations he examined than something akin to a capacious articulation of the ways that race and colonization operated in the production and reproduction of humanism. Wright's conception of what we might think of as the space of race and empire was at once flat and broad. While much of the rhetoric of *Pagan Spain* turns on his naming what amounts to Spanish exceptionalism in relation to the rest of Europe, the work is relentless in its depiction of Spanish paganism as largely indistinct from the primitivism so often associated with the African and the black.

Richard Wright had been attempting to draw seamless connections between Spaniards and (African) Americans since at least 1937, when he worked as a writer for several Communist Party–affiliated journals. In a September 20, 1937, essay in the *Daily Worker* entitled "Harlem Spanish Women Come Out of the Kitchen," Wright describes a meeting of one of the party's all-female Pasionaria cells, named for Isidora Dolores Ibárruri Gómez, a Communist militant whose bracing speeches in defense of Republican Spain often included the defiant slogan *¡No pasarán!* (They will not pass!), earning her the sobriquet "La Pasionaria."

> Each Wednesday at 1 P.M. some 70 women in Spanish Harlem lay aside their aprons, turn off the gas in their cook stoves, tell their children to be good (or better, take them with them), and go to a small, dingy meeting at 84 West 111th Street. They are not going to a women's sewing circle, or to a temperance meeting or to a Bible class; these dark-haired, bright-eyed women are about much more serious business. They are members of the Communist Party and the ideal in their hearts is la Pasionaria, the heroine of the Loyalist Spanish masses. Some of the women are elderly; some are young; almost all of them have children; eleven of them have husbands in the Loyalist trenches. . . . They assemble in the room and wait for their comrades. The room is quiet. Soon is heard a faint humming; it grows louder, then finally breaks into song. NO PASARÁN![8]

One of the things that make it easy to admire Richard Wright is that regardless of his public disavowal of Communism and the Communist Party, he continued throughout his life to think of himself as a radical advocate for working-class and poor people in their struggles against the most severe forms of capitalist domination. Moreover, as is well known, he was particularly forceful in his critiques of colonization and the ways that capitalism and white supremacy are mutually constitutive. At the same time, it is obvious that at even this earliest point in his efforts to fashion rhetorical structures equal to the task of bridging what many might take to be yawning differences of race and language, Wright's descriptions remain surprisingly bland. None of the Spanish women whom he describes are named. With their aprons, cook stoves, and slightly less than well-behaved children, they are all of a type, all creatures of the flesh. Their actions are measured and repetitive, recurring with a devoted regularity each Wednesday at 1:00 p.m. What he takes to be their normal business—sewing, temperance, and Bible study— quickly gives way to the serious matters at hand, all of which seem to turn on either their reproductive abilities ("Some . . . are elderly; some are young; almost all of them have children") or the status of their men ("eleven of them have husbands in the Loyalist trenches"). What Wright describes are not women per se, but instead reflections of what he imagines women ought to be.

I must remind myself to be generous toward Wright, to remember that much of what he was after was the disarticulation of what he took to be the common sense of space, race, and human subjectivity. As Wright pushes his female protagonists out of their kitchens, he is less concerned to deliver them to West 111th Street than to have them enter into the expansive, worldwide terrain that he imagines La Pasionaria inhabits. It is obvious, however, that Wright fails in these efforts to the extent that he simply reverses the terms of the very gendered conceptions of space that he attempts to attack. Stereotypical notions of proper femininity are hardly disrupted in this passage. Instead, these beliefs were stolen wholesale from the ideological larders of capitalism, white supremacy, and patriarchy, then delivered without fanfare to the cause of the multinational struggle against fascism.

It behooves us to turn again to the idea of the war archive that I developed in the first chapter. While much of that discussion pivoted on drawing attention to the ways that theaters of war might be understood as sites of aesthetic intervention, places where breaks in established aesthetic and ideological structures might be at once acknowledged and sutured, I do not want to limit myself to consideration of only the mechanics of military combat. Even in the absence of guns, bombs, planes, and gas, practices of violence and domination are constantly reiterated and refined in domestic spaces. The ideological assemblies binding war and the domestic are the very structures that produce a necessary and inevitable pairing of Man and anthropophorous animal. The viciousness of the war theater is not so much disappeared as domesticated at the end of official hostilities.

Acknowledging this fact gets us a bit closer to understanding why in the previous passage Wright works so hard to relate the celebrated bloodletting of the Spanish Civil War to what we might think of as the naïve activities of Communist women. The homes that these women promptly exited at 1:00 p.m. each Wednesday were themselves sites of war, locations at which the complex work of absorbing and redirecting violence was accomplished. Wright's investment in Spain was part of an effort to disturb the ways that the transnational, complex, and mul-tivalenced structures of white supremacy could be so readily misnamed in local contexts. The scene of "Spanish" women attending meetings in West Harlem might be dismissed as females going about their inconse-quential business, perhaps pausing for a moment to sigh over the fact of their country's ever-present racism and its crushing hostility to females. What Wright attempts to do, however, is sharpen the critical faculties of his audience. He wants to rip through the veil of misrecognition that obscures the obvious connections between La Pasionaria and her Har-lem doppelgängers. What is vividly demonstrated in *Pagan Spain* is that even on the European continent, the realities of white supremacy and capitalist exploitation are ever present. What is lacking, however, is a fully developed language of anticolonialism that might allow Spaniards (and the many other Europeans whom presumably they represent) to acknowledge not only their complicity with slavery and colonization but also the ways that the overvaluation of the fantasy of whiteness retards the ability of Spaniards—and other "white" Europeans—to acknowledge the basic facts of their own exploitation and submission; that is to say, the very many ways that their own flesh has been forced to endure the never fully articulated horrors of (white) Western humanism.

I direct you now toward the awkward approach that Wright forces his readers to make toward *Black Power*, his study of the Gold Coast in the days immediately prior to its achieving independence and be-coming Ghana. Wright, at once an unmistakably American and yet self-consciously European (black) intellectual, cannot seem to make his way "back" to Africa except through Spain. Traveling as the sole American passenger aboard the *Accra* from one notorious slaving city, Liverpool, to another, Takoradi, his copy of Eric Williams's masterful work, *Capitalism and Slavery*, ever at hand, Wright was keenly aware of the fact that he was retracing a key portion of the Atlantic trade. He writes of Liverpool, "This was the city that had been the center and focal point of the slave trade; it was here that most of the slavers had been organized, fitted out, financed, and dispatched with high hopes on their infamous but lucrative voyages" (Wright, *Black Power*, 22).

What surprises, however, is that even as he outfits *Black Power* with all the trappings of anticolonialist gravitas, he seems in no way allergic to the inclusion of a bit of sophomoric and vaguely pornographic farce. Also traveling aboard the *Accra* was one Justice Thomas of the Nigerian Supreme Court, a character Wright uses to demonstrate what Frantz Fanon describes as the national bourgeoisie, that thin layer of colonial elites who bristle at the usurpation of power and resources by armies of often less than impressive civil servants sent from European metropoles, but who greedily claim (and protect) the positions vacated by these so-called whites once formal independence is gained.[9] "We are Creoles," boasts Justice Thomas. "It's from us that the English draw their best African leaders, teachers, doctors, lawyers. If we didn't have the help of the English, we'd be swamped by the natives" (32).

Later, as Wright, Thomas, and a minor character whom Wright labels "Mr. Togoland" disembark from the *Accra*, anchored off Las Palmas in the Canary Islands, the justice casually mentions, "Once, when I was passing through Las Palmas . . . someone offered to take me to a house of prostitution."

> "Did you go?"
>
> "I refused," Mr. Justice said with moral indignation. "I never let anybody take me to places like that. Things like that are to be found by yourself. I pity the man who can't find a woman." (39)

What is rich about this passage is how effortlessly Wright seems to rehearse the most commonplace fantasies and phobias about the (necessary) mingling of black, white, African, European, English, and Spanish in the articulation of colonialism. The theatrics of border crossing are so broadly drawn that the first thing to which the wide-awake reader must attend is the simple question, "Where are we?" Las Palmas, the largest city in the European Union to exist *outside* the continent, is one of the two co-capitals of the Canaries, an archipelago of thirteen islands lying some one hundred kilometers off the coast of Morocco. (Two Spanish cities, Ceuta and Melilla, are located *on* the African continent itself.) European colonists began arriving in the Canaries during the fourteenth century. By 1495, the resistance of the native Guanches had been overcome and the Canaries were absorbed into the Kingdom of Castile, eventually becoming important sites for sugar production and the outfitting of Spanish galleons for the Atlantic crossing. Thus large numbers of enslaved Africans both worked the plantations and passed through the islands' forts and prisons. Considering these facts, it becomes nearly impossible to deny the complexity and depth of a seemingly humdrum statement of misogynist braggadocio such as "I pity the man who can't find a woman."[10]

That the three men do eventually make their way to a house of prostitution, an institution that I prefer to refer to by the more colloquial title "house of girls" or "girls' house" (*casa de chicas*), forces us to reconsider some of the most well-established methods by which we have conceptualized the ideas of transnationalism. Paul Gilroy, writing in his epoch-making treatment of Atlantic culture, *The Black Atlantic: Modernity and Double Consciousness*, argues,

> The image of the ship—a living micro-cultural, micro-political system in motion—is especially important for historical and theoretical reasons. . . . Ships immediately focus attention on the middle passage, on the various projects for redemptive return to the African homeland, on the circulation of ideas and activists as well as the movement of key cultural and political artifacts.[11]

Gilroy's language here represents a singularly precise rendering of the situation aboard the *Accra*. Wright self-consciously names the ways the ship's passengers are representative of the calcified structures of control and domination that the British erected for their colonies. The ship is full of "men and women going to Africa to assume civil service jobs or returning from a few months' leave in England. . . . a mediocre lot to administer the destinies of millions of blacks" (Wright, *Black Power*, 35).

Moreover, Wright's status as an (African) American "returning" to the continent can be said to approximate one of the "projects of redemption" to which Gilroy gestures. Regardless, Wright seems bored by life aboard the *Accra*, describing it as a vault of "self-conscious stodginess" that he negatively compares with the "simplicity, honesty, and straightforwardness" of the house of prostitution (42).

What neither Gilroy nor Wright names, however, is the fact that our conceptions of life aboard ship are often erroneously keyed toward romantic notions of men alone at sea. Though the metaphor of the ship as "a living micro-cultural, micro-political system in motion" is put to the service of exploding the idea that culture, politics, and economics can be understood within narrowly defined national boundaries, it nonetheless gains its own rhetorical vigor from the idea of the presumed social isolation of those on board. Stated slightly differently, as many of the "civilizing" practices in our societies are necessarily absent onboard ships, one might see which of the presumably most common, most "natural" aspects of human social interaction will be called upon to take their places. As we saw in Langston Hughes's chilling description of a young girl's gang rape by the all-male crew of the *Malone*, the ship was not simply the vehicle of an ill-defined and transcendent modernity. It was also a location in which the ugly work of putting human flesh in service to humanism's basic ideological structures was enacted. Once we recognize this fact, we can move beyond a precious understanding of ships and sailing in order to examine the many places at which flesh, particularly black and female flesh, is attacked, "tamed," processed, and made ready for proper utilization as a vehicle of anthropophorous (non)subjectivity.

Immediately after disembarking from the *Accra*, Wright and his companions set a straightforward land course toward the girls' house. Part of what Wright accomplishes with this extremely evocative interlude is the disruption of the fantasy of the sea in favor of what one might think of as a much more holistic understanding of the mechanics of racialism and colonial contact. Hurrying toward what I take to be the most significant of my claims in this chapter, I argue that the house of prostitution, the girls' house, is hardly peripheral to the articulation of humanism. Its primary role in the articulation, rearticulation, maintenance, denial, and dissemination of the common sense of colonialism, white supremacy, and capitalism is bolstered by the fact that it exists as a thing that everyone knows, but never names. It is always approached via side streets and back entrances. Its inmates have no social presence, and even the value of their labor is acknowledged only haphazardly in the more respectable precincts of society. "The girls" are never understood to be laboring at all. Instead, they are always at rest. Dressed in party wear or lingerie, they linger, pose, and coo, apparently oblivious to the often brisk flow of dollars, pesetas, and pounds through the currents of their bodies. The very strength of the girls' house, the reason that it can operate as such a potent ideological apparatus, is that it is imagined as existing outside the social. It is at its best an answer to a set of base/basic desires that are decidedly *pre*-social.[12] I would add to this that Wright's heavy reliance on farce and slapstick in his description of the house further obscures the complexity of the ideological work being accomplished.

I hope that the rather striking structural and ideological parallels between the girls' house, the hold, the baracoon, and the market are readily apparent. In each case we encounter a closed environment in which the most basic architecture has been designed to refine and reiterate the Man/human distinction. Much of what I have attempted to accomplish in this book has been to nominate these presumably dead spaces as potent locations of meaning, key archives in the articulation of posthumanism, the disruption of the Man/anthropophorous animal binary. Tellingly, Wright's description of the sociality of the girls' house remarks it as a place literally brimming with humanity, full of bodies, but with apparently very few actors. The girls, lost and sinful, pretty and always receptive, remain largely silent and inactive throughout the scene, pausing only to fill drinks or rise promptly to service less taciturn customers in one of the house's back rooms. Conversation takes place almost exclusively between men and *about* men. The very fact that neither Wright, "Mr. Togoland," nor the justice spoke anything more than the most rudimentary Spanish sets a scene in which the point seems to be to ignore what is happening in front of them in favor of using this experience as a platform to name and celebrate their newly achieved status as (black male) cosmopolitans.

"Let me tell you a personal story," Mr. Justice said, relaxing, smiling. "Years ago, when I was young man, I went into one of those houses. When I presented my card, the madam said: 'Why your name is familiar

to me. Wait a moment; I'll find a card with a name on it like yours. . . ?
The madam pulled out from a closet a big glass bowl in which calling
cards were kept. She fished around in it and a few minutes later she pulled
out my father's calling card, all yellow and dusty. . . . Boy, oh, boy was I
proud!" (41)

This passage stretches the concept of homoerotic triangulation to
new limits. Justice Thomas encounters his father through the offices of
a bright-eyed, friendly madam. She presents him with his father's calling card, a sanitized emblem of sexual exploits that is nonetheless yellow
and full of dust, suggesting that hidden animality/primitivism/paganism
has reasserted itself in the very fiber of the text. Moreover, the catalyst
for the woman's impressive acts of cataloging and retrieval is presumably
the strangeness of the dark face presenting itself in her parlor as well as
the incongruity of the names that both father and son carry. They are
black and African, yet their cards, carriage, and ready access to British
pounds mark them as men of distinction. The justice enters looking for
a girl but leaves carrying with him Manhood's many accoutrements. The
entire scene is narrated by Wright, who, though seemingly unimpressed
by the idea of entering a house of prostitution in the company of two
other men, nonetheless continues to present himself as the very paragon
of sobriety, assigning the stigma of greediness, hypocrisy, and pretension
to the judge. Wright revels in making Justice Thomas uncomfortable
and thwarting his desires, writing, "I could have easily put him at ease,
could have spoken a sentence and released him from the high-flown
sentiments of honor and Christianity and he could have done what he
wanted to do, but I was perverse enough to make him sit there on top of
his platitudes and grin nervously" (43). Wright is absolutely aware that
though ritualized violence against women is a central reality, a necessity,
of humanism, it is important to behave as if nothing is happening, as if
the production of the Man/anthropophorous animal binary involves no
force at all. Instead, it exists as an elemental reality to which our intellectual procedures and social structures are more or less attuned.

The corralling of human bodies, including female bodies, was perhaps the most widely utilized means with which to control and extract value from enslaved Africans. I suggest, therefore, that we ought
to pay very close attention to the theatrics of the encounter between

men and market-ready women that Wright describes. We should dare to see those male buyers braced with alcohol, capital, and impressively effective powers of self-deception. We ought to strive to recognize the women as self-aware participants, eagerly attempting to judge and influence their prospective clients. Dress, demeanor, those few words of English and Spanish nonchalantly bandied about, were all designed to facilitate the exchange of flesh and cash as well as to announce and revivify a set of protocols with roots deep in the practices of the Atlantic trade. The farce that Wright narrates took place in the context of a set of ideological and discursive assemblies in which the notion of a disembodied Western Manhood was established through the production—and immediate disavowal—of anthropophorous animality. Here in the city of Las Palmas on the island of Gran Canaria, where the notion of an absolute distinction between Europe and Africa ceases to be strange and becomes ridiculous, not only was the slave trade once practiced, but also those traditions binding together white supremacy and capitalism structured the most basic, most intimate aspects of (Atlantic) society and culture.

Though I am grateful for the insights left to us by Wright in *Black Power* and *Pagan Spain*, I am also extremely frustrated by his consistent tendency to steer his readers away from a full appreciation of the radical potential inherent in treating enslavement and the enactment of slave culture as realities that have structured the basic realities, the basic aesthetics, of Western humanism. Wright's tendency is to remain too firmly fixed on surfaces, too eager to advance rather underdeveloped arguments about human psychology where a thoroughgoing treatment of the history underwriting the societies that he examines would be more in order. In my more generous moments, I can see that part of what motivated Wright was his desire to move away from Communist-inspired forms of cultural analysis that were at once much too derivative and far too prescriptive. Where his efforts chafe, however, are in those many locations at which the considerable power of his voice overshadows the complexity and the preciousness of the often extremely interesting scenes that he narrates. One of the most regularly repeated maneuvers in *Pagan Spain* is one in which Wright produces often quite satisfying rhetorical effect by flattening the elements that he has available to him. We have seen several examples of his tendency to produce two-dimensional, thin caricatures, particularly of women. We will see others as we continue in this chapter. Instead of simply castigating him for his presumed misogyny, however, I would like to suggest that Wright, who took hundreds of photographs in both the Gold Coast and Spain, was fascinated by the aesthetic/ideological possibilities available within the two-dimensional graph, that place at which the complexities of the flesh are compressed, fixed in time, and made redundant yet infinitely available for circulation as symbols of humanism's breadth and stability. For Wright, the female lacks both aggression and ability. As a consequence, her presence does not inhibit the explorer, secure in his newly found Manhood, from moving forward. The girls he encounters have no need, no pathos; their lives are not inextricably bound to his. The loveliness that they inhabit is all of a moment, even if their shoes are scuffed and their dresses torn. As a consequence, their savage fecundity might be noted and approached without threatening the most significant conventions of Manhood.

Wright's biographer Hazel Rowley relates the details of an affair the author had in 1959 with "German Jewish, blue-eyed and bottle blond" Celia Hornung. In the course of his seduction, Wright apparently asked Hornung whether she had ever slept with a black man and whether she was a member of the Communist Party. She had not and was not. Rowley then reports that Hornung's relationship with Wright was largely built around their rehearsal of a sort of peek-a-boo aesthetics of sexuality:

> Wright liked to tell her about seducing other women. He would describe the scene in graphic detail. Hornung was never jealous—personally she did not think him much of a lover—but she thought it bad taste. Sometimes he bought pornographic photos at Pigalle, and they used to look at them together. He preferred to take his own. Hornung enjoyed being his model. (Rowley, *Richard Wright*, 500)

What startles me in this passage is the phrase "graphic detail." Wright's description of the activities that presumably took place between him and his lovers is already removed from the activities themselves. The erotic charge that passes between Wright and Hornung is built upon Wright's articulation of more and more complex procedures of graphing. In lieu of actual human coupling, he introduces pornographic photographs into the equation, suggesting that the action of the erotic scene always takes place at the site of re-presentation.

Following the lead of Maurice Wallace, who himself takes inspiration from Susan Sontag and Charles Johnson, I argue that Wright's aesthetic in *Black Power* and *Pagan Spain* articulates an "ethics of seeing the world" in which all of everyday life is seen as a potential photograph. Value is a product of reproduction and fungibility. Thus the sexual act has little importance in and of itself. (Wright was not much of a lover, they say.) Instead, pornography works at exactly the level of titillation. The heat is produced from the knowledge that there is a necessary and insurmountable divide between image and act. The continual return to the pornographic image is motivated by the self-conscious awareness that the two-dimensional scenes before us are never equal to the real thing. Likewise, the value of the widely circulated lynching postcards that Shawn Michelle Smith examines in *Photography on the Color Line: W. E. B. Du Bois, Race, and Visual Culture* was built upon the recognition that some Negro somewhere was murdered, tortured, burned, and dismembered while the basic elements of the viewers' worlds remained intact.[13]

There is nothing particularly natural nor inevitable about the ability and will to graph the largely unspoken ways that we live in our animal bodies. Even more to the point, these processes of representation exist in history and are structured at the deepest levels by methods of representing the human form developed in and by colonization, enslavement, and the Atlantic trade. The pornographic aesthetic that Rowley associates with Wright is made coherent by the suffocating presence of slavery and colonization that suffuses all relations—even and especially erotic relations—bounded by Western humanism. Wright, fleeing from American-style white supremacy, approaches his Jewish lover, fleeing German-style white supremacy, well armed with camera and film. It is almost as if his efforts as a photographer are designed to produce a new archive of white supremacy. His practice seems almost talismanic. He attempts to appease the vicious beast of racial representation by feeding it, attending to its needs in an effort to turn it, ever so slightly, toward less noxious projects. What he achieves is the articulation of the simple fact that the slave culture that has been so clumsily narrated as having a rather proscribed existence (among the blacks on the plantations of America) is very much alive and well in the heart of Europe.

After receiving the nearly six-hundred-page manuscript for *Pagan Spain*, Wright's editors at Harpers extracted from the author a number of painful concessions designed to address the length and unwieldiness of the document. Wright had omitted already his discussions of both "Gypsies" and Spanish exiles. To further appease the press, he shortened the discussion of his stays in Madrid, Barcelona, Seville, and Granada, cut the chapter on Protestantism by half, and eliminated altogether a chapter on the annual Las Fallas (The Faults) festival in Valencia.[14] Even with these cuts, it is fair to say that *Pagan Spain* is a text that is at times needlessly rambling, and sometimes surprisingly shallow. Nonetheless, one wonders whether the editors ever allowed themselves to hear clearly Wright's many provocations. He understood that at the level of everyday culture, at those many sites of unexamined ritual, even the most casual of observers might see that at the center of Spanish culture there stood a transnational, cross-racial cultural exchange in which Spaniards pressed against the unstable border separating "white" Europe from "black" Africa. *Pagan Spain* might be seen, in fact, as Wright's attempt to produce a sort of aesthetic palliative to this state of affairs. Like a woman alone in her rooms fingering the edges of some socially proscribed image, Wright produces in *Pagan Spain* a sort of diagnostic and therapeutic template that allows the viewer to remember traumatic experience without exactly reliving it.

It is in this sense that the excision of the Las Fallas chapter from Wright's text seems a particularly ill-considered act. It is here that Wright most clearly demonstrates what were for him the most important of his aesthetic/ideological insights.

The origin of *Las Fallas* stems from the time when the father of Jesus—No, that's not the way to say it. But how does one say it? Let's see, Joseph, the father of Jesus, but who did not sire Jesus,—yes, that's the way to say it and not hurt anybody's feelings, was a carpenter, so relate the Good Christian citizens of the city of Valencia. And, legend tells us, on that day of spring when the evening sky became bright enough so that no artificial light was needed in Joseph's carpenter shop, Joseph, in celebration of the lengthening of the day and the nearness of summer, amassed all the shavings, sawdust, and the odd, unusable bits of wood and piled them in a heap in an open space in front of his shop and set fire to them while he and his neighbors sang and danced about the roaring flames.[15]

As with his description of women attending a Pasionaria cell meeting, Wright's tone in this passage evinces a healthy portion of tongue-in-cheek derision and belittles the history advanced by "the Good Christian citizens of the city of Valencia." Instead of simply enjoying the festival, in which professional artists created massive sculptures that lampooned religious, political, and economic elites only to be burned on the final day of the festival, Wright remains focused on his own interpretive talents. His flippant description of Joseph as "the father of Jesus . . . who did not sire Jesus" alerts his readers to the improbable distinction between ideality and flesh that stands at the heart of both Christianity and the forms of Western humanism that presumably eclipsed it. Much of what Wright hopes to do is deepen the community's narrative (suggesting that the origin of the festival was pagan sun worship) while also modernizing it, telling us that "inhibitions expected from men in the name of civilization . . . stimulated the population to seek emotional release in the making of these bonfires." He adds that the sculptors "fashioned images . . . embodying thoughts and ideas forbidden by the State and Church, images into which one poured the illicit longings of one's heart" (Wright, "Las Fallas"). For Wright, the Las Fallas sculptures amplified realities of the human animal that predate the structures of historical narrative announced by Foucault while somehow remaining firmly entrenched in the everyday actualities of modern life. At the same time, however, Wright's commitment to humanist protocols often led him away from full consideration of the ways religious notions of transcendence and disembodiment function in modern aesthetic practices.

We have seen that Wright obsessively depicted his own presumably vibrant masculinity in relation to highly manicured images of exploited and cloistered women. From postcards bought at Pigalle to prostitutes demurely attending to the needs of their clients, Wright liked his women tame. The master's manipulation of a thin, two-dimensional female figure allowed for the articulation of fully formed masculinity while simultaneously inoculating him against the threat of undisciplined female-initiated reproduction, the "law of the mother," to borrow Hortense Spillers's apt phrase.[16] One thinks of the way that Picasso obsessively imaged his lovers and wives, extracting from them some feminine essence that overshadowed the social realities of the actual individuals. Intimately attached to this are the ways that each of the artists seemed fascinated by the (necessarily) fetishistic function of the best modern art. Picasso's large collection of African and Oceanic statues and masks was certainly an inspiration for the experiments with form, perspective, and scale that secured his dominant position in twentieth-century painting and sculpture. At the same time, the famously superstitious artist was fascinated with the idea of the beautiful object that was not simply decorative, but also talismanic. He attempted to produce works that not only referenced some exterior world but also existed for themselves, producing effect from within their very being. While Wright evinced no such metaphysical leanings, he did believe that the weeklong Las Fallas celebration was less a modern cultural event than the articulation of a complex worldview in which the physical, the emotional, the erotic, and the religious were indistinct. "These safety-valves are widely known in primitive societies," he writes. "Some African tribes set aside one day in the year in which everybody has the right to say exactly what he pleases to or about anybody else, with no punitive measures attached" (Wright, "Las Fallas").

Again, what I find most fascinating about Wright is how effortlessly he reverses the rhetorical and ideological codes that maintain the clumsy notions of "the Western" and "the modern," by reserving for himself status as a privileged, cosmopolitan interloper among (white) natives. Moreover, he is relentless in his efforts to assign to Spain many of the stereotypes of primitive society:

> My primary reaction to the revealed sculptures was one of amazement at the amount and degree of assertive nudity that they contained; it was odd that, in a nation where the human body was a shameful and loathsome object, the first opportunity given its artists and citizens for public self-expression resulted in so demonstrative a preoccupation with the naked human form and its physiological functioning. (Wright, "Las Fallas")

That is to say, Spaniards were as hopelessly controlled by their fascination with the limits and possibilities of human flesh as were native Africans.

I will repeat that for Wright, when one shouts the word "Spain," one hears "Africa" as its echo. More to the point, what Wright seems to be able to forgive neither Africans nor Spaniards is their lack of reserve, the ways their emotional lives are presumably lived entirely at the surface, creating societies that are at once vibrant and brittle, coyly reserved and surprisingly lurid. In making these arguments, I am struck by the similarities in the ways that street celebrations were narrated by Wright in both *Pagan Spain* and *Black Power*. Describing the final night of the Las Fallas festival, in which the prizewinning statue was set ablaze, he writes,

> There sounded a series of tremendous explosions that stilled every voice. It was crushing, with a promise of menace to it. A mob of about five thousand stood in a vast ring. . . . When the explosions died, a band struck up a blare of music. A young man stepped forward and tossed a match onto a keroscene [*sic*] -soaked statue. A tiny flame licked uncertainly, then with a *poof*, a huge red blaze leaped toward the sky and screams of awed delight went up from the mob as it backed fearfully away. (Wright, "Las Fallas")

Compare this with a quote from *Black Power* describing an Akan funeral procession:

> The parade or procession or whatever it was called was rushing past me so rapidly that I feared that I would not get the photograph that I wanted; I lifted my camera and tried to focus and when I did focus I saw a forest of naked black breasts before my eyes through the camera sight. I took the camera from my eyes, too astonished to act; passing me were about fifty women, young and old, nude to the waist, their elongated breasts flopping loosely and grotesquely in the sun. Their faces were painted with streaks of white and sweat ran down their foreheads. They held in their hands a short stick—taken from packing boxes—and they were knocking these sticks furiously together, setting up an unearthly clatter, their eyes fixed upon the revolving coffin of brass. (Wright, *Black Power*, 164)

The most obvious thing that one can say about these passages is that in both cases Wright is startled by the fleshy excessiveness of what he encounters. The crowds, the fire, the music, the clatter all seem to work together to stretch the idea of human being to its limits. As Manhood is defined by its limitations, that breaking, ripping, tearing, and discomfort to which the human animal is subject, Wright sees in these scenes an overabundance of both human physicality (that forest of breasts) and human affect (those screams of awed delight) that work together to disrupt the clear distinction between Man and animal.[17] The camera is rendered useless in such situations. The author's graphic abilities are simply too severely taxed. The spectacles are too large, too noisy, too primitive, too unabashedly human to be captured by the artist and properly reproduced for his audience. As with the discursive structures created by imprisoned Africans crossing the Atlantic, narratives of Manhood are disrupted by the copiousness of both human flesh and those many sublingual expressions (the tremendous explosions, the blare of music, the unearthly clatter) that reassert the presence of an untamed and untutored human animality darting alongside the practice of Western humanism.

Beating a fast conceptual/aesthetic retreat, Wright regains his balance by assigning to both Spain and Africa the label "pagan." In neither location has the work of civilization been accomplished. Instead, as a fully formed Western Man, Wright stands face to face with his primitive kin, sensing something less than the comforting shock of human simplicity. Spain represents a site of failure, a place at which the terror of Franco, the repressiveness of the Catholic Church, and the social domination of the Falange act as necessary bulwarks against an unchecked animality that might be read as abject not so much because it represents a threat to civilization but instead because it disrupts all of the most sacrosanct of our modern social boundaries.[18] For Wright, the true conceptual problem is that while he sees in Spain much evidence of just how tired the notion of a clear distinction between Europe and Africa actually is, he also recognizes a potentially radical challenge to the entire edifice on which so-called Western humanism rests. In response, he not only turns to images of cloistered and exploited women, but also unleashes a mocking narrative voice that domesticates the Spanish/African threat by lampooning it.

It is in this manner that I suggest we approach one of the most jarring of the snapshots that Wright took on his trip to Valencia (see figure 5.1). The black and white photograph of one of the Las Fallas sculptures offers a breathtakingly accurate graphic representation of the historical, psychological, and ideological structures that Wright was at pains to demonstrate in *Pagan Spain*. It is, in fact, a study of the many similarities that presumably exist between Spanish and African culture. At its center are two kings attended by emaciated servants. The one is black, fat, and dressed only in a crown and grass loincloth. The second is white, also fat, and dressed smartly in a top hat and fashionable business suit. The African king sits outside a hut topped by a thatch roof and adorned with a human skull. The Spanish king sits in front of his mantle, over which hangs a tasteful piece of modernist art. Both men are eating. It appears, moreover, that the African king has the remains of a human hand nonchalantly pressed between arm and chest, while the object that he rips with his teeth appears decidedly phallic. Regardless, a small sign, written in Catalan, alerts the sculpture's audiences that in both cases what we are witnessing is a species of cannibalism: *Hi ha mes d'un pobre caníbal emigrat i desmenjat, estos pobres cobren fama però mireu al costat.* (There is more than one poor, emigrated, and listless cannibal; these poor ones steal all the attention, but look to the side.) The white king of commerce consumes his fellow humans just as readily as the African savage. The motivation for the accumulation of wealth, including the accumulation of such markers of sophistication and cosmopolitanism as modern art, is imagined as not particularly modern at all. Instead it is again an expression of an ancient, elemental bloodlust that civilization presumably works to mitigate. The sculpture—and Wright's photograph of it—provide remarkably clear illustrations of the great conceptual strain that accompanies the reproduction of ideologies of Manhood and anthropophorous (non)subjectivity. The kings represent both the pinnacle of human possibility and the vulgar/comic strain of human corporeality/animality necessary to achieve this state. Attending them are servants whose physical desiccation demonstrates the actual price of the kings' elevation to Manhood. Wright forces a properly social consideration of the master/slave dialectic. The very clumsiness and grotesqueness of the graph prove how limited our understanding of the mechanics of dominance and repression, subjectivity and (counter)subjectivity can be.

Figure 5.1. Las Fallas photograph by Richard Wright. Copyright © 1957 by Richard Wright. Reprinted by permission of John Hawkins & Associates, Inc., and the Estate of Richard Wright.

I am not simply attempting to name the androcentric and Western-focused nature of Wright's criticism. Instead, the "post" of this work's post-humanism represents not a new methodology per se, but instead a refined skepticism regarding the possibility of defeating white suprem-acy and woman hating through recourse to ever more "liberal" forms of critique. Instead, I invite my readers to join in an exploration of al-ternative modes of thought and inquiry in which (human) flesh is no longer disavowed. In articulating these arguments, I make a great deal of Wright's failures in *Pagan Spain*. I suspect, in fact, that the crucial silence around the work stems from the clear clumsiness and unwieldiness of the text as well as from the fact that Wright does such a bad job of hiding his tracks as he reiterates humanism's racialist and masculinist conceits.

One of the many challenges Wright faced while writing a book that ostensibly dealt with the ungainly topic of "the Spanish character" was the matter of how to arrange and pace the work. As he was forced seriously to edit his discussions of life in the country's major cities, Wright had necessarily to look for other structuring schemes with which to hold together his text. What he hit upon was the insertion of long passages from a book of fascist catechism issued by the national government and directed at girls and young women. The quotes he selected worked perfectly as he attempted to demonstrate the ways that Spanish culture was rigidly hierarchical, excessively religious, and rather impressively vexed about the proper role of women in modern society.

> Are there cases of women dying while fighting like men?
> Yes, in the War of Independence against France, but it is unusual.
> So what is the real heroism of women?
> Giving up the pleasures of life when we feel we have to do a duty
> over and above them.
>
> What do "pleasures of life" mean?
>
> All that is pleasant in life, beginning with life itself. (Wright, *Pagan
> Spain*, 90)

The female becomes in this configuration less a marker of human distinction than a key resource for the articulation of state and society. The heroism of women is always framed negatively. The only action open to the girl being hailed by this text is to "give up." Like the African mother in Cabrera's *De español y negra, mulata*, her strength is in her passivity, the aloof stance she takes in relation to life itself. Females are most powerful, most heroic when they are (socially) dead. I remain confused, however, about the matter of how Wright positions himself in relation to this conservative line of thought. On the one hand, he offers vivid descriptions of the ways that females are particularly oppressed under Spanish fascism. At the same time, the very consistency and vibrancy of his discussions suggest an author who is more than a bit titillated by the sequestration of the female form. As I suggested earlier, Wright the porno-grapher, with his collection of naughty photos, postcards, and female accomplices, cannot be easily distinguished from Wright the cosmopolitan intellectual eager to create new arenas of action for black men in a frankly white supremacist world. What is most attractive about *Pagan Spain*, then, is in fact that unwieldiness of which I have just spoken. Wright attempts to broach the question of the black's exclusion from the main precincts of Western humanism by placing Spaniards and females into supporting positions. As a consequence, *Pagan Spain* becomes overburdened with images of cloistered Spanish femininity. The indelicacy of Wright's prose demonstrates those many aesthetic/ideological cleavages where one might properly initiate the critical archival project that I believe must stand at the heart of an anti–white supremacist and anti-misogynist post-humanism.

The enforced frailty and enclosure of Spanish women that so fascinate Wright are nowhere better articulated than in the character of Lola, a young Catalan woman living with her mother, their housekeeper, and their vicious dog, Ronnie, in a large Barcelona apartment. Wright met the family when he boarded with them soon after arriving in the city. While settling himself into his room, he was interrupted by Lola, carrying Ronnie in her arms. In the course of their conversation, Lola asks Wright whether he is a Communist, then explains that her father had been taken by party members and that she and Ronnie would not return "home" until he was returned. We later find that the girl's father had been shot during the war and that the ensuing trauma forced Lola into a life of stoic passivity, while the ever-volatile Ronnie acts as the avatar of those parts of her that are hysterical, raging, and animal. Trapped in a household lacking paternal authority, the girl cannot be reborn as a social being capable of negotiating the complexities of modern, postwar Spain.

Wright deftly uses the character of Lola to continue the articulation of his problematic relationship to the presumed liberation of females in Communist political and ideological structures. The members of the La Pasionaria cell are noble but indistinguishable one from the other. La

Pasionaria herself was an abstraction of a living, multifaceted woman, Isidora Dolores Ibárruri Gómez. Wright's attraction to Celia Hornung was partially motivated by the fact that she was *not* Communist. And in the case of Lola, we see a girl who is ill precisely because of (anti-paternalist) Communist intervention. I would like to suggest that part of what this pattern demonstrates is not only Wright's fraught relationship to the self-consciousness with which Communists attempted to resist—or at least restructure—hierarchies of race and gender, but also his hesitant approach to the project of critiquing forms of humanist discourse in which the black—and the female—are always already repressed. When Wright asked Hornung about her party affiliation, he complained that he was tired of interactions with white Communist women eager to sleep with black men in order to prove that they were not prejudiced (Rowley, *Richard Wright*, 499). He was not yet prepared to give up on the "necessity" of a repressed femininity. Even so, the females approaching Wright turn the tables, producing him as a fetish while also de-romanticizing sexual desire, placing it decidedly in the realm of politics and ideology.

I have used the term "Manhood" throughout *Archives of Flesh* in order to represent the ways that processes of globalization begun after 1492 produced rigid ideas about the essentially hierarchical nature of human being such that to be a member of the species *homo sapiens* is never enough, in and of itself, to mark one as a "Man." Moreover, though most females lack the ability to achieve this status, I do not claim that the Man/human distinction is exclusively a matter of gender. Instead, what rankles Wright is that there is no easy way to cleanly distinguish the disabilities of the black from those of the female. While Manhood status may be understood to adhere to only a small minority of persons, humanity is a conceptual category literally overflowing with possibility. As within the darkness of the slave hold, the question of where "I" begin and "you" end can never be fully resolved for the human. One of the most common slurs of the white supremacist as he surveys the sea of black, yellow, red, and brown faces before him is that he cannot distinguish one from the other. Much within *Pagan Spain* is specifically directed at rectifying this issue. The graphic procedures that dominate the text work specifically to produce an aesthetics of categorization in which the (black) Man might gain social presence by producing documents capable of idealizing, aestheticizing—and disrupting—messy practices of human assemblage.[19] In this context, the female becomes a desperately important stabilizing device. As with an incongruously feminine Gertrude Stein, the female helps to steady systems unsettled by the opening of Manhood status to formerly disqualified humans such as Wright.

Understanding this allows us to wrestle more effectively with Wright's extremely complicated interaction with Lola and Ronnie. Taking place in Wright's small room, a place overcrowded with animal and human presence, the scene recycles the themes of compression and enclosure that are not only shot through *Pagan Spain* but are also some of the primary tropes in the various literatures that narrate Western humanism. "I hope that you won't be like all the others who come to live here," Lola states with tearful aggression.

> "They go away. Always, they go away. . . . I don't like that. Why do people always leave?" She beamed a sudden smile upon Ronnie, who sat watching her face. "We don't like that, do we, Ronnie?" she asked. Then she lifted appealing eyes to me. "But you'll stay, won't you?" (Wright, *Pagan Spain*, 60)

We see both the horror and the promise of human frailty and complexity. Wright, hemmed within a space dominated by women, finds himself in a carnival of boundary crossings. Lola disturbs his manly privacy. She stays in constant physical contact with Ronnie, erasing the line between girl and dog. Together they charge Wright with ontic disloyalty. He threatens to leave, to break the overdetermined communality that underwrites the expression of a steadily disintegrating/reintegrating character like Lola. Wright attempts to dismiss the girl's peculiarity by naming it as a factor of the trauma she experienced during the war. "For Lola there had been no peace, no armistice. The bullets had long since stopped whining, and the bombs were bursting no more, but memories of violence and horror lived on and kindled mental and emotional pain" (Wright, *Pagan Spain*, 61). What he misses, however, is that the structures of violence and domination that sparked the Spanish Civil War were in no way peculiar to the Iberian Peninsula. Instead, domestic space, the girls' house, is a key site in the management of the ever-present violence of colonialism, white supremacy, and patriarchy. The rage directed at Wright, the way Ronnie's eager greeting of the stranger turns to vicious barks and bites at the moment of his departure, can be understood as nothing less than a militant's response to a traitor. He might leave to seek his noble Manhood elsewhere, but it is not incumbent upon those he has left behind to celebrate his exit.

One of the things that most troubles me about *Pagan Spain* is the sheer repetitiveness of Wright's descriptions of bewildered virgins and world-weary prostitutes. The master is almost obsessive in his reiteration of the idea that any female character might be read as *every* female character. They are all "Woman," the fleshy repository of Spanish society's breath-stealing fears and its tawdry, if only half-acknowledged, desires.

> I had the feeling that, if I had said: "All right, now, pull off your clothes and lie there on that couch!" she would have been momentarily shocked, but would have obeyed at once. The girl was the living personification of sexual consciousness; one could have scraped sex off her with a knife. (99)

The girl, another character to whom Wright never speaks directly, is not quite there; or better put, she is only "there" as a reflection and echo of his own consciousness. Wright never imagines that what he reads as her sexual desire could have arisen from anything other than the most elemental drives. She does not want Wright per se. Indeed, to place the words "girl" and "wanting" side by side in one's sentences would risk the commission of the most horrendous of syntactical errors. Instead, modes of aspiring and choosing developed by thousands of years of "Spanish history" course through and around her. She may smell of sex, but it is not a thing that emanates from within. Instead, sex adheres only to her exterior, where it reflects Richard Wright, ready if necessary to scape the substance off with his knife.

Part of what it is to be a slave, part of what Hegel himself reminds us, is to possess no interiority, to exist only as a reflection of the master's desires.[20] No matter the many trappings that may litter one's prose, when we speak of the slave's desire, our efforts always return us to the master's wanting. Thus much of what motivates my efforts here is my profound frustration with the fact that the discursive and ideological complexities of the master/slave, Man/human divide are so deeply embedded in our social and cultural practices that they have become invisible, nearly unimaginable. When the liberal scholar approaches the subjects of kidnapping, enslavement, forced migration, and human trading (if he approaches them at all), all too often the result is a sort of teary regret in which Africans and their descendants continue as thin, voiceless subjects, specters of a guilty white imagination only now coming to scratch their marks onto the planet. The even greater insult, however, is that though these conceptual habits continue to organize our societies at the most basic, most obvious levels, so much within our cultural studies seems ill-suited to note this most rudimentary fact. The culture of Western humanism is slave culture. It is held firmly in place by a willed—and viciously defended—clumsiness in relation to our understandings of society and aesthetics in which our most cherished cultural artifacts, the precious markers of European and American Manhood, are only very infrequently understood to continue the discursive structures established during centuries of colonization and bondage.

Wright refers to a "wall of flesh," the scores of female prostitutes whom he encounters "in bars, cafes, pensions, hotels, sidewalks, churches, parks, etc." (177). And he rightly indicts poverty and illiteracy as the primary motivations for women's entry into the profession. What he avoids, however, is any consideration of the stunning feats of discursive and ideological gaucherie necessary to maintain the assumption that this overwhelming presence represented either the backwardness of the Spanish psyche or the feebleness of the Spanish economy but not the continuation of the very legacies of flesh peddling that produced the writer himself. The history that Wright evokes is never longer than a single human lifetime. Instead, he continually stresses narratives of psychological development that suggest that all problems in Spanish society stem from a childish petulance brought about by the essentially inward-focused nature of the culture. "Girls quickly develop traits of wild jealousy," he opines.

> They cultivate tantrums of protest, practice the imperious policy of being the sole objects of amorous solicitation. They learn to bedeck themselves with flowers, earrings (I've seen earrings six inches long!), develop the arts of gesturing sensually with their arms, shoulders, and fingers; they

master the violent, sexual contortions of flamenco dancing and singing; in short, being a woman in Spain means being mistress of all the tricks of sexual seduction and almost nothing else. (180)

What Wright seems unwilling to imagine is anything approaching what one might think of as gendered social interlocution. The seductiveness of the Spanish woman seems all of a piece, a thing established as part of an inevitable process of self-alienation. If she moves at all, she moves for him. Her jealousies, tantrums, and solicitations have but one motivation. Yet even within this rigid schema, there seem to be moments of awkwardness, places at which the rigid elegance of the Spanish women whom Wright describes unravel.

Sitting in a hotel room in Seville, stunned and irritated by the baroque rituals of Semana Santa, Wright confided to his diary about the feelings of distress brought about by his encounter with a young Spanish girl who had approached him, begging for money.

> She upsets me. I shook my head at her; it is not that I don't want to give her anything, but I don't want to encourage this kind of begging in a tiny little girl who looks as though she would grow up into a pretty young woman. I tried not to look at her, I kept my eyes on my book. . . . Then she did something that made me ill somewhat; she lifted her tiny little dress and pointed to her vagina. . . . She knows everything. I'm hardboiled, but not that hard. (Quoted in Rowley, *Richard Wright*, 460–61)

Where elsewhere Wright maintained a studied aloofness, presenting himself as a disinterested chronicler of a complicated culture, here the emphasis is on concern and stress. There are dozens of sentences in *Pagan Spain* in which the prostitution of girls is noted without the least furrowing of the brow. Here, however, some previously unbreachable boundary appears to have been crossed. The girl is not simply young, but also tiny and little. And though Wright seems to have resigned himself to the notion that in Spain female children quickly developed baldly provocative schemes of sexual seduction, here it seems that the matter has been taken one step too far. It is the child's sophistication and self-consciousness that bother Wright. She demonstrates an alternative form of intellectualism. She knows everything. She is infinitely aware that not only might she trade sex for food and money, but also that in the eyes of the traveling man, the individual caught up in the complexities of border crossing, any female of any age is a potential prostitute and a fungible commodity. It seems, in fact, that the sense of unease that accompanies the figure of the girl selling sex is motivated by the half-formed awareness that within routes of exchange established by capitalism and white supremacy, her status as quintessential modern subject is much more certain that that of the intrepid intellectual.

Perhaps the most usefully provocative thing I can say at this juncture is that Atlantic cosmopolitanism is much more weighted toward the human than the Man. Where Wright is to be celebrated is in his hardheaded articulation of the ability of an elite black to wear comfortably the mantle of intellectual sophistication so long monopolized by elite whites. What he largely ignores, however, is that much of the rhetoric of cosmopolitanism represents a retreat from the lived reality of Atlantic travel and cultural exchange. The social and discursive assemblies that define humanism have been produced through the interposition of itinerants whose journeys have been taken in the dark, whose forms of knowledge have necessarily involved, indeed privileged, the enclosure and close contact of bodies, not so much the relentless erosion of the mind/body split as subordination of flesh to dream. To imagine the Atlantic, one must embrace one's ignorance and concede the fact that established rhetorics of self and other are woefully inadequate to the procedures at hand. The confident and aloof intellectualism that Wright models in both *Black Power* and *Pagan Spain* is first and foremost a celebration of a willed blindness, the fetishization of a rigidly narrow intellectualism that represents at its core a will to ignore the base, poorly delineated, undecided, and animal aspects of humanity in favor of a pristine Manhood.

One of the most startling moments for Wright in his travels was when he met a pimp, S., gathering together a group of women in order to install them in Moroccan houses of prostitution. Again Wright describes a scene in which, surrounded by prostitutes, he self-consciously covers himself in a (theatrically presented) veil of ignorance. Wondering aloud why the women seemed so solicitous toward him, he hears from S.,

"Boy, these girls'll do anything on earth for you. They think you're the boss from Africa. . . . You don't look like a sailor. So I wanted to see how they would receive you."

"They think I'm the one they would work for in Africa?" I asked.

"They think you own the cathouses in Casablanca," he guffawed. . . .

"White slavery?" I asked him haltingly, leaning forward and speaking into his ear.

He looked at me mockingly.

"No. Not white slavery," he chuckled. "Olive-skinned slavery." (Wright, *Pagan Spain*, 216–17)

If you can bear the insult for a moment, I will submit that what disables Wright in this passage is his status as a Man. S.'s sneering response to Wright is an announcement of his awareness that the great author's status as an intellectual is brought into focus not so much by his erudition as his ignorance. S. stands in for those many readers who, having waded through dozens of pages describing prostitutes and prostitution, find Wright's incredulousness difficult to swallow. That Wright immediately seeks to sanitize the scene before him, to place it within already well-established, continually marshaled narrative structures, is itself an indication of just how inadequate and indeed frail many of our most cherished constructions for articulating Atlantic society and culture are. The notion of "white slavery" is useful only to the extent that it signifies a break with "black slavery." This is while the methods put into place to carry on the respective trades are one and the same. Wright asks coyly, "You smuggle them out of the country?" S. answers, "Hell, no! They travel on the train and ferry. I buy their tickets." Just as Wright had described Liverpool as a city in which slaving ships had been "fitted out, financed, and dispatched with high hopes on their infamous but lucrative voyages," we might see in Seville a city infinitely available for the support of the contemporary trade (Wright, *Black Power*, 22). "This was white slavery," Wright reflects. "How simple and jolly it was!"

If there is any lesson that can be drawn from the failures of Wright's critical practice in *Pagan Spain*, it is less that we need to develop even more sophisticated critical apparatuses and more that we need simply to pay attention. You will have noted that once again, Wright never directly engages the women who so fascinate him. As with much of the knowledge that we have of the transportation of enslaved Africans to Europe and the Americas, the archive that we consult is one primarily constructed and controlled by slavers. Thus, as Stephanie Smallwood brilliantly argues, the lived realities of kidnapped humans is graphically represented in neat columns of logs and ledgers, creating marks where human beings once stood.[21] All too often, notions of cosmopolitanism, modernity, and "the imaginary" gain meaning precisely to the extent that they represent pure abstraction. To do otherwise would risk breaking with the logics of colonialism, white supremacy, and Western humanism such that the distinction between slave history and world history would become unsustainable, ultimately forcing one to the conclusion that a Man is nothing more than a broken human.

Conclusion

If you are planning to travel to the Museo Nacional Centro de Arte Reina Sofía in Madrid to see Picasso's 1937 masterpiece, *Guernica*, don't bother. The famed painting is not visible, nor has it ever been. Though impressive amounts of space have been given over to the display of the monumental mural, commissioned as the Republican government's submission to the Exposition Internationale des Arts et Techniques dans la Vie Moderne, there is not a single space in the grand room that houses it where one might gain enough distance, enough composure, to see the work (see figure C.1). Instead, against a backdrop of familiar, if alarmingly disconnected, elements that catch the eye like pieces of landscape viewed from a window seat aboard a speeding train, one encounters a sea of tourists anxiously pressing against boundaries maintained by notices, alarm wires, and irritated guards. They have fought their way to this place, bought tickets, packed bags, bundled themselves into uncomfortable transports, and waited in endless queues for the express purpose of capturing quick photographic memories of their obligatory visits to this most sacred relic of Spanish national culture before they exit for afternoon tapas and sangria. In Sala 206, where *Guernica* is presumably housed, it is the tourists themselves who are visible. It is their desire to see something, something important and historic, that hits like a wave of Iberian summer heat as one enters the room. Here is the great work of Picasso! Its reference to the April 26, 1937, German bombing of a Basque village might be briefly noted by guides trooping their exhausted charges through impressive exhibitions, but mere facts cannot trump the confusion and splendor of what stands before the Reina Sofía's visitors. We are stunned by the grand spectacle of seeing and being seen that Picasso's work has somehow made possible. The vulgar truths of the Spanish Civil War and the profound accomplishment of the maestro's art are beside the point. We ourselves are what we have come to experience and witness.

Figure C.1. Pablo Picasso, *Guernica* (1937). Museo Nacional Centro de Arte Reina Sofía.

What draws me to *Guernica*, what has fueled my many returns to the site where I am told it is hung, is that I suspect that it represents Picasso's attempt to image the always already deterritorialized nature of violence and war. Without attempting to deny the lived reality of death and suffering, it is key that we understand that warring is also a representational practice, a concatenation of methods by which to challenge established geopolitical and conceptual boundaries through keen manipulation of those narrative strategies by which individuals and communities name and resist commonsensical articulations of human subjugation. My turn to the work of Picasso at this late point in our journey is designed in part to expand the idea of the war archive by noting again the systematic violence and exploitation that arrange the ideologies of Western humanism. Or to turn to the specific rhetoric of these concluding remarks, the protocols of seeing/not seeing that choreograph our approach to a work like *Guernica* are articulations of the deeply embedded scholasticism to which so much within the practice of the humanities and human sciences pays obeisance. These protocols represent forms by which the antihuman violence that the work chronicles are rendered innocuous and mute. Thus what I am attempting to encourage in this book is a radically suspicious approach to what I have called the war archive, but which I might as easily have named the archive of Man. I call for a vigorous articulation of the disloyalty and displeasure I noted in the introduction, a recommitment to aesthetics that rejects Man in favor of the human.

I hope that it is clear that much of my fascination with Spain stems from the key role that it has played in the articulation of the concept of Western humanism. There is no way in which the African American on the hunt for the social and ideological bases of the constant rehearsal of his presumed cultural deficiency and biological deformity can avoid engagement with Spain and the Iberian Peninsula. For both Spaniards and African Americans alike, modern understandings of space and human being are mediated through a complex of representational strategies that were themselves dependent upon ideological and aesthetic forms established by and through the systems of exploitation and *dehumanization* perfected and modernized within the structures of colonization and enslavement. More important still, I have argued that one of the most important tasks of the scholar of arts and aesthetics is to reimagine our critical procedures so as to make it that much more possible to discern the functioning of violence within even and especially the most rarefied precincts of culture.

Located just off the lovely Plaza Merced in Málaga lies the childhood home of Pablo Picasso. Inside the small row house one might find a modest collection of memorabilia from the artist's youth as well as the offices of the Fundación Pablo Picasso. Prominently displayed on a second-floor wall of the building is a 1936 quote from the artist:

Yo he nacido de un padre blanco y de un pequeño vaso de agua de vida andaluza. Yo he nacido de una madre hija de una hija de quince años nacida en Málaga en los Percheles el hermoso toro que me engendra la frente coronada de jazmines.

(From a white father and from a small glass of water of Andalusian life was I born. Born from a mother, daughter of a daughter of fifteen years old born in Málaga in "Los Percheles," the beautiful bull that engenders my forehead crowned with jasmines.)

Half statement of primogeniture, half impressionist prose poem, this spiritedly performative statement operates for the administrators of the foundation as evidence of the artist's abiding relationship to a city that he left as a child and only very infrequently visited after that. The point is to place Picasso not so much within the history of Málaga as above it. He has been formed from the very water of the city and the bull of a neighborhood that gave birth to his grandmother. But what of that white father? Why such an awkward detail in an otherwise whimsically evocative statement of Picasso's origins?

The word "white" (*blanco/a*) at once obscures and reiterates the history of colonialism and mercenary violence that gave rise to the complex visual vocabularies of Picasso. It names a long history of aesthetic development in which the more brutish arrangements of capitalism and white supremacy were integrated into aesthetic practice and then obscured, turned into inert modes that might be approached through self-consciously formal critical practices in which the black might be treated as at best an awkward, ill-placed (non)subject. Thus working against the sedimented logics that surround the artist, I will read him not as a master but instead a student. The potent representation of *dis*articulation that we find in *Guernica* would not be possible without the brooding expression of masculine anxiety in José de Ribera's 1631 composition *Maddalena Ventura, con su marido,* or Miguel Cabrera's lushly decorative and self-consciously white supremacist eighteenth-century celebrations of the racialist protocols underwriting Spanish colonization. "White" is the name that we give to that complex of procedures designed to break tradition, to murder, plunder, rape, and exploit, but also to rehabilitate, recuperate, and repurpose. "White" is the sign of not simply cannibalism, parasitism, destruction, and waste, but also reproduction, innovation, rehabilitation, and conservation.

This catabolistic dynamism is the very thing evoked by Picasso's impolitic quote. It is the power evoked by images of enslaved Africans trapped in cells, cages, and holds. It is that dis-ease that we see tepidly confronted in the on-again, off-again liberal fretting about black incarceration and police violence. It is the grand problem that plagues and severely delimits the practice of cultural studies, the obscuring of the Man/human/anthropophorous animal ideological nexus that underwrites the whole of the Western humanist project. The result is not only the reiteration of a grotesquely segregated set of disciplinary apparatuses, but also the proliferation of practices and procedures in the humanities and human sciences that work less to illuminate the aesthetic structures of the various works that we examine than to obscure the conditions of their production and consumption.

Throughout *Archives of Flesh* I have used Orlando Patterson's masterful work, *Slavery and Social Death: A Comparative Study*, as a touchstone. Concerning himself with the macroeconomic, macro-social concept of enslavement, Patterson reveals the binding common sense of the institution. Alienated from the rituals and etiquettes of its birth and rendered "socially dead," the slave became an addition to the master's identity, a prosthetic. "In his powerlessness the slave became an extension of his master's power. He was a human surrogate, recreated by his master with god-like power in his behalf."[1] Where I have departed from Patterson is in my concern with the everyday procedures and practices that might allow such a strange pairing of master and slave to occur; that is to say, where Patterson privileges social death, I focus on social (re)birth. I recognize that the ties that bound the enslaved to the logics of slavery were never so tight or secure as the masters assumed. Thus my call for a post-humanist archive, an archive of flesh, is an attempt to access those many moments of slippage and uncertainty in the master/slave dynamic in order to make plain the dominant logics of humanism and hopefully to corrode further the Man/anthropophorous animal binary. This is why I return again and again to the fact that enslaved persons had by necessity to work actively to calibrate the stitching that Patterson describes. The notion of the slave as "human surrogate" is maintained through the deployment of often impossibly complicated ideological/aesthetic conventions, the very conventions that support the efforts of all modern intellectuals, even an artist with the talents of Picasso.

I would like to look toward a set of works in Picasso's oeuvre that vividly demonstrate the aesthetic procedures that I have been at pains to name. Located at the Museu Picasso in Barcelona, *Las meninas* is a suite of fifty-eight paintings produced by the master in 1957, forty-five of which reiterate and reinterpret Diego Velázquez's famed 1656 painting of the same name (see figure C.2).

It is the over-the-top theatricality of Velázquez's masterwork that Picasso worries in his own series. He stretches the figure of the Infanta, producing not so much a caricature as a deft commentary on the fact that her image came ready-made as an infinitely reproducible product. To approach one of the portraits in Picasso's *Las meninas* is to seek instruction in the mechanics and protocols of the Velázquez cottage industry. The conceit of a young royal attended by her servants and looked

Figure C.2. Diego Velázquez, *Las meninas* (1656). © Museo Nacional del Prado.

on admiringly by her parents has been stripped away. What is left is pure light, color, line, and perspective (see figure C.3). In the process, Picasso reiterates Federico García Lorca's fear that images of artists are useful only to the extent that they are deadened and made available for (re) production.

Facsimiles of *Las meninas* were produced by both Botero and Dalí, who famously dispensed with any semblance of human imagery alto-

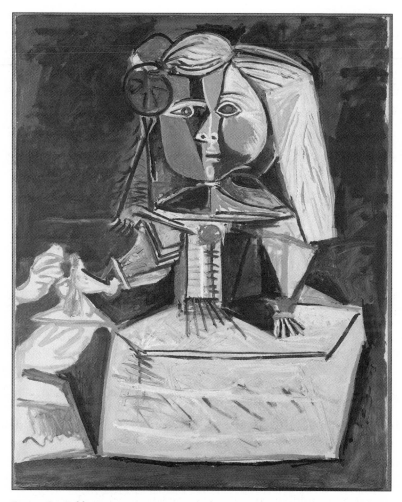

Figure C.3. Pablo Picasso, *Las Meninas (Infanta Margarita María)*, Museu Picasso, Barcelona. Photograph, Gasull Fotografia.

gether and instead substituted numbers for the painting's characters. In addition, artists as disparate as Robert Llimos, Isabel León, Carmen Aguado, Franca Pacetti, José Terrero, Francisco Crespo, Alvaro Paz, Luis Blanco, Francisco Marín, Eve Sussman, Alexandru Racu, Federico Navarra, Ying Feng, Cristóbal Toral, and Manolo Valdéz all produced successively more abstract, mischievous, and iconoclastic images of the Infanta and her attendants.

Foucault famously understood the great value of Velázquez's master-work to be that the painting epitomized a key moment in the history of representation, the place at which classical ideas of human subjectivity were confronted by the aggressive claims of modern Man. "Representa-tion undertakes to represent itself here in all its elements," he writes of *Las meninas*.

> But there, in the midst of this dispersion which it is simultaneously group-ing together and spreading out before us, indicated compellingly from every side, is an essential void: the necessary disappearance of that which is its foundation—of the person it resembles and the person in whose eyes it is only a resemblance. This very subject—which is the same—has been elided. And representation, freed finally from the relation that was impeding it, can offer itself as representation in its pure form.[2]

Where this precious insight is justly critiqued is in the way that Foucault's elegant prose points away from the practical means by which representation "freed itself" from its impeding foundational relations in favor of pure form. The maestro's attempt to historicize the conceptual-ization of Man and humanism devolves into metaphysics to the extent that it cannot contain radical disruptions in the history of philosophy alongside radical disruptions in the political and economic structures of seventeenth-century Spain. Infanta Margarita Teresa was in the midst of a war room. Her fulsome presence was attended by effectively defeated persons. The fawning gazes of her maids are perfect replicas of the over-drawn masks taken up by slaves. And if the rigid protocols of (theatrical) domination should fail, one might always hail that bodyguard stand-ing badly lit and nonchalantly menacing behind the bright tableau of women and children.

Our ability to announce, without giggling, something as ethereal as "pure form" is itself the continuation of a set of discursive practices de-veloped in the contexts of slavery and colonization, structures in which the obvious violence represented in *Las meninas* becomes invisible to contemporary audiences. If the original subjects of the Spanish throne were Isabella and Ferdinand, architects of capitalism and the modern nation-state, then this cartoonish image of the Infanta represents their "necessary disappearance." The young royal's puckering redundancy is given all our attention. The focus is not so much on sovereignty as splendor. Even so, one senses something akin to a parlor trick, a momentary dispersal of the viewer's attention away from the range of structures that made the painting possible.

My ability to read the processes of *Las meninas*' iconographic dispersal is much improved when I consider the complexities of African American playwright Lynn Nottage's distressingly underappreciated play *Las Meninas*. The work repeats the widely believed rumor of an illicit affair between the Spanish-born wife of Louis XIV, Queen Marie-Thérèse, and her African servant, Nabo, a dwarf from Dahomey. The couple is said to have produced an illegitimate, never acknowledged child, Louise Marie-Thérèse, the so-called Mauresse de Moret or Black Nun of Moret, a handsome portrait of whom hangs in the Bibliothèque Saint-Geneviève in Paris (see figure C.4). Born on November 16, 1664, the child was presumably removed from the Louvre palace soon after her birth and placed in an abbey of Benedictine sisters in the nearby town of Moret-sur-Loing.

Set in 1695 on the eve of thirty-one-year-old Louise's final vows, *Las Meninas* operates as a gossipy articulation of the facts of her birth. The truths that she holds have barely enough time to slip through the quickly closing cracks of possibility still available to a novitiate not yet securely sealed into the disciplinary structures of the Church. The young nun's alleged mother, Marie-Thérèse of Spain, the daughter of King Philip IV and his wife, Elisabeth of France, was six years old when her own mother died in 1644. Marie-Thérèse's half-sister, Margarita Teresa, was born seven years later, in 1651, to King Philip and his second wife, Mariana of Austria. Margarita Teresa was just short of five years old when Velázquez finished her portrait in *Las meninas* and about nine when Marie-Thérèse (née Maria Teresa) left Spain to marry King Louis of France.

Every detail of these women's histories is an emblem of the self-conscious ways early modern elites worked to create seamless aesthetic/discursive ties between the micro-level biopolitics of their families and the articulation of (modern) sovereignty. Marie-Thérèse arrived in France to disrupt martial competition between Spain and France and to invigorate the extra-national colonialist structures that would allow for the production of the modern European nation-state. Margarita eventually departed Spain for Austria, marrying her uncle and cousin

Figure C.4. Pierre Gobert, *La Mauresse* (*The Black Nun of Moret*) (early 18th century). © Bibliothèque Sainte-Geneviève, Paris. Used by permission.

Leopold I, Holy Roman Emperor. The newly enthroned empress would eventually give birth to four children, only one of whom survived. In both instances the trick is to read these women's implication within the geopolitics of early modern Spain in relation to the extremely complex iconographic codes embedded within the representational history of the nobility. Bending my comments once again toward this book's dominant rhetorics, I would argue that Margarita Teresa and Maria Teresa (Marie-Thérèse) were at once architects and products of a set of discursive structures designed to control and manipulate the profundity of the flesh. Their reproductive abilities were met by a set of aesthetic conceits designed to effect the complex transmogrification from animal to Man. In both cases, however, their physical bodies proved less than fully useful to the project at hand.

The mischievousness of Nottage's play is built on the fact that she so successfully weaves questions of doubt, dissimulation, desire, and violence into that history. The work is stuffed with visual and aural cues designed to encourage consideration of the human corporeality that supported the statecraft of eighteenth-century Europe. Her reputation for great piety notwithstanding, Marie-Thérèse is played as a lusty woman eager for entertainment, the attentions of her husband, and chocolate, a reality revealed most poignantly by the state of Her Majesty's teeth. The queen's suspect heritage is demonstrated by the pidgin language she uses to translate herself into French. "Ay Dios mío. Es un African. A little one at that. Look Luis, es fantastic."[3] Moreover, she is fully aware of the parallels between her status and that of her fool, Nabo. "You were shipped in a box, I, a carriage," she confides to the black dwarf. "When you first peered over the edge of that little box I recognized you" (Nottage, *Las Meninas*, 311).

What plagues and burdens the young monarch are the gratingly complex techniques that she must develop in order to maintain her own thickly embodied desires alongside the disciplinary protocols of royal iconography. "I am the vessel of empires to come," she reminds Nabo with equal measures of joy and lamentation (311). She knows that this particular gambit, this willingness to sacrifice one's animal self to the exigencies of representation, must always culminate in tragedy. The queen's inability to reproduce with Louis is met by the readiness with which she and Nabo create a child. Where with her husband Marie-Thérèse set about to open the gates to possibility, with Nabo she was willing, however briefly, to celebrate "presence." It was this openness to interstitiality and experimentation that created the cloistered unspeakable entity known as Louise Marie-Thérèse. But a dark-skinned child appearing incongruously in the queen's bedchambers at the Louvre could never be properly explained within the colonialist and white supremacist conventions that dictated the behavior of Louis's court.

Nottage insists that within the complex of techniques available to the actors in *Las Meninas*, there were few that might grant safe harbor to any form of human subjectivity that had not already been sacrificed to the exigencies of representation and replication. "I was explaining to Her Majesty that when I first arrived in France, I'd never seen white powdered makeup or a wig," Nabo tells a half-amused Louis in a joking conversation about his former patron.

> So you can imagine my surprise one evening when I went into his sleeping chamber to say good night and found an old balding man tucked in my patron's bed. "Who are you?" I demanded. For what was this shriveled old man doing there? I tried to pull him out of my patron's bed. But he refused to budge, insisting that he was my patron. "Oh no," I said, "my patron is a beautiful man with a full head of hair, a man who is still in his golden years." He slapped my face, I slapped his. "Fool!" he said. "Indeed!" I said. So I found my patron's sword and drove this man triumphantly from the house. That evening as I was searching for signs of my patron's disappearance I came upon his wig placed lovingly in a cradle as if a child. Next, I found my patron's face in a jar of rouge and a compact of powder. O dear. I could still hear the old man yelling from the cold. I thought, Should I let him in to give me a thorough beating or should I let him freeze to death and claim he went mad? (277)

The complexity of the aesthetic/ideological work that Nabo does is remarkable. He must be careful never to insult his patrons. (The old man whose pretensions he unveils is an absent former employer and not the king himself.) At the same time, he announces the very representational instability that Louis and Marie-Thérèse so awkwardly and ostentatiously negotiate. Both the nobleman whom Nabo unmasks and the king himself must submit their own human bodies to the protocols of Manhood. Formally mirroring their slaves and servants, they operate as a species of the anthropophorous. Their own "selves" are old, shriveled, easily driven from their homes, and prone to early deaths. Thus they quickly resort to violence when the fiction of a clear distinction between human and Man is unveiled. That slapping to which Nabo's employer turns is a necessary part of the apparatus that maintains Man's centrality in the dominant discursive and ideological structures of Western humanism. The presence of the black dwarf demonstrates not only his presumably comic nature, but also a history of kidnapping, theft, and coercion that is reiterated each time the little man makes his unlikely entrance.

As with Picasso's efforts in *Guernica*, we see violence represented not as solemn but instead farcical. The everyday visual protocols to which one might refer when attempting to unpack the works of either the great painter or the great playwright are so overdetermined, so weakened and deracinated, that it becomes nearly impossible to see an image of a kidnapped and abused dwarf or a representation of a human body mutilated by falling bombs as anything other than pure representation, a graph, a set of signs that exist separately from the complexities of history.

As I have said, you are unlikely to encounter *Guernica* in Sala 206. The complex codes necessary to decipher the work have been too severely obfuscated to allow the many spectators who visit the Reina Sofía to experience anything other than a pleasantly displayed carcass. Picasso's obsessive reiterations within the *Las meninas* suite ought to be read, then, as a form of self-defense, the efforts of the artist to resist the deadening of meaning and affect that accompanies the disciplining protocols of humanism. Like Lynn Nottage, he returns to the iconographic structures embedded within Velázquez's painting in order to jolt his audiences out of their complacency, to remind them that art is at its best less concerned with decoration than destabilization. The repetition imaged by Velázquez, Picasso, and Nottage is an essential practice within the aesthetic/ideological matrices that support the deadly fiction of Manhood. Drawing attention to this fact, continually repeating the logic of repetition, forces our cultural studies back toward the historical and the social. We become, like Nabo and the pregnant Marie-Thérèse, nothing more than simple, always changing, and inevitably damaged individuals struggling to shape our histories with only the most improbable of tools at our disposal.

Coda

On the day that I decided to undertake the project that has become *Archives of Flesh*, I left the small apartment I had rented close by the "mixed" *madrileño* neighborhood of Lavapiés and set myself walking toward the riotously elegant Parque del Buen Retiro in Madrid's city center. I had just announced to myself that I preferred African Madrid to European Barcelona, that I valued the crush of immigrants from Colombia, Ecuador, Morocco, Senegal, and Nigeria gathered around the cafés and flower stalls in the Plaza de Tirso de Molina more than the warm, if smug and casually racist, bourgeois nationalists whom I had befriended in Catalonia. I came to Spain years before in search of something larger and more open than the provincialism of the United States. I found relief in the Spanish language from the everyday stupidity and mediocrity that are perhaps the most crushing aspects of American-style white supremacy. The Spanish saying *El cuerpo no tiene la culpa de na'* seemed an apt summation of my haphazardly developing sense of the proper relation between politics, intellectualism, and aesthetics. In Madrid, free in the forgiving brightness of mid-morning, I was released. Dressed sparsely in tee-shirt, shorts, and running shoes, I left each morning before my lessons in grammar and vocabulary to make a thick-thighed hop through the Retiro's sand trails, feasting on the grand visages of statues and manicured gardens that are among the city's most generous gifts.

At the park's edge, tripping up the small bank of steps of an elegant side entrance, I encountered a policeman, dressed from head to toe in tight-fitting green, hiding himself beside a clump of bushes. A strange image, but the type of thing that a tourist out for a morning jog is best advised to leave unremarked. Turning into the park and puffing a ways down the path, I encountered an African immigrant, his back heavily loaded with a sheet filled with counterfeit belts and handbags. We looked tense and uncomprehending at one another, the complexities of diaspora palpable in the terrible silence attending the strangeness we saw reflected in each other's eyes. I spoke first.

"Que hay policía."

"Where?" he answered in English, quickly coming to recognize that I might not be as useless as my behavior and clothing seemed to suggest. I turned my head in the direction of the entrance. He immediately trotted off through the bushes. Two, three, four beats later, a crash of perhaps ten blue-skinned men broke through the woods that bordered the path, all burdened with sacks of imitation Coach, Gucci, and Hermes purses, each larger than the next. They scattered around me as I stood stock-still, my face turned toward my recently escaped interlocutor, acting like an unlikely brown-skinned beacon of retreat. Two Spanish policemen followed immediately upon their heels, huffing and very clearly irritated that a clumsy, inexplicably (non)African tourist had helped to spring their trap.

The thought came to me without warning. Humans were herding humans. In a burlesque of the sorry history that binds Europe, America, and Africa, the exigencies of petty commerce drove Wolof, Fula, Hausa, and Fulani scattering like panicked gazelles into mid-morning traffic. The war was here. Our ancestors had succeeded in modulating the etiquette of conflict, produced for many of us zones of (relatively) safe withdrawal. But the terms of armistice have yet to be ratified. Especially within this most precious site of Spanish civilization, this monument to the legacies of Isabella and Ferdinand, situated close by the Museo Nacional del Prado, the Real Jardín Botánico de Madrid, the Reina Sofía, the Plaza del Sol, and the Biblioteca Nacional, one might easily encounter the most commonplace violence against Africans and their descendants while oblivious tourists clutch cheap treasures and poorly examined fantasies of European exceptionalism to their chests. It was not lost on me that a little more than a century earlier, crowds of *madrileños* had gathered in this same park to ogle collections of Ashanti, Filipinos, and Inuits in specially designed exhibition spaces, many of which continue to service the needs of the park's many pleasantly distracted visitors.[4] It is this willingness not only to assault and abuse but also to ignore and obfuscate that supports the most rarefied, most obscene cultural projects of Western humanism. It is what makes so much of the work in the humanities and human sciences so shockingly hermetic and disconnected. What I have attempted to demonstrate in *Archives of Flesh* is not simply that as a matter of both ideology and aesthetics Africans must be scattered from about the environs of the white kings, but instead that these theatrical dispersions, these nonsensical images of police chasing human men through well-manicured woods, are absolutely necessary devices in the articulation of the vague and reedy concepts of nobility and Euro-American "civilization" with which so much in the practice of contemporary literary and cultural studies is so unapologetically concerned. My response has been to follow the only half-discernible paths prepared for me by a generation of intellectuals who have asked not only that we radically expand the foci of our inquiries, but also that we resist the manufactured tone deafness that stands at the heart of the increasingly irrelevant practices of our cultural studies. My face, narrowed by distress, is turned in the direction of the African's retreat. I resist those commonsense ideological structures that privilege the nativity—and nobility—of "white" Europeans and their American look-alikes. I openly question the proprietary claims to culture and cultivation that are choked down the throats of successive generations of not always willing supplicants at the altar of civilization. I have lost all proper respect for the essentially segregationist disciplinary structures to which many in my profession desperately cling. With each improbable stoke of this indelicate pen, I announce the inevitability of a coming revolt of ideas, politics, and culture in which the fictions of Europe and Africa will finally be dismantled. With each clumsy step, I attempt as best I can to reject Man's allure in favor of humanity's promise.

NOTES

INTRODUCTION

1. See Ann Helms, "Judge Accuses CMS of 'Academic Genocide,'" *Charlotte Observer*, May 24, 2005; Ann Helms, "Threat to Close Schools Lifted," *Charlotte Observer*, August 19, 2006.
2. See Institute of Education Sciences, "Race/Ethnicity of College Faculty," n.d., http://nces.ed.gov.
3. Cary Wolfe, *What Is Posthumanism?* (Minneapolis: University of Minnesota Press, 2010), xv.
4. Frank B. Wilderson III, *Red, White, and Black: Cinema and the Structure of U.S. Antagonisms* (Durham: Duke University Press, 2010), 6.
5. Sara Ahmed argues that the diversity rhetoric that is so prevalent in some American and European universities is itself deeply implicated in the foreclosure of new modes of thought in which black subjectivity might be recognized as something other than marginal or supplementary. See Sara Ahmed, *On Being Included: Racism and Diversity in Institutional Life* (Durham: Duke University Press, 2012).
6. Orlando Patterson, *Slavery and Social Death: A Comparative Study* (Cambridge: Harvard University Press, 1982).
7. W. E. B. Du Bois, *Black Reconstruction in America, 1860–1880*, intro. David Levering Lewis (1935; reprint, New York: Free Press, 1998); C. L. R. James, *The Black Jacobins: Toussaint L'Ouverture and the Santo Domingo Revolution* (1938; reprint, New York: Vintage, 1989); John W. Blassingame, *The Slave Community: Plantation Life in the Antebellum South* (New York: Oxford University Press, 1979); Deborah Gray White, *Ar'n't I a Woman? Female Slaves in the Plantation South* (1985; reprint, New York: Norton, 1999).
8. Alexander G. Weheliye, *Habeas Viscus: Racializing Assemblages, Biopolitics, and Black Feminist Theories of the Human* (Durham: Duke University Press, 2014), 1–2.
9. Hortense Spillers, "Mama's Baby, Papa's Maybe: An American Grammar Book," in *Black, White, and in Color: Essays on American Literature and Culture* (Chicago: University of Chicago Press, 2003), 203–29.
10. See Cedric J. Robinson, *Black Marxism: The Making of a Radical Tradition* (1983; reprint, Chapel Hill: University of North Carolina Press, 2000).
11. María DeGuzmán, *Spain's Long Shadow: The Black Legend, Off-Whiteness, and Anglo-American Empire* (Minneapolis: University of Minnesota Press, 2005).

12. Sylvia Wynter, "On How We Mistook the Map for the Territory, and Reimprisoned Ourselves in Our Unbearable Wrongness of Being, of *Desêtre*: Black Studies toward the Human Project," in *Not Only the Master's Tools: African American Studies in Theory and Practice*, ed. Lewis R. Gordon and Jane Anna Gordon (Boulder, CO: Paradigm, 2006), 107–69. See also Michel Foucault, *The Order of Things: An Archaeology of the Human Sciences* (1970; reprint, New York: Vintage, 1994); and Jacob Pandian, *Anthropology and the Western Tradition: Toward an Authentic Anthropology* (Prospect Heights, IL: Waveland, 1982).

13. Marcus Rediker, *The Slave Ship: A Human History* (New York: Penguin, 2007); Stephanie Smallwood, *Saltwater Slavery: A Middle Passage from Africa to American Diaspora* (Cambridge: Harvard University Press, 2007).

14. Frantz Fanon, *Black Skin, White Masks* (New York: Grove, 1967), 217.

15. Giorgio Agamben, *The Open: Man and Animal*, trans. Kevin Attell (Stanford: Stanford University Press, 2004), 12.

16. For a very interesting discussion of the transformation of Colombo/Colón into the U.S. national hero Columbus, see Michel-Rolph Trouillot, *Silencing the Past: Power and the Production of History* (Boston: Beacon, 1995).

17. For more on Cabrera, see Ilona Katzew, *Casta Painting* (New Haven: Yale University Press, 2004).

18. See Peter Pierson, *The History of Spain* (Westport, CT: Greenwood, 1999), 18–19.

19. See Debra Blumenthal, "'La Casa dels Negres': Black African Solidarity in Late Medieval Valencia," in *Black Africans in Renaissance Europe*, ed. T. F. Earle and K. J. P. Lowe (Cambridge: Cambridge University Press, 2005), 225–46.

20. Jeremy Lawrance, "Black Africans in Renaissance Spanish Literature," in Earle and Lowe, *Black Africans in Renaissance Europe*, 7–93.

21. See Foucault, *The Order of Things*; and Robinson, *Black Marxism*.

CHAPTER 1. WAR ARCHIVE

1. Brent Hayes Edwards, *The Practice of Diaspora: Literature, Translation, and the Rise of Black Internationalism* (Cambridge: Harvard University Press, 2003).

2. For a very useful treatment of the racialist and white supremacist impulses compelling the Spanish-American War, see Nell Irvin Painter, "The White Man's Burden," in *Standing at Armageddon: A Grassroots History of the Progressive Era* (New York: Norton, 1987), 141–59.

3. Between 1898 and 1919 the U.S. military invaded not only Cuba, Puerto Rico, and the Philippines, but also Mexico, the Dominican Republic, and Nicaragua.

4. See Willard B. Gatewood Jr., *"Smoked Yankees" and the Struggle for Empire: Letters from Negro Soldiers, 1898–1902* (Fayetteville: University of Arkansas Press, 1987).

5. The *Plessy* decision was part of a group of racialist decisions by the court designed to ratify the country's developing status as an imperial power while guarding against the threat of racial mixture. I specifically have in mind the series of Supreme Court decisions regarding the political status of Puerto Rico, Guam, and the Philippines as "foreign in a domestic sense." There are a fair number of

works that treat this matter in depth. Among the best is Christina Duffy Burnett and Burke Marshall, eds., *Foreign in a Domestic Sense: Puerto Rico, American Expansion, and the Constitution* (Durham: Duke University Press, 2001). See also Amy Kaplan, *The Anarchy of Empire in the Making of U.S. Culture* (Cambridge: Harvard University Press, 2005).

6. See Donna Haraway, "A Cyborg Manifesto: Science, Technology, and Socialist-Feminism in the Late Twentieth Century," in *Simians, Cyborgs and Women: The Reinvention of Nature* (New York: Routledge, 1991).

7. Paul Gilroy, *Against Race: Imagining Political Culture beyond the Color Line* (Cambridge: Harvard University Press, 2002). Tellingly, the work was published in the United Kingdom in 2000 as *Between Camps*.

8. "Negro Leaders Call Conference on Spain and Fascist Menace," *Daily Worker*, December 30, 1938.

9. The Fifteenth International Brigade would ultimately number approximately forty thousand troops from fifty-two countries. See Peter N. Carroll, *The Odyssey of the Abraham Lincoln Brigade: Americans in the Spanish Civil War* (Stanford: Stanford University Press, 1994), 12.

10. James Yates, *Mississippi to Madrid: Memoir of a Black American in the Abraham Lincoln Brigade* (Greensboro, NC: Open Hand, 1989), 115.

11. As with most chroniclers of the participation of American militants in the war on behalf of the Republican government in Spain, Peter N. Carroll refers to the collective body of persons who served as the Abraham Lincoln Brigade. This name is technically incorrect as, in fact, the soldiers, ambulance drivers, doctors, nurses, and others mainly served in the Abraham Lincoln Battalion, which was part of the Fifteenth International Brigade of the Spanish Republican Army. This brigade was made up of troops from countries around the world, particularly Europe. One of the reasons for continuing with the inaccurate title Abraham Lincoln Brigade is to bring together those individuals who served in the actual American battalion along with those individuals who served either with Spanish troops or with other, non-American forces. At the same time, the use of the term "brigade" obscures the fact that no more than three thousand Americans served in the Republican army.

12. "International Letter from Paul Robeson, Jr.," *Daily Worker*, April 26, 1938.

13. "Spain, 1938: Guillen and Robeson Meet," *World Magazine*, July 24, 1976.

14. Quoted in Jonathan Scott, *Socialist Joy in the Writing of Langston Hughes* (Columbia: University of Missouri Press, 2006), 36.

15. Roughly, "the silly reign of the house of Borbón": Borbón + *nada* (nothing).

16. Giorgio Agamben, *Homo Sacer: Sovereign Power and Bare Life*, trans. Daniel Heller-Roazen (Stanford: Stanford University Press, 1998). Where I differ with Agamben, however, is not so much in his deployment of the idea that much within the practice of modern biopolitics is specifically designed to distinguish "bare life" from "qualified life"—or what I label here "human" from "Man"—but instead that he demonstrates so little interest in the multifarious methods utilized

by humans identified as objects, automatons, and chattel to refuse this same sovereignty. Like most of his predecessors, Agamben speaks *of* the slave but not *to* him. He attempts a critique of the most vulgar aspects of so-called Western humanism without once noting that there are very many alternatives to even the most sacred of these presumably universal intellectual traditions.

17. Here I am referring primarily to the complex history of the Spanish Protectorate in Morocco, a location in the extreme north of Morocco that as late as 1955 held as many as one million persons, or perhaps a tenth of Morocco's population. Today the remnants of the protectorate comprise primarily the poor "garrison cities" of Ceuta and Melilla. See Tony Hodges, *Western Sahara: The Roots of a Desert War* (Westport, CT: L. Hill, 1983); and John Mercer, *Spanish Sahara* (London: Allen and Unwin, 1976).

18. Salaria Kea Application to the Army Nurse Corp, Frances Patai Papers, Abraham Lincoln Brigade Archive (ALBA), Tamiment Library and Robert F. Wagner Labor Archives, New York University (hereafter cited as Frances Patai Papers).

19. Negro Committee to Aid Spain and the Medical Bureau and North American Committee to Aid Spanish Democracy, *Salaria Kee: A Negro Nurse in Republican Spain* (1938; reprint, San Francisco: Bay Area Post of the Veterans of the Abraham Lincoln Brigade, 1977). In reference to Kea's last name, I will spell it Kea, which she preferred at the end of her life, rather than Kee, which appears in most of the documents that discuss her. For ready access to this pamphlet, see the website Ireland and the Spanish Civil War, http://irelandscw.com.

20. Howard Rushmore, "Fascists Won't Win, Declares Negro Nurse," *Daily Worker*, May 18, 1938.

21. Salaria Kea O'Reilly, "While Passing Through," Frances Patai Papers.

22. Michel Foucault, *The Order of Things: An Archaeology of the Human Sciences* (1970; reprint, New York: Vintage, 1994), 297.

23. Bob August, "Salaria Kea and John O'Reilly: Volunteers Who Met and Wed in Spain, 1938," *Cleveland Magazine*, 1975, available at Ireland and the Spanish Civil War, http://irelandscw.com.

24. Martin Balter to Frances Patai, December 7, 1990, Frances Patai Papers.

25. Frances Patai to Martin Balter, December 7, 1990, Frances Patai Papers.

26. For more on the history of African American women in the nursing profession, see Darlene Clark Hine, *Black Women in White: Racial Conflict and Cooperation in the Nursing Profession, 1890–1950* (Bloomington: Indiana University Press, 1989).

27. Most of these individuals were part of the Fuerzas Regulares Indígenas (Indigenous Regular Forces) recruited from the Spanish Protectorate in Morocco. For more, see Hugh Thomas, *The Spanish Civil War* (New York: Penguin, 2003); and Antony Beevor, *The Battle for Spain* (New York: Penguin, 1982).

CHAPTER 2. LORCA'S DEATHLY POETICS

1. I am of course punning on Fanon's notion of "the fact of blackness." See Frantz Fanon, *Black Skin, White Masks* (New York: Grove, 1967).

2. See Henri Lefebvre, *The Production of Space*, trans. David Nicholson-Smith (Malden, MA: Wiley-Blackwell, 1992).

3. Michel de Certeau, *The Practice of Everyday Life*, trans. Steven Randall (Berkeley: University of California Press, 1984).

4. Walter Johnson, *Soul by Soul: Life inside the Antebellum Slave Market* (Cambridge: Harvard University Press, 1999), 164–65.

5. James C. Scott, *Weapons of the Weak: Everyday Forms of Peasant Resistance* (New Haven: Yale University Press, 1987).

6. Quoted in Maggie Montesinos Sale, *The Slumbering Volcano: American Slave Ship Revolts and the Production of Rebellious Masculinity* (Durham: Duke University Press, 1997), 100.

7. Even Ángel del Río, Lorca's friend and one of his most sensitive critics, believed that Lorca had been born in 1899. His biographical essay "Federico García Lorca, 1899–1936" was singularly important in securing Lorca's status as one of the most significant poets and playwrights of the twentieth century. See Ángel del Río, "Federico García Lorca, 1899–1936," *Revista Hispánica Moderna* 6, nos. 3–4 (July–October 1940): 193–260.

8. See Leslie Stainton, *Lorca: A Dream of Life* (London: Bloomsbury, 1998); and Ian Gibson, *Federico García Lorca: A Life* (New York: Pantheon, 1989).

9. Federico García Lorca, "El niño Stanton" ("Little Stanton"), in *Collected Poems: A Bilingual Edition*, ed. Christopher Maurer (New York: Farrar, Straus and Giroux, 1991), 688, 689.

10. See Orlando Patterson, *Slavery and Social Death* (Cambridge: Harvard University Press, 1985).

11. Nowhere was this more obvious than in the Spanish military, which had been so soundly defeated by the Americans. In response, King Alfonso XIII attempted to save face by redeploying troops to the Spanish protectorate in Morocco, where they engaged in an endless series of bloody "cleanup" operations against rebellious Berbers. Among the soldiers who were deployed to Morocco was a young officer known for both his cruelty and ultra-conservative politics who would later figure with great prominence in the lives of both García Lorca and the country as a whole, Francisco Franco. See Stainton, *Lorca: A Dream of Life*, 54, 387–88.

12. Federico García Lorca, "Play and Theory of the Duende," in *In Search of Duende*, ed. Christopher Maurer (New York: New Directions, 1998), 64.

13. Bob Kaufman, "Like Father, Like Sun," in *The Ancient Rain: Poems, 1956–1978* (New York: New Directions, 1981), 35.

14. Albert Camus, *The Plague*, trans. Stuart Gilbert (1947; reprint, New York: Vintage, 1991).

15. Antonio Machado, "Españolito," in *Poesías Completas*, with prologue by Manuel Alvar (Madrid: Espasa-Calpe, 1975), 229. Translation mine.

16. See Paul Julian Smith, "New York, New York: Lorca's Double Vision," *Tesserae: Journal of Iberian and Latin American Studies* 6, no. 2 (December 2000): 169–80.

17. Jonathan Mayhew, *Apocryphal Lorca: Translation, Parody, Kitsch* (Chicago: University of Chicago Press, 2009), 29–30.

18. See Robert F. Reid-Pharr, *Once You Go Black: Choice, Desire, and the Black American Intellectual* (New York: New York University Press, 2007).

19. A typical example of this tendency to create Lorca as a sort of primitive fetish can be found in Cyrus Cassells's poem "Lament for Lorca": "Federico, at seventeen, I became possessed / By your voice in Andalucía, in Nueva York. / I loved you then / As the chronicler of the gypsies, / As the visionary traveler / Who mourned for Harlem." See Cyrus Cassels, "Lament for Lorca," *Callaloo* 32 (Summer 1987): 380–84.

20. Federico García Lorca, "Scene of the Lieutenant Colonel of the Civil Guard" ("Escena del teniente coronel de la Guardia Civil"), in *Collected Poems*, 155, 157.

21. The reference here is to Gayatri Spivak's essay "Can the Subaltern Speak?" in *Marxism and the Interpretation of Culture*, ed. Cary Nelson and Lawrence Grossberg (Chicago: University of Illinois Press, 1988), 271–316.

22. Federico García Lorca, "Ballad of the Three Rivers" ("Baladilla de los tres ríos"), in *Collected Poems*, 97, 99.

23. Ángel Sahuquillo, *Federico García Lorca and the Culture of Male Homosexuality*, trans. Erica Frouman-Smith (Jefferson, NC: McFarland, 2007).

24. Federico García Lorca, "Dialogue of Amargo" ("Diálogo del Amargo"), in *Collected Poems*, 161, 163, 165.

25. Federico García Lorca, "Song of Amargo's Mother" ("Canción de la madre del Amargo"), in *Collected Poems*, 164, 165.

26. Federico García Lorca, "Ode to Walt Whitman" ("Oda a Walt Whitman"), in *Collected Poems*, 731, 733.

27. My understanding of primitivism owes much to the work of Hal Foster. See Hal Foster, *Recodings: Art, Spectacle, Cultural Politics* (New York: New Press, 1998).

28. George Hutchinson, *In Search of Nella Larsen: A Biography of the Color Line* (Cambridge: Belknap, 2006), 3.

29. See Thadious M. Davis, *Nella Larsen, Novelist of the Harlem Renaissance: A Woman's Life Unveiled* (Baton Rouge: Louisiana State University Press, 1994).

30. Federico García Lorca, "Streets and Dreams" ("Calles y sueños"), in *Collected Poems*, 661, 663.

31. The literature surrounding the practice of "New World African religions" is both diverse and rich. There are any number of works, moreover, that speak to the belief on the part of practitioners that they are not simply emulating the gods during possession, but instead that they actually *become* the gods. For examples of two classic works, see Zora Neale Hurston, *Tell My Horse: Voodoo and Life in Haiti*

and Jamaica, intro. Henry Louis Gates (1938; reprint, New York: Harper and Row, 1990); and Katherine Dunham: *Island Possessed* (1969; reprint, Chicago: University of Chicago Press, 1994).

32. Federico García Lorca, "El rey de Harlem" ("The King of Harlem"), in *Collected Poems*, 650–58.

33. Federico García Lorca, "Son de Negros en Cuba" ("Blacks Dancing to Cuban Rhythms"), in *Collected Poems*, 742, 744.

CHAPTER 3. LANGSTON'S ADVENTURES IN THE DARK

1. Albert Memmi, *The Colonizer and the Colonized* (1965; reprint, Boston: Beacon, 1991), 134.

2. Arnold Rampersad writes in his introduction to Hughes's *The Big Sea*, "In a genre defined in its modern mode by confession, Hughes appears to give virtually nothing away of a personal nature." See Arnold Rampersad, introduction to *The Big Sea*, by Langston Hughes (New York: Hill and Wang, 1940), xvii.

3. Langston Hughes, *I Wonder as I Wander* (New York: Hill and Wang, 1956), 331.

4. Karl Marx, *The Eighteenth Brumaire of Louis Bonaparte*, trans. Daniel de Leon (1852; reprint, New York: New York Labor News Company, 1951), 14.

5. Langston Hughes, "Song of Spain," in *The Collected Poems of Langston Hughes*, ed. Arnold Rampersad and David Roessel (New York: Vintage, 1994), 195–97.

6. Norris was convicted and then sentenced to death in 1933. His case eventually reached the Supreme Court, which ordered a retrial. In 1937 he was tried again and reconvicted, again with a sentence of death. This was later commuted to life in prison. He eventually was paroled in 1946, whereupon he fled the state of Alabama. In 1976 his conviction was overturned. He died in 1989, "the last of the Scottsboro Boys." See Clarence Norris, *The Last of the Scottsboro Boys* (New York: Putnam, 1979).

7. Langston Hughes, "August 19th . . . A Poem for Clarence Norris," in *Collected Poems*, 204–6.

8. Langston Hughes, "Too Much of Race," in *Langston Hughes in the Hispanic World and Haiti*, ed. Edward J. Mullen (Hamden, CT: Archon, 1977), 94.

9. Langston Hughes, "Broadcast on Ethiopia," quoted in Arnold Rampersad, *The Life of Langston Hughes*, vol. 1, *1902–1941: I, Too, Sing America* (New York: Oxford University Press, 2002), 322.

10. Frantz Fanon, *The Wretched of the Earth*, trans. Richard Wilcox (1963; reprint, New York: Grove, 2004), 135.

11. Langston Hughes, "Advertisement for the Waldorf-Astoria," in *Collected Poems*, 143–46.

12. Langston Hughes, "Cubes," in *Collected Poems*, 175–76.

13. Seth Moglen, "Modernism in the Black Diaspora: Langston Hughes and the Broken Cubes of Picasso," *Callaloo* 25, no. 4 (Autumn 2002): 1188–1205.

14. At an April 2010 reading of a shorter version of this essay at Addis Ababa University, one of my Ethiopian interlocutors pointed out to me that the word "disease"

is composed of only five letters, the *s* and the *e* repeating themselves. I thank her now for her clever intervention.

15. See Rampersad, *The Life of Langston Hughes*, vol. 1; and Arnold Rampersad, *The Life of Langston Hughes*, vol. 2, *1941–1967: I Dream a World* (New York: Oxford University Press, 2002).

16. Nicolás Guillén, "Conversación con Langston Hughes," in Mullen, *Langston Hughes in the Hispanic World*, 172–75. Translation mine.

17. See Vera Kutzinski, "Yo También Soy América: Langston Hughes Translated," *American Literary History* 18, no. 3 (2006): 550–78. See also Vera M. Kutzinski, *The Worlds of Langston Hughes: Modernism and Translation in the Americas* (Ithaca: Cornell University Press, 2012).

18. Langston Hughes to Noel Sullivan, in *Selected Letters of Langston Hughes*, ed. Arnold Rampersad and David Roessel (New York: Knopf, 2015), 172–73.

19. José Antonio Fernández de Castro, "Presentación de Langston Hughes," in Mullen, *Langston Hughes in the Hispanic World*, 169–71. Translation mine. A very similar set of procedures was utilized in an appreciation of Hughes by the Spaniard Miguel Alejandro in a 1936 issue of the radical journal *Nueva Cultura*. Alejandro writes of Hughes,

> Ha sido universitario, chofer, repartidor de flores, marinero de viejos y lentos pataches, y de navíos de alto bordo. Pensó una noche ascender a todos los balcones de Verona, y ha paseado las charcas venecianas, y se emborrachó de vinos y mujeres en nuestra Valencia.
>
> Carl Van Vechten que le conoce muy bien, dice de él ¡Ojalá que este joven negro, se decida a confiar al papel, en sus mas mínimos detalles, las corridas de toros de México; la ebria alegría del Gran Duc; la delicada y exquisita gracia de las negritas de Burutu; la exótica languidez de las mujeres españolas de Valencia; los viles bárbaros al son de jazz, en Harlem, en el corazón de Nueva York.
>
> (He has been a university student, driver, flower delivery boy, sailor of old and slow schooners, and of oceangoing ships. He thought one night to climb all the balconies of Verona, and has walked the Venetian ponds and gotten drunk off of wine and women in our Valencia.
>
> Carl Van Vechten, who knows him very well, says of him, Hopefully this young black will decide to trust to paper, in their most minute details, the bullfights in Mexico, the drunken joy of the Gran Duc, the delicate and exquisite grace of the black girls of Burutu, the exotic languor of the Spanish women of Valencia, the wild dances to the sound of jazz in Harlem in the heart of New York.)
>
> Miguel Alejandro, "Langston Hughes," *Nueva Cultura*, no. 10 (January 1936): 9. Translation mine.

20. Langston Hughes, "Tomorrow's Seed," in *Collected Poems*, 431.

CHAPTER 4. PRIMITIVE AT THE PLANTATION'S EDGE

1. The deep connections between especially the most elite American universities and slavery is becoming ever more clear. Brown University, the College of William and Mary, Harvard University, Emory University, the University of Maryland, the University of North Carolina at Chapel Hill, the University of Virginia, Yale University, and Columbia University, among many others, either held slaves directly, utilized slave labor in the building of their campuses, traded slaves as commodities, greatly supported the work of slavery apologists (and later apologists for colonization and segregation), or more likely some rich combination of all these things. For more on this matter, see Craig Steven Wilder, *Ebony and Ivy: Race, Slavery, and the Troubled History of America's Universities* (New York: Bloomsbury, 2013).

2. Sylvia Wynter, "The Ceremony Must Be Found: After Humanism," *boundary 2*, vol. 12, no. 3–vol. 13, no. 1 (Spring–Autumn, 1984): 47.

3. In addition to the two autobiographies, information on Himes and Lesley Packard in Spain can be found in James Sallis, *Chester Himes: A Life* (New York: Walker, 2000); and Edward Margolies and Michel Fabre, *The Several Lives of Chester Himes* (Jackson: University Press of Mississippi, 1997).

4. Chester Himes, *The Quality of Hurt: The Early Years; The Autobiography of Chester Himes* (New York: Thunder's Mouth, 1971), 301.

5. Chester Himes, *The End of a Primitive* (1955; reprint, New York: Norton, 1990).

6. Jodi Melamed, "The Killing Joke of Sympathy: Chester Himes's *End of a Primitive* Sounds the Limits of Midcentury Racial Liberalism," *American Literature* 80, no. 4 (December 2008): 769–97.

7. See Cary Wolfe, *What Is Posthumanism?* (Minneapolis: University of Minnesota Press, 2010).

8. Chester Himes to Mrs. Roslyn Targ, July 29, 1975, Chester Himes Papers, box 22, folder 227, Beineke Rare Book and Manuscript Library, Yale University (hereafter cited as Chester Himes Papers).

9. Chester Himes to Mrs. Roslyn Targ, July 17, 1976, Chester Himes Papers, box 22, folder 227.

10. The details that Himes offers about this affair in *The Quality of Hurt* are largely confirmed by the discussion of the relationship in Edward Margolies's and Michel Fabre's biography, *The Several Lives of Chester Himes*. They identify Alva as Willa Thompson Trierweiler, whom Himes met onboard a France-bound ship and who at the time of their meeting was seeking a divorce from her husband, a Luxembourg dentist with whom she had four children.

11. For more on Haywood, see Lawrence Jackson, *The Indignant Generation: A Narrative History of African American Writers and Critics, 1934–1960* (Princeton: Princeton University Press, 2010).

12. Jacques Derrida, *The Animal That Therefore I Am*, ed. Marie-Louise Mallet; trans. David Wills (New York: Fordham University Press, 2008), 5.

13. Octavio Paz, *Conjunctions and Disjunctions*, trans. Helen R. Lane (1969; reprint, New York: Arcade, 1990), 20.

14. Franz Kafka, "A Report to an Academy," in *The Basic Franz Kafka*, intro. Eric Heller (New York: Pocket Books, 1946), 245.

15. For more on Carl Hagenbeck and his shows, see Hilke Thode-Arora, "Hagenbeck's European Tours: The Development of the Human Zoo," in *Human Zoos: Science and Spectacle in the Age of Colonial Empires*, ed. Pascal Blanchard, Nicolas Bancel, Gilles Boëtsch, Eric Deroo, Sandrine Lemaire, and Charles Forsdick (Liverpool: Liverpool University Press, 2008), 65–173.

CHAPTER 5. RICHARD WRIGHT IN THE HOUSE OF GIRLS

1. Richard Wright, *Pagan Spain* (1957; reprint, Jackson: University Press of Mississippi, 1995), 4.

2. For a very good discussion of Stein's influence over other modernist intellectuals, see Michael North, *The Dialect of Modernism: Race, Language, and Twentieth-Century Literature* (New York: Oxford University Press, 1994).

3. In his March 3, 1957, review of *Pagan Spain* in the *Chicago Sunday Tribune Magazine of Books*, Roi Ottley wrote,

    When a novelist of Richard Wright's stature pauses in his fictional chores to turn journalist and report on a foreign nation's social fabric, one always wonders whether he merely is indulging himself in a writing exercise.
    I am an admirer of Wright's novels, but do not think he has the talents of a skilled reporter, or indeed has he developed and [*sic*] subtle understanding necessary to accurately report the social and cultural nuances of the Spanish people.

    Roy Ottley, "Review of *Pagan Spain*," in *Richard Wright: Critical Perspectives Past and Present*, ed. Henry Louis Gates and K. A. Appiah (New York: Amistad, 1993), 56.

4. Richard Wright, "An Outline Tracing the Treatment of Material on a Proposed Book on Spanish Life, Tentative Title, *Lonesome Spain*," Richard Wright Papers, 1927–1978, box 53, folder 652, Beineke Rare Book and Manuscript Library, Yale University (hereafter cited as Richard Wright Papers).

5. See Hazel Rowley, *Richard Wright: The Life and Times* (New York: Henry Holt, 2001), 475.

6. Richard Wright, *Black Power: A Record of Reactions in a Land of Pathos*, in Richard Wright, *Three Books from Exile: Black Power; The Color Curtain; and White Man, Listen!*, intro. Cornel West (New York: Harper Perennial Modern Classics, 2008).

7. Granville Hicks, reviewing *Pagan Spain* in the *New York Post*, amplifies Myrdal's thinking, telling us that for Wright, "Spain was not so much a landscape to be looked at as a problem to be solved." Granville Hicks, review of *Pagan Spain*, *New York Post*, February 24, 1957. See also Saunders Redding, review of *Pagan Spain*, *Afro Magazine*, March 9, 1957.

8. Richard Wright, "Harlem Spanish Women Come Out of the Kitchen," *Daily Worker*, September 20, 1937.

9. See Frantz Fanon, *The Wretched of the Earth* (1961; reprint, New York: Grove, 2005).

10. See William D. Phillips, "The Old World Background of Slavery in the Americas," in *Slavery and the Rise of the Atlantic System*, ed. Barbara Solow (New York: Cambridge University Press, 2003), 43–61.

11. Paul Gilroy, *The Black Atlantic: Modernity and Double Consciousness* (Cambridge: Harvard University Press, 1994), 4.

12. My thinking here is heavily indebted to those feminist critics whose efforts to reevaluate sentimental fiction turned on the ways that the seemingly non-ideological nature of sentimental novels made them perfect vehicles for the articulation of various political ideologies. See, for example, Nancy Armstrong, *Desire and Domestic Fiction: A Political History of the Novel* (New York: Oxford University Press, 1987).

13. Maurice O. Wallace, *Constructing the Black Masculine: Identity and Ideality in African American Men's Literature and Culture* (Durham: Duke University Press, 2002); Shawn Michelle Smith, *Photography on the Color Line: W. E. B. Du Bois, Race, and Visual Culture* (Durham: Duke University Press, 2004).

14. Michel Fabre, *The Unfinished Quest of Richard Wright* (1973; reprint, Chicago: University of Illinois Press, 1993), 414.

15. Richard Wright, "Las Fallas: A Pagan Celebration, draft," Richard Wright Papers, 1927–1978, box 5, folder 84.

16. See Hortense Spillers, "Mama's Baby, Papa's Maybe: An American Grammar Book," in *Black, White, and in Color: Essays on American Literature and Culture* (Chicago: University of Chicago Press, 2003), 203–29.

17. Octavio Paz, *Conjunctions and Disjunctions*, trans. Helen R. Lane (1969; reprint, New York: Arcade, 1990).

18. See Julia Kristeva, *Powers of Horror: An Essay on Abjection*, trans. Leon S. Roudiez (New York: Columbia University Press, 1982).

19. My thinking here owes a great deal to Jasbir Puar. See Jasbir Puar, *Terrorist Assemblages: Homonationalism in Queer Times* (Durham: Duke University Press, 2007). See also Darieck Scott, *Extravagant Abjection: Blackness, Power, and Sexuality in the African American Literary Imagination* (New York: New York University Press, 2010).

20. See G. W. F. Hegel, *Phenomenology of Spirit*, trans. A. V. Miller (Oxford: Clarendon, 1977).

21. Stephanie Smallwood, *Saltwater Slavery: A Middle Passage from Africa to American Diaspora* (Cambridge: Harvard University Press, 2007).

CONCLUSION

1. Orlando Patterson, *Slavery and Social Death: A Comparative Study* (Cambridge: Harvard University Press, 1982), 4.

2. Michel Foucault, *The Order of Things: An Archaeology of the Human Sciences* (1970; reprint, New York: Vintage, 1994), 16.

3. Lynn Nottage, *Las Meninas,* in *Crumbs from the Table of Joy and Other Plays* (New York: Theater Communications Group, 2004), 253.

4. See Neus Moyano Miranda, "Exhibiting People in Spain: Colonialism and Mass Culture," in *Human Zoos: Science and Spectacle in the Age of Colonial Empires,* ed. Pascal Blanchard, Nicolas Bancel, Gilles Boëtsch, Eric Deroo, Sandrine Lemaire, and Charles Forsdick (Liverpool: Liverpool University Press, 2008), 353–68.

INDEX

Abd-al-Rahman, 23

Abraham Lincoln Brigade, 44–46, 56, 62, 64–65, 67

Abraham Lincoln Brigade Archive (ALBA), 44

"academic genocide," 3

Accra, 189, 190–91

adolescent sexuality, 98

"Advertisement for the Waldorf-Astoria," 135

aesthetics: colonization and, 113; of Himes, 156, 175; of Hughes, 118, 147; of Lorca, 74, 81, 97, 100, 109, 117; naïveté, 20; of Picasso, 218, 219; slavery and, 113; war and, 48, 187; of Wright, 196, 197, 205, 206–7

Africa, 152, 176, 194, 200, 201, 202

African American intellectuals, 26; human subjectivity and, 42; Lorca and, 75, 82; Spanish Civil War and, 43; Spanish intellectuals and, 11, 13, 131; struggle of, 88; white supremacy and, 36

African Americans: artists, 26, 155; avant-garde, 35; culture, 26, 46, 106; Hughes on oppression of, 130; identity, 106; internationalism of, 34, 35, 45, 46; labor, 134; masking practices of, 147; modernity, 108–10; paternity, 37; perception of, 34; in U.S. broadcasting, 174; violence and, 164; women, 68

African American studies, 154

African culture, Spanish culture and, 202

African Diaspora Studies, 7, 33, 35, 171

African essence, 105

Africans, 8, 22, 144, 229

Afro-Asian Conference, 185

Against Race (Gilroy), 41

Agamben, Giorgio, 14, 119

Agta, 39–40

"Air Raid: Barcelona," 130

AIT. *See* Asociación Internacional de los Trabajadores

Akan funeral procession, 200

ALBA. *See* Abraham Lincoln Brigade Archive

Alberti, Rafael, 52

Alcalá, Duque de, 15

alcohol, 172

Alejandro, Miguel, 52

Alfonso, King, XII, 52

Alfonso, King, XIII, 52, 53, 54–56

American culture, 119

American folk culture, 88

American Nurses Association (ANA), 68

American radicalism, 64

Amistad, 77

ANA. *See* American Nurses Association

anarchism, in Spain, 50

ancient norms, 78

animals: anthropophorous, 14–15, 70, 119, 154, 170, 173, 174–75, 192–93, 218, 219; aspect of humanity, 211; Disability Studies and Animal Studies, 6; Himes on black/animal, 165–66; humans and, 168; imagery of Himes, 165; man and, 12–14, 15, 30, 161, 201, 225; man/ anthropophorous animal nexus, 154, 192–93, 218, 219; nature, 172; studies, 6; subjectivity, 174

anthropology, zoology and, 173
anthropophorous animal, 14–15, 70, 119, 154, 170, 173, 174–75, 192–93, 218, 219
anti-black violence, 157
Arabs, 23–24
art, 50, *51*, 94–95, 147, 222
artists, 19, 26, 88, 155, 220
Asociación Internacional de los Trabajadores (International Association of Workers, or AIT), 50, *51*
Atlantic culture, 24
Atlantic slavery, 15, 23, 77, 80–81, 117, 152, 175
"August 19th . . . A Poem for Clarence Norris," 130

"Ballad of the Three Rivers" ("Baladilla de los tres ríos"), 92–93
Balter, Martin, 65–67
baptism, 67
Barneveldt, Alva Trent Van Olden. *See* Trierweiler, Willa Thompson, 155, 159–61
Barnum, P. T., 173
Batista, Fulgencio, 114
The Bearded Woman. See Maddalena Ventura, con su marido
Berlin Society for Anthropology, Ethnology, and Prehistory, 173
Berrueta, Domínguez, 85
bestiality, 10, 156, 165, 166
black, white conception of, 174
"Black and American, 1982," 150
black/animal, Himes on, 165–66
black artists, 88
The Black Atlantic: Modernity and Double Consciousness (Gilroy), 190–91
Black Boy (Wright), 181
black culture, 49, 73
black history, 148, 150
black identity, 36, 68
black incarceration, 218
black intellectualism, 150

black liberation, 14
black literature, 150
The Black Nun of Moret. See La Mauresse
Black Power (Wright), 183, 185, 188, 189, 194, 196, 200, 211
black progressive thought, 43
black scholars, 150–51, 153
Black Skin, White Masks (Fanon), 1
black soldiers, 26, 32, 35–37, 38, 40, 45, 49, 70, 71, 114
Black Studies, 9, 13, 15, 76, 119, 130, 150–51, 152–54, 175
black subjectivity, 8, 10, 151
black/white sexual congress, 155
black women, violence against, 69–70
Boabdil, Prince, 17
body, 10, 27, 171, 193
Botero, 220–21
Bradley, David, 150, 157
British Gold Coast colony, 185, 188, 195
broadcasting, 174
"Broadcast on Ethiopia," 132
Brooklyn, 29, 70
Brown, Edward, 39
Brown v. Board of Education, 2, 185
Buffalo Soldiers, 38
bufones, 40

Cabrera, Miguel, 20, *21*, 22, 204, 218
"Calles y sueños." *See* "Streets and Dreams"
camp mentality, 41–42
Campos de Castilla (Machado), 85
Camus, Albert, 84
"Canción de la madre del Amargo." *See* "Song of Amargo's Mother"
cannibalism, 202
cante jondo. See deep song
capitalism, 12, 27, 40, 44, 123; colonialism and, 131; exploitation and, 130, 156; legacy of, 175; racialism and, 12; slavery and, 131; subjectivity and, 75; white supremacy and, 43, 49, 186, 194, 211, 218

"The Unthinkable," 155
U.S. *See* United States

Valencia, 202
Van Vechten, Carl, 145
Velázquez, Diego, 219, 220, 222, 223, 227
Ventura, Maddalena, 15, *16*, 17, 18, 20, 22
Villa Paz, 59, 66
violence, 10, 13, 28, 29–30, 125, 178;
    African Americans and, 164; against
    Africans, 229; anti-black, 157; black
    peoples and, 36; against black women,
    69–70; colonialism and, 207–8; Euro-
    pean superiority and, 173; homosexu-
    ality and, 95; in literature, 84; Lorca
    and, 78, 83–84; Manhood and, 164;
    modernity and, 41; nature of, 216; po-
    lice, 218; silence surrounding, 69–70;
    in Spain, 43
voodoo practitioners, 110–11

Walker, Peter, 106
Wallace, Maurice, 196
war: aesthetics and, 48, 187; black soldiers
    and, 35–37; domesticity and, 63–64,
    187–88; gender and, 49–50, 56, 63–64;
    Lorca and, 84; narratives of, 31–32;
    nature of, 216; slavery and, 34
Warmsley, W. C., 35–36
wealth, 12, 19, 202
The Weary Blues (Hughes), 145
Weheliye, Alexander, 10
Western humanism, 5, 7, 10, 13, 28, 179,
    183, 196, 207, 209
Western Man, 201
Western philosophical traditions, 5, 9
What is Posthumanism?, 5, 6
"While Passing Through," 60–61
White, Steven, 80
white bourgeois domesticity, 160
white Christian identity, 11
white conception of black, 174
white identity, 19

white paternalism, 45
"white slavery," 212
white supremacy, 2, 4, 23, 27, 28, 30, 44,
    122, 168; African American intellec-
    tuals and, 36; American-style, 228;
    capitalism and, 43, 49, 186, 194, 211,
    218; colonialism and, 131; coloniza-
    tion and, 43; culture of, 13; Hughes
    on, 141; humanism and, 9, 154; legacy
    of, 175; Lorca and, 91; protocols of,
    70; slavery and, 131; Wright and, 203,
    205
white Western homogeneity, 23
Whitman, Walt, 98–102
Wilderson, Frank, 7–8
Williams, Eric, 189
Wolfe, Cary, 5–7, 156
women, 30; African American, 68; fas-
    cism and, 204; heroism of, 204; history
    of, 223; liberation of, 205–6; Lorca
    and, 87; modern society and, 204; op-
    pression of, 121–23; poverty and, 209;
    repressed femininity, 206; sexuality
    of, 208, 209–10; of Spain, 188, 209–11;
    violence against black, 69–70; Wright
    and, 182, 187, 195, 198–99, 200, 204–5,
    207–13
world history, slave history and, 213
World War I, 68, 83–84
World War II, 41, 68
Wright, Richard, 27–28; aesthetics of, 196,
    197, 205, 206–7; affair with Hornung,
    195, 206; on Akan funeral proces-
    sion, 200; Christianity and, 197–98;
    colonialism and, 189–90; Communism
    and, 205–6; editors of, 197; Las Fallas
    festival and, 197–202, *203*; Las Fallas
    sculptures and, 198, 202, *203*; human-
    ism and, 204; Manhood and, 181, 194,
    206–7; masculinity of, 198–99; minor-
    ity status of, 181; pornography of, 195–
    96, 198, 205; prostitution and, 190–94,
    208, 209, 210–12; self-consciousness

of, 206; sexuality of, 195–96, 208; slapstick and farce of, 192; slave culture
and, 194, 196–97; slavery and, 212; social consideration of the master/slave
dialectic, 202; Spain and, 183–84, 188,
199–200, 204; Spanish Civil War and,
184, 188; Stein and, 180–81, 207; stereotypes of, 187, 199–200; trip to Valencia,
202; Western humanism and, 183,
207; white supremacy and, 203, 205;
women and, 182, 187, 195, 198–99, 200,
204–5, 207–13
Wynter, Sylvia, 12, 62, 150, 152, 153, 157,
164, 168

zoology, anthropology and, 173

ABOUT THE AUTHOR

Robert F. Reid-Pharr is Distinguished and Presidential Professor of English and American Studies at the Graduate Center of the City University of New York. A specialist in African American culture and a prominent scholar in the field of race and sexuality studies, he has published three books: *Conjugal Union: The Body, the House, and the Black American* (1999); *Black Gay Man: Essays* (New York University Press, 2001); and *Once You Go Black: Choice, Desire, and the Black American Intellectual* (New York University Press, 2007).